South African Cinema

This book is dedicated to Leon Van der Merwe, a soul mate for more than 30 years, and Hubert Dethier, a great scholar, humanist and friend.

South African Cinema

1896-2010

Martin Botha

intellect Bristol, UK / Chicago, USA

First published in the UK in 2012 by
Intellect, The Mill, Parnall Road, Fishponds, Bristol, BS16 3JG, UK

First published in the USA in 2012 by
Intellect, The University of Chicago Press, 1427 E. 60th Street,
Chicago, IL 60637, USA

A catalogue record for this book is available from the
British Library.

Cover designer: Sarah Newman
Copy-editor: Macmillan
Production manager: Jelena Stanovnik
Typesetting: Mac Style, Beverley, E. Yorkshire

ISBN 978-1-84150-458-2

Printed and bound by Hobbs, UK.

Contents

Acknowledgements

This book is the culmination and consolidation of 30 years of my own personal research into the South African film industry, from my post-graduate studies to professional research at the Human Sciences Research Council of South Africa and film projects at the University of Cape Town. This book is also a product of the African Cinema Unit (ACU) at the University of Cape Town. The ACU is committed to promoting the study of African Cinemas, taking account of the richness and diversity of the film cultures that have emerged from the countries that make up this vast and complex continent.

Since 1988 I have been involved in the South African film industry in a multiplicity of roles. From 1990 to 1992 I was involved in extensive research for the Film and Allied Workers' Organisation (FAWO) regarding the restructuring of the South African film industry. For this project I studied the film industries of Canada, New Zealand, West Africa, Iceland, Australia, Germany and Italy. From 1993 to 1995 further studies were conducted into the film industries of China, France, Great Britain, Argentina, Mexico, Brazil and Cuba. I worked closely with the Film and Television Federation on the establishment of a South African Film Foundation for the administration and funding of the local film industry. During April and May 1995 I was co-opted onto the Film Subcommittee of the new democratic government's Ministry of Arts, Culture, Science and Technology's Task Group regarding post-apartheid film policy. At the end of July 1995 I was seconded to the Ministry of Arts, Culture, Science and Technology to co-write the white paper for a future South African film industry. The draft was completed at the beginning of 1996.

I had also the opportunity to serve as a council member of the National Film and Video Foundation of South Africa (between 1999 and 2007), a sub-committee member of the National Film and Video Foundation (NFVF) regarding the establishment of a National Film School and a director (representing the NFVF and formal training institutions) of the Cape Film Commission (1999–2003). I was also a board member of the Community Video Education Trust in Cape Town, a community-based training institution. These roles provided me with an insider's perspective on the film industry of South Africa. The monograph has also been enhanced by personal diaries with entries on more than 9000 films, including many South African films, which I wrote between 1975 and 2010.

During the past three decades numerous people had an impact on my research into South African cinema. On the academic side Prof. Hubert Dethier from Belgium, with whom I co-authored a book on the late South African director Manie Van Rensburg, has been a great colleague and friend for more than 18 years. On the side of film critics the late William Pretorius's essays and reviews on South African and world cinema, as well as our lengthy conversations, remain a great source of inspiration. I am also deeply indebted to Prof. Pieter Fourie, Braam Muller, Johan Blignaut, Jans Rautenbach, Ross Devenish, Tobie Cronjé, Lionel Ngakane, Louis du Toit, Regardt Van den Bergh, Manie Van Rensburg, Lucia Saks, Ricardo Peach, Moonyeen Lee, Katinka Heyns, Zulfah Otto-Sallies, Jacky Lourens, Mike Dearham, Adri Van Aswegen, Astrid Treffry-Goatley, Gerhard Uys and Keyan Tomaselli for discussions on South African cinema during the past two decades.

Considerable assistance was given to me by innumerable film industry professionals, academics and other individuals, and while it is impossible to mention them all individually, I am particularly indebted to Prof. Jan Uhde, Grant Appleton, Evert Lombaert, Damon and Craig Foster, Michael Auret, Steven Markowitz, Richard Green, Ross Garland, Jeremy Nathan, Johan Nel, Regardt Van den Berg, Peter and Zaria Lamberti, Garth Meyer, Jason Xenopoulos, Inger Smith, Bryan Little, Harold Holscher, Gustav Kuhn, Minky Schlesinger, Thabang Moleya, Neil Brandt, Francois Verster, John Warner, Pierre Crocquet, Hein Devos, Nilesh Singh, Helena Spring, Paul Raleigh, Monica Keys, Douw Jordaan, Tim Greene, Freddy and Sue Ogterop, Trevor Moses, M-Net's Jan du Plessis and Bonolo Modisakwane, Ingrid Thomson, Kenneth Kaplan, Oliver Schmitz, Julie Frederikse, Dirk de Villiers, Grethe Fox, Marina Bekker, Wilma Stockenström, Roy Armes, José Gatti, Angela Van Schalkwyk, Michael Rogosin, Johan de Lange, Darrell Roodt, Trevor Steele Taylor, Aryan Kaganof and Oscar Phasha.

I have been continuously indebted to Leon Van der Merwe for sustained encouragement regarding my career.

I would also like to thank Braam Muller for his invaluable input as copy-editor of the revised manuscript and Jelena Stanovnik from Intellect Publishers for her encouraging words to ensure that the final book is as strong as possible.

I wish to express my gratitude to Prof. Ian Glenn and Prof. Paula Ensor from the University of Cape Town for the opportunity to take research leave and finish this book.

Many individuals and organizations provided stills. In particular I would like to thank M-Net, kykNET and the African Film Library for their major contribution.

Introduction

A
lthough 1994 saw the birth of democracy in South Africa, the South African film industry is much older; in fact, its great documentary film tradition dates back to 1896 as well as the Anglo-Boer War or South African War. Surprisingly only a few books have been published regarding the history of one of the oldest film industries in the world and one of the largest in the African continent. Between 1910 and 2008 as many as 1434 features were made in South Africa (Armes 2008). The majority, 944 features, were shot in the short period between 1978 and 1992 (Blignaut & Botha 1992).

South African film history is captured in a mere 13 books. Developments in early South African cinema (1895–1940) have been chronicled in Thelma Gutsche's *The History and Social Significance of Motion Pictures in South Africa: 1895–1940* (1946/72). Other significant studies include Keyan Tomaselli's *The Cinema of Apartheid: Race and Class in South Africa* (1989), Johan Blignaut and Martin Botha's *Movies Moguls Mavericks: South African Cinema 1979–1991* (1992), Martin Botha's edited volume, *Marginal Lives and Painful Pasts: South African Cinema After Apartheid* (2007), Jacqueline Maingard's *South African National Cinema* (2007), André le Roux and Lilla Fourie's *Filmverlede: Geskiedenis van die Suid-Afrikaanse speelfilm* (1982), Peter Davis's *In Darkest Hollywood: Exploring the Jungles of Cinema's South Africa* (1996), Martin Botha and Adri Van Aswegen's *Images of South Africa: The Rise of the Alternative film* (1992), Tomaselli's compilation of revised and reworked papers and chapters published elsewhere, *Encountering Modernity: Twentieth Century South African Cinemas* (2006), Isabel Balseiro and Ntongela Masilela's edited volume, *To Change Reels: Film and Film Culture in South Africa* (2003) as well as Lucia Saks's *Cinema in a Democratic South Africa: The Race for Representation* (2010).

In the 113-year history of South African cinema only two books have been devoted to South African film directors: Martin Botha and Hubert Dethier's *Kronieken van Zuid-Afrika: de films van Manie van Rensburg* (1997) and Martin Botha's *Jans Rautenbach: Dromer Baanbreker en Auteur* (2006c). Veteran directors such as Jans Rautenbach (*Jannie Totsiens*, 1970), Ross Devenish (*Marigolds in August*, 1979), Manie Van Rensburg (*The Fourth Reich*, 1990) and the younger generation of the 1980s challenged moral and political censorship during apartheid, a severe lack of audience development and inadequate film distribution to shape progressive texts, which became the foundation of a new, critical South African cinema during the 1990s.

Even after several decades Gutsche's book (1972) remains a pioneering study and virtually the only reference for all studies dealing with early South African film history (1895–1940). Gutsche examined the social, cultural, economic and political history of early South African cinema as well as some of the significant technological advances.[1] Gutsche, however, approached the production of South African cinema as a historian of social and cultural institutions, rather than a film historian of artistic processes or from a concern with aesthetics of form.

Although producing significant studies on the representation of class and/or race in South African cinema, scholars such as Tomaselli (1989), Davis (1996) as well as Balseiro and Masilela (2003) were also more occupied with the social, cultural, economic and political histories of South African cinema before and during the apartheid years than artistic processes. As a result the artistic achievements of film directors, cinematographers, actors, art directors, composers, editors and other members of the production teams received little scholarly attention.

Recent attempts to rework the history of South African cinema such as Isabel Balseiro and Ntongela Masilela's edited volume, *To Change Reels: Film and Film Culture in South Africa* (2003) as well as Jacqueline Maingard's *South African National Cinema* (2007) devoted entire chapters to the ideological analysis of films such as *De Voortrekkers* (1916), *Cry, the Beloved Country* (1951) and *Come Back, Africa* (1959), but in the process they

Cry, the Beloved Country. Videovision

10

ignored the significant oeuvres of directors such as Ross Devenish, Manie van Rensburg, Jans Rautenbach, Katinka Heyns and Darrell Roodt as well as many of the directors of the 1980s. Surprisingly Heyns and Roodt, and other significant (and internationally acclaimed) post-apartheid directors such as Gavin Hood, Mark Dornford-May, Rehad Desai, Francois Verster, Ramadan Suleman, Madoda Ncayiyana, Craig Matthew, Craig and Damon Foster, Jack Lewis, Liz Fish and Ntshaveni Wa Luruli, are absent from the list of 25 film-makers and cultural leaders whom the American scholar Audrey Thomas McCluskey interviewed for her recent publication on post-apartheid cinema titled *The Devil You Dance With: Film Culture in the New South Africa* (2009).

The exciting revival of short-film-making in South African cinema since the 1980s has also received little attention by academic scholars. Among the above-mentioned books on South African film history only Botha (2007) and Maingard (2007: 157–66) focused on this very significant development in post-apartheid South African cinema. Hundreds of short fiction and non-fiction films have been made in South Africa since 1980. The themes of most of these films were initially limited to anti-apartheid texts, which were instruments in the anti-apartheid struggle (Botha 2009). During the late 1980s and early 1990s short-film-makers have also explored themes other than apartheid, for example, equal rights for gay and lesbian South Africans. Many short-film-makers have since 1994 experimented with form and aesthetics as well as various narrative structures, including oral storytelling. Future studies of post-apartheid cinema need to take the revival of short-film-making in South Africa into account. Exciting directorial voices such as Garth Meyer, Dumisani Phakhati, Willem Grobler, Teboho Mahlatsi, Justin Puren, Inger Smith, Johan Nel, Nina Mnaya and John Warner hold immense promise for future feature film-making in post-apartheid South Africa.

Among the decades of film escapism, racist films and government propaganda, South African cinema produced cinematic jewels. This monograph is an attempt to describe, contextualize and analyse the aesthetic highlights of South African cinema from 1896 to 2010 by focusing on the use of film form, style and genre.

Chapter 1 briefly chronicles the early history of South African cinema. Early projection devices were used around the Johannesburg goldfields from 1895 onwards. The first ever newsreels were filmed at the front during the Anglo-Boer War (1889–1902). As many as 43 films of good technical quality were made between 1916 and 1922 by I.W. Schlesinger's company, African Film Productions Ltd. In the 1930s the company was also responsible for features with sound, including the first Afrikaans-language productions. Schlesinger, however, was unable to secure a foothold in either the British or US markets for the screening of South African films.

Chapter 2 deals with a few independent British and American film-makers, such as Eric Rutherford, Donald Swanson and Lionel Rogoson, who attempted to make films about the black majority in apartheid South Africa. Film production, however, was still dominated by Schlesinger. A 30-year lull was broken in the 1950s by Jamie Uys, who succeeded in attracting Afrikaner-dominated capital for independent production. He was instrumental in persuading the Afrikaner Nationalist Party government to provide a subsidy for the making of local films. Indirectly this step led to the severe fragmentation of the country's film industry, the topic of Chapter 3.

In a nutshell, one could say that the apartheid policy together with the ineffective state-subsidized film structures contributed to the severe fragmentation of the South African film industry in the 1960s (Nathan 1991; Tomaselli 1989). Since 1956, when a regulated subsidy system was introduced, government and big businesses have collaborated to manipulate cinema in South Africa. Ideology and capital came together to create a national cinema that would reflect South Africa during the Verwoerdian regime of the 1960s. However, it was initially a cinema for whites only and predominantly Afrikaans. The white Afrikaans audience for the local cinema was relatively large and very stable, guaranteeing nearly every Afrikaans film a long enough run to break-even as long as it provided light entertainment and dealt with Afrikaner reality and beliefs (Davies 1989; Tomaselli 1989).

But for a few exceptions, the films were unremarkable. Fourie (1981) attributes this to the conservative attitude of contemporary Afrikaners towards the films. Afrikaners wanted their ideals visualized in these films. This idealistic conservatism was characterized by an attachment to the past, to ideals of linguistic and racial purity and to religious and moral norms. Homosexuality, for example, had no place in this world view. The films had to subscribe to these conservative and homophobic norms in order to be successful at the box office. The films seldom attempted to explore a national cultural psyche. As such, they were a closed form, made by Afrikaners for Afrikaners, with little or no attention to their potential to say something important about their society to an international audience. The type of realism that could have analyzed Afrikaner culture in a critical manner was avoided. Instead folk stereotypes that showed the Afrikaner as chatty, heart-warming and lovable in a comedy tradition, or as beset by emotional problems that had little to do with society but much to do with the mainsprings of western melodrama about mismatched couples overcoming obstacles on the path to true love, were employed (Blignaut & Botha 1992).

The films by Jans Rautenbach and Emil Nofal, namely *Die Kandidaat*, *Katrina* and *Jannie Totsiens*, were successful alternatives to the numerous Afrikaans escapism fare of the 1960s and early 1970s (Botha & Van Aswegen 1992). After the introduction of South African television in 1976, some Afrikaans film-makers such as Manie Van Rensburg made brilliant dramas and series for local television. In fact, Van Rensburg became a chronicler of the Afrikaner psyche in revisionist dramas such as *Verspeelde Lente, The Fourth Reich* and *Die Perdesmous*. The oeuvre of Rautenbach is discussed in Chapter 4, and the impressive work by Van Rensburg is examined in Chapter 5. The attempts of director Ross Devenish to make meaningful films about the socio-political realities of South Africa during the 1970s are analyzed in Chapter 6.

Another contributor to the fragmentation of South African film industry was the creation of a so-called *Bantu* film industry during the 1970s. This boost to films for black South Africans resulted in the making of a large number of shoddy films in Zulu, Sotho, Xhosa and other South African languages, and these films were screened in churches, schools and community and beer halls. It was contrary to government policy to allow black cinemas in the urban white areas, as this would have been tantamount to conceding citizenship to urban blacks. The urbanization of blacks was portrayed as uniformly negative and homeland life as more fitting (Gavshon 1983; Van Zyl 1985). At this stage, black and white audiences were treated differently. Audiences were separated each with its own set of rules and operations, films and cinemas. Any film that managed to be made reflecting in any way the South African society in turmoil was banned by the state, or received no distribution whatsoever, and thus did not qualify for any film subsidy. A true national film industry did not, therefore, develop through the *Bantu* film industry – only a few inferior paternalistic films for blacks were made, chiefly by whites. These developments are briefly discussed in Chapter 7.

During the mid-1980s the industry was further fragmented. By means of substantial tax concessions that made investing in film an attractive option, a boom occurred in the commercial industry (Accone 1990a; 1990b; Blignaut & Botha 1992; Powell 1990; Schoombie 1990; Silber 1990a; 1990b). Several hundred films were made, mostly inferior imitations of American genre films (Blignaut & Botha 1992). The majority of these tax-shelter films did not reflect any recognizable socio-political reality. At the end of the 1980s, the tax-shelter scheme collapsed and this industry was virtually wiped out. Developments during the 1980s are discussed in Chapters 8 and 9.

The history of film distribution in South Africa has sadly been one of racism and segregation (Tomaselli 1989). Only in 1985 did the distributors manage to desegregate some cinemas, and for the first time the existence and importance of the majority of South Africans, deprived both socially and economically of the chance to be part of a cinema-going public, were acknowledged.

Since the late 1970s and early 1980s a group of film and video producers who were not affiliated to the established film companies in the mainstream industry made films about the realities of the majority of South Africans (Botha & Van Aswegen 1992). Most of these were shown at film festivals, universities, church halls, trade union offices and in private homes of interested parties. The majority of the films experienced censorship problems during the state of emergency. The films had small budgets and were either financed by the producers themselves, by progressive organizations or with the assistance of the tax-benefit system of the 1980s (Tomaselli 1989). The films were chiefly the product of two groups that emerged jointly: a group of white university students opposed to apartheid and black workers who yearned for a film form using indigenous imagery that would portray their reality in South Africa and would give them a voice and space in local films. Chapter 9 examines some of these features and documentaries.

This remarkable process led to a mass movement of workers, students and members of youth, sport and church organizations who united in their opposition to apartheid. It also contributed to the formation of the Film and Allied Workers' Organisation (FAWO) in September 1988. One of the aims of FAWO was to unite all film-makers within South Africa to establish a democratic society (Currie 1989; Metz 1990).

Together with numerous documentaries, community videos and the rise of short fiction and animation film-making, full-length films such as *Mapantsula* marked the beginning of a new, critical South African cinema. Botha and Van Aswegen (1992) referred to this cinema as the alternative film movement of the 1980s. It is evident that this new cinema is based on audio-visual material that reflects the realities of the black majority. It constitutes a valid part of South Africa's national film industry. It is from these films that the symbols and iconography of a national film industry can be drawn, rather than from the diversions produced by the Afrikaans-language cinema of the 1970s, the *Bantu* film industry and the tax-shelter films discussed in Chapters 3 and 7.

An estimated 944 features were shot between 1979 and 1992 as well as nearly 998 documentaries and hundreds of short films and videos (Blignaut & Botha 1992). Although most of the features were of mediocre value, at least 20 remarkable local feature films were made. They included *Mapantsula* (which participated in the Un Certain Regard section at the Cannes Film Festival), *Marigolds in August* (a winner of two Silver Bears at Berlinale), *On the Wire*, the brilliant *The Road to Mecca* (which was highly applauded at film festivals in India and Canada), the interracial drama *Saturday Night at the Palace*, the Mannheim Jury prize winner *Shotdown*, the evocative Afrikaans dramas *Fiela se Kind* and *Die Storie van Klara Viljee*, Manie Van Rensburg's 4-hour director's cut of *The Fourth Reich* about Afrikaner nationalism and the Darrell Roodt trilogy (*Place of Weeping*, *The Stick* and *Jobman*). In the 1990s co-productions led to six local films receiving international attention: Darrell Roodt's *Sarafina!* and *Cry, the Beloved Country*; Elaine Proctor's *Friends*; Les Blair's *Jump the Gun*; Shyam Benegal's *The Making of the Mahatma*; and Katinka Heyns's *Paljas*.

Although apartheid was officially still in place during the making of films such as *Mapantsula*, *Jobman*, *On the Wire* and *The Stick*, these features, together with numerous community and resistance videos, became vital instruments in the anti-apartheid struggle. The exhibition and distribution of these films, especially the community videos and documentaries on the evils of apartheid were one great problem area. *Mapantsula* and *The Stick*, for example, were only unbanned after 1990, and *Jobman* has still not been commercially released in South Africa. Most of these films were screened at alternative venues like community halls, churches in the townships, selected progressive film festivals and even private homes.

These films can be described as progressive film texts in the sense that all of them are consciously critical of apartheid, either in a historical (*Fiela se Kind, Jobman*) or a more contemporary context (the South Africa of the 1980s in *Mapantsula*). They deal with the lives and struggle of people in a developing country and are mostly allied with the liberation movements for a non-racial South Africa.

Mapantsula is an example of local film-making that represents a voice of resistance, which echoes in the popular culture, and memory of the majority of South Africans. The existence and experience of township life was severely censored and withheld from the media before 1990. The workings of the Publication Control Act, coupled with the state of emergency and the regulations accompanying it, were just two of the more obvious means to achieve this media silence. Features such as *Mapantsula, Jobman* and *On the Wire* were a critical and necessary intervention in the representation of this usually hidden reality on South African screens. These films, like the short film *Come See the Bioscope*, try to recover popular memory. They deal with events which were conveniently left out in official South African history books or in a contemporary context in actuality programmes on national television. Therefore, they became guardians of popular memory within the socio-political process in South Africa.

A positive development during the early 1990s was the perception from all sectors of the South African film industry that cinema has a vital role to play in the forging of social cohesion and the process of democratization and development that so urgently needs to take place. In 1991 the Film and Broadcasting Forum (FBF) was established to address the challenges faced by the film industry. It was widely considered to be an important step in the consultation process that resulted in the creation of a single body during 1993, motivated by mutual interests. In composition, the FBF represented the widest possible cross-section of industry interests, from producers to directors, writers, actors, musicians, technicians, agents, managements and studios. It also included both progressive and more establishment-oriented groupings, some of which have hitherto not been overly co-operative. The creation of an environment in which its members could address strategic issues of common interest and discuss such strategies with the state, political parties, cultural groups, broadcasters, distributors, exhibitors and others was the FBF's prime objective. The main aim was the establishment and development of a representative South African film culture which would redress the political imbalance of the past to ensure equal access to film structures for all South Africans. From this consultative process, an interim consensus document emerged, which tried to address the restructuring of the local film industry.

This resulted in the creation of the Film and Broadcasting Steering Committee, in 1993, representing the eight major film organizations in local cinema. The Film and Broadcasting Steering Committee painstakingly worked on proposals for a South African Film Foundation for more than a year. The proposed structures were modelled on the French film structures in France and Burkina Faso. By mid-1994 the Film and Television Federation emerged from the Broadcasting and Film Steering Committee. This process is discussed in Chapter 10.

Another important development was the historic democratic elections of 1994. The year 1994 could also be regarded as a landmark for the South African film industry. A comprehensive study by the Human Sciences Research Council (HSRC) on the restructuring of the entire South African film industry was completed and forwarded to the newly formed Department of Arts, Culture, Science and Technology (DACST; see Botha et al. 1994). The 400-page report received widespread praise throughout the local film and television industry. The HSRC research team recommended that state aid to the local film industry should be administered by a statutory body referred to as the South African Film and Video Foundation (SAFVF). Commercial viability should not be the sole criterion for government support of locally made films. All types of films, including short films, should benefit, and a developmental fund should be used to support first-time film-makers from previously marginalized communities. A government-appointed task group extensively used this report in 1995 to draft the white paper regarding a post-apartheid film industry. The white paper was completed by 1996, and the National Film and Video Foundation Bill was accepted by the South African Parliament in 1997.

Chapters 11 and 12 focus on developments in post-apartheid cinema. Post-apartheid cinema in general is characterized by the emergence of new voices and a diversification of themes. The monograph concludes with the challenges faced by the South African film industry. Thanks to digital technology the post-apartheid cinema is currently enjoying a revival and substantial international acclaim. The industry, however, also faces major challenges. Despite the establishment of the National Film and Video Foundation (NFVF), local film-makers are still struggling to find funding for their work and, in many cases, an audience for their films.

A film industry or, in more ambitious terms, a national cinema is ultimately dependent on the number of people who are willing to pay for it. Without a paying audience, whether it is cinema, television, video or new media exhibition, there can be no industry to speak of. With a total population of approximately 49 million people South Africa has a tiny cinema-going audience, measured at approximately 5 million persons with a rapidly growing television-consuming public penetrating approximately 49% of the total number of South African households.

Audience development will become more and more crucial to build audiences for the post-apartheid cinema. South Africa's film industry has been held to ransom for decades by the developed markets' funding and exhibition models, content and distribution strengths and worldwide dominance of the Hollywood studios. It has been estimated that Hollywood product dominates 99% of screen time in South African cinemas. Local film-makers have to compete with films by independent American, British and Australian film-makers as well as films from the Middle East and Asia for the remaining 1%.

Other challenges facing the South African film industry are the inaccessible film exhibition sites that are outside the reach of the majority of South Africans, the limited concentration of theatres in metropolitan areas and the general lack of culturally specific, community-based film exhibition points and products. According to research by the NFVF, audience attendance at South African cinemas is decreasing at an alarming rate to the extent that exhibitors have had to close down cinemas, especially in townships. Some independent cinemas in townships have been converted to churches. Various factors contributing to this decline include the increase in the range of entertainment media, especially a wider range of television content, door price increases, unemployment, crime and a lack of effective marketing strategies.

Some theatrical distributors such as UIP (United International Pictures) owned by international studios merely serve as a 'courier service' between international studios and local exhibitors. They do not have a quota system for local content distribution and exhibition, and the rationale that informs their decision on whether to acquire and exhibit a product is based on the commercial viability of the product. Criteria used to determine viability is sometimes out of touch with South African and African realities, especially if one studies the cultural role of cinema within African communities. In this regard one could also look at the South Korean cinema regarding its struggle to fight American dominance. The unfair competition and massive marketing budgets of Hollywood's studio-backed film releases reduce the chances of South African box-office success at cinema level. The introduction of incentivized screen quotas for domestic and African film theatric releases thus becomes a necessary intervention. France and South Korea are important case studies in this regard.

Through audience development programmes South African distributors and exhibitors can ultimately create a demand for local content on the screen, video hire, video sell thru, pay TV, free TV and public broadcasters, both locally and internationally. There is a definite need for aggressive marketing of South African films in people's home communities and the generation of local media enthusiasm around promotion of local product. Local film journalists and critics are also to be encouraged to support South African films. It is a fragile film industry, especially in the face of globalization.

Note

1. Mangin (1998) also provides a documentation of advances in technological developments in southern African cinema from the 1940s to 1960s.

Chapter 1

Early South African cinema: 1895-1948

In order to understand the state of cinema in South Africa after the end of apartheid in 1994, one needs to contextualize the recent developments in our film industry against a brief history of film production during the colonial and apartheid years.[1] The South African film industry is one of the oldest in the world. The kinetoscope, invented by Thomas A. Edison, had reached Johannesburg by 4 April 1895, only six years after its introduction in New York (Gutsche 1972: 8). It was opened to the South African public on 19 April 1895.

Wow!

The first projected motion pictures were shown in May 1896 in South Africa at the Empire Palace of Varieties, which was managed by Edgar Hyman. Between 1896 and 1909 mainly British and American films reached many parts of South Africa by means of mobile bioscopes. The term 'bioscope' became the standard term for anything to do with moving pictures (Gutsche 1972: 27).

From 1896 to 1899 Hyman shot short non-fiction films for the Warwick Trading Company of London, many of which were shown in Johannesburg and throughout the world. These short films consisted mostly of images of Johannesburg taken from the front of a tram. Hyman also shot images of the then-president of the Transvaal Republic, Paul Kruger, leaving his home. The footage was sent to England to be processed and printed and was included in the Warwick Trading Company's catalogues. Other Hyman films of this period included *A Rickshaw Ride in Commissioner Street*, *The Cyanide Plant on the Crown Deep* and others. Hyman shot film footage wherever he went.

Two independent Boer republics at the time (Transvaal and Orange Free State) and two British colonies constituted the geographical area referred to as South Africa today. A fierce war between the British Empire and the two Boer states erupted after Cecil Rhodes came to know that the two sovereign republics were the owners of potentially the world's richest gold and diamond mines. The Anglo-Boer War or South African War (11 October 1899 to 31 May 1902) was systematically documented by various companies in Britain, including the Warwick Trading Company. Edgar Hyman served as its war correspondent (Gutsche 1972: 42). The nature of the military conflict, however, gave cameramen little or no opportunity to film anything other than troop movements or military installations (Barnes 1992). In this war there was no front line in the accepted sense, such as existed in the First World War. Military action consisted of brief and swift skirmishes of the type usually associated with modern guerrilla warfare. This situation made the actual conflict nearly impossible to film unless the camera person happened to be in the right place at the right time by chance. As a result film-makers in England began to produce reconstructions purporting to be based

Feast of the Uninvited. Garth Meyer, M-Net

on actual incidents in the South African War (Barnes 1992). The former head of the South African National Film, Video and Sound Archives, Johan de Lange (1991), produced a valuable catalogue of the films shot during the war period, indicating which films were 'real' and which mere reconstructions. The potential for propaganda was enormous. The traumatic memory of this war was to become an important theme in several post-apartheid productions such as Herman Binge's documentary *Scorched Earth* (2001), which examines the British concentration camp strategy during the war period, as well as director Katinka Heyns's *The Feast of the Uninvited* (2008). Both productions are discussed in Chapter 12.

Film historians consider *The Great Kimberley Diamond Robbery* (1910) to be the first feature to be produced in South Africa (Gutsche 1972). It was shot by the Springbok Film Company, which was based outside South Africa. The country was a British Dominion with General Louis Botha as prime minister. According to Thompson (2001) the population of the Union of South Africa included 4 million Africans, 300,000 'coloureds', 150,000 Indians and 1,275,000 whites. The film was the first of many to be produced by non-South African directors and companies during the 113-year history of South African cinema.[2]

The first permanent cinema was built in 1909 by Electric Theatres Limited in Durban, and it opened on 29 July 1909. In December 1909 another cinema was opened on the corner of Grey and Alice streets in Durban for 'non-white' audiences. Racial segregation, which was a reality of South African cinemas till 1985, was now part of the exhibition system. Over the next 5 years several film distribution companies built cinemas across the country, which led to serious competition (Gutsche 1972). By the end of the 1930s a widespread circuit of cinemas existed all over South Africa, including in small towns (Gutsche 1972: 256). Sadly, since the 1990s many of these venues have disappeared (Blignaut & Botha 1992), and currently exhibition sites are characterized by a limited concentration of theatres in metropolitan areas, especially in the form of multiplexes in shopping malls.

Isadore William Schlesinger and African film productions

By 1913, New York-born Isadore William Schlesinger brought all film distributors under the control of his company, African Theatres Trust Ltd. Schlesinger was born in 1877 and at the age of 17 sailed from the United States to South Africa. He arrived in 1894 practically penniless, and after various challenges he succeeded in establishing himself in the insurance business. From 1904 onwards he managed to become a significant figure in the insurance world (Gutsche 1972). Schlesinger developed massive investments in land and real estate. Although the first ever newsreels were filmed at the front during the Anglo-Boer War (1899–1902), Schlesinger started a tradition of newsreel production in the form of *The African Mirror*, the world's longest running newsreel (1913–1984). In the course of the next six decades *The African Mirror* captured current affairs in South Africa, but in a rather superficial manner, and from 1948 it was used as a propaganda tool to support the dominant practice of apartheid.

Schlesinger was also responsible for the building of extensive and substantial studios at Killarney, a suburb of Johannesburg and at that time located outside an urban milieu (Gutsche 1972). Several feature films, some of them epic in scope, were also made between 1916 and 1922 by Schlesinger's production company, African Film Productions Ltd. These films included *De Voortrekkers/Winning a Continent* (1916), *Allan Quartermain* (1919), *King Solomon's Mines* (1918) and *Symbol of Sacrifice* (1918). The financial success of African Film Productions Ltd, however, was largely contingent on the market outside South Africa. The country itself offered far too small a cinema-going public to guarantee anything but the production costs of a film (Gutsche 1972: 320). *The Blue Lagoon* (1923) marked the end of local fiction film production in the 1920s by Schlesinger's company because of the film's poor performance at the South African box office. Between 1910 and 1925 as many as 43 features were shot in South Africa.

De Voortrekkers (1916) has received substantial attention by various academic scholars (Davis 1996; Gutsche 1972; Hees 2003; Maingard 2007; Tomaselli 2006; Van Zyl 1980). This historical epic is based on the so-called Great Trek. A small group of white Afrikaner

Symbol of Sacrifice. M-Net

farmers of Dutch descent who were known as the Voortrekkers migrated from British rule at the Cape Colony during the 1830s.[3] Harold Shaw, producer for Vitagraph and London Films, was hired to direct the film and he came to the Union of South Africa, while an Afrikaner historian, Dr. Gustav Preller, wrote the script based on his interpretation of the events that had led to the Battle of Blood River, a clash between Voortrekkers and Zulu warriors in the nineteenth century. *De Voortrekkers* deals almost exclusively with the last years of the Voortrekker leader Piet Retief, who signed a land treaty with the Zulu King Dingaan. After the murder of Retief and his men by Dingaan's warriors, the Voortrekkers vowed to avenge Retief's death. They also vowed to commemorate the day of their victory over the Zulus. On 16 December 1838 the Battle of Blood River resulted in victory for the Voortrekkers under the leadership of Andries Pretorius. For more than 150 years the Day of the Covenant or Dingaan's Day was a religious public holiday in South Africa. Even after the 1994 democratic elections some white Afrikaner groups still celebrate it, and in many ways it is one of the foundations of Afrikaner nationalism.[4] According to Hees (2003), the screenwriter Gustav Preller created the popular image of the Great Trek by giving it a heroic,

De Voortrekkers. M-Net

mythical and even sacred dimension. Preller regarded the migration of the white farmers away from imperial control at the Cape Colony as an act of Afrikaner nation-building. In Preller's account the viewer experiences the conquest of black 'barbarism' by the noble forces of a white, Christian civilization (Hees 2003: 53).

De Voortrekkers created and sustained the myth of the Voortrekkers as the founding fathers of a new nation. The film also used black people to represent the negative qualities against which whiteness and real civilization are defined (Hees 2003: 55). Dingaan, for example, is presented as the archetypal savage ruler.

Preller insisted on absolute 'realism' in his account of the historical events. Attempts were made to ensure authenticity; for example, 20,000 assegais and other Zulu war paraphernalia, as well as 500 rifles from the period, were collected. As many as 40 wagons and costumes were specially made for the production (Gutsche 1972). From an artistic viewpoint the sheer logistics, as well as the art direction and costume design, are impressive. The script, however, reduced the Great Trek to a few scenes where Voortrekkers try to cross a river, the events in Dingaan's camp, the massacre of Voortrekkers at Weenen and the Battle of Blood River.

De Voortrekkers. M-Net

The first screening of *De Voortrekkers* took place on 16 December 1916 in Krugerdorp. General Louis Botha and an audience of Afrikaners greeted the film with 'wholehearted acclamation' (Gutsche 1972: 315). Subsequently the film was screened throughout the Union of South Africa to large audiences. 'Thence onwards the showing of *De Voortrekkers* on Dingaan's Day of every year became a national institution' (Gutsche 1972: 316).

For the next 43 years Schlesinger had the monopoly of film distribution from the Cape to the Zambezi. By 1930 Schlesinger owned African Consolidated Theatres Ltd and African Consolidated Films Ltd after having temporarily lost control of distribution when sound films were introduced in South Africa (Gutsche 1972).

The growth of Afrikaner nationalism and birth of the apartheid state

Sarie Marais, the first South African film with sound, was produced by African Film Productions Ltd in 1931, after which local films gained in popularity. *Sarie Marais* as well as *Moedertjie* (1931) heralded the beginning of a decade in which Afrikaner[5] nationalism would grow in Afrikaans-language films (Maingard 2007; Van Staden & Sevenhuysen 2009). *Sarie Marais* could be described as a featurette that tells the story of a Boer sent as

Sarie Marais. M-Net

prisoner of war to Ceylon. *Moedertjie* is based on a one-act play *In die Wagkamer/In the Waiting Room* by J. F. W. Grosskopf, a well-known playwright. The film was directed by Joseph Albrecht and featured the talented young actor Pierre De Wet. The plot is set in a waiting room at a railway station, where an Afrikaner couple is waiting for their son's arrival. When the son (played by De Wet) finally makes his appearance the viewer learns that he has been involved in crime. At the end of the film he commits suicide. *Moedertjie* has also received substantial academic attention (Maingard 2007). The portrayal of white, poor Afrikaners, their sometimes painful migration from family farms to the city and subsequent disintegration of the Afrikaner family during the 1930s are major themes in director Manie Van Rensburg's work, which will be discussed in Chapter 5.

A full-length propaganda film *They Built a Nation – Die Bou van 'n Nasie*, commissioned by the South African government, was released in 1938 as part of the Voortrekker Centenary Celebrations (Le Roux & Fourie 1982). The film was produced by Schlesinger's African Film Productions Ltd for the Publicity and Travel Department of the South African Railways, Harbours and Airways. The director Joseph Albrecht's *Die Bou van 'n Nasie* attempted to

Moedertjie. **M-Net**

depict the history of the white Afrikaner people and was made to be used as part of the celebration of the centenary of the Great Trek and the Battle of Blood River. The centenary included a re-enactment of the Great Trek, with ox wagons starting from Cape Town on a symbolic 800-mile journey to Pretoria. As was intended the event was a great outpouring of patriotic sentiment, with the political goal to celebrate white Afrikaner nationalism. The resulting mood of nationalistic euphoria provided much of the dynamism for the National Party election victory in 1948 on its apartheid platform (Hees 2003: 53). The narrative of *Die Bou van 'n Nasie* also includes a brief reference to the Anglo-Boer War, but nothing is said about the concentration camps and the death of over 26,000 Afrikaner women and their children. The film ends with artistic shots of South African farmers working on the fields. lyrical shots of farmers working on the fields of the Union of South Africa. It represents a pastoral beauty that would dominate Afrikaans cinema for the next few decades.

In July 1940 Afrikaner nationalists established a film production organization known as the Reddingsdaadbond-Amateur-Rolprent-Organisasie (RARO) (which, roughly translated, means Rescue Action League Amateur Film Organisation). As an alternative film industry, RARO objected to the Anglo-American cultural imperialism prevailing in

Die Bou van 'n Nasie. South African National Film & Video Archives

South Africa as a result of the showing of numerous overseas films.[6] South African cinema was almost completely dominated by films from the United States during the 1920s and 1930s (Gutsche 1972: 173).

Just as in the 1980s, when South Africans made alternative films to promote the struggle against the apartheid government (a resolution taken during the Culture and Resistance Conference in Gaborone, Botswana, in 1982), in the 1940s RARO saw promoting Afrikaner nationalism as one of its key functions. Dr. Hans Rompel led RARO, and in his book *Die bioskoop in die diens van die volk* (1942) he criticized the Anglo-American dominance on South African screens as a form of cultural imperialism. Rompel played a significant role – theoretically and production-wise – in the shaping of an alternative film industry that favoured Afrikaner nationalism (Eckardt 2005).

In 1939 RARO produced its first film, *'n Nasie hou Koers*. RARO films dealt with emotionally charged political events such as Dingaan's Day celebrations on 16 December. By 1940 *'n Nasie hou koers* had been shown 285 times in 144 venues to at least 50,000 people. Audiences grew larger when Afrikaner nationalism grew. During the 1940s, thus, Afrikaans-language films became politicized to promote Afrikaner nationalism.

Die Bou van 'n Nasie. South African National Film & Video Archives

The Afrikaner nationalists also set up an alternative film distribution network called Volksbioskope Maatskappy Beperk (People's Bioscopes or VOB). The aim was to distribute RARO films on 16mm. Ironically, however (given Hans Rompel's attacks on American and British cultural imperialists), VOB was ultimately forced to distribute Hollywood studio films to stay solvent (Gutsche 1972: 264). When the National Party came into power in 1948 there was no further role for RARO and Volksbioskope, and both ventures ceased to exist.

Another notable documentary of the 1930s was *The Golden Harvest of the Witwatersrand* (1939), which celebrated the mining industry in South Africa. It won a Special Mention Award at the 1939 Venice Film Festival. Only five features were shot during the 1930s. Eleven features constituted the total output of the 1940s until the National Party came into power in 1948.

By 1930 the Entertainments (Censorship) Bill had been introduced in South Africa. It was a lengthy document to

> regulate and control the public exhibition and advertisement of cinematograph films and of pictures and the performance of public entertainments and provided for the institution

of a national board of censors whose approval was necessary before any film or film advertisement could be publicly shown.

(Gutsche 1972: 298)

By 1934 amendments had been made to the bill to include the screening of films at the emerging film societies. It now covered all performances to which the South African public was admitted. Some films were also allowed for screening to white audiences only (Gutsche 1972: 303). Films considered blasphemous, indecent or obscene, or which were likely to be injurious to morality or to encourage or incite crime, became the target of the censors. Films that were likely to be offensive to the people of any friendly nation or the British Empire also ran the risk of being banned. It was the beginning of a repressive era in South African cinema, which would last till the early 1990s.

Notes

1. Publications by Gutsche (1972), Le Roux and Fourie (1992), Maingard (2007), Balseiro and Masilela (2003), Botha and Van Aswegen (1992), Blignaut and Botha (1992), Botha and Dethier (1997), Davis (1996), Louw and Botha (1993) and Tomaselli (1989) documented developments in South African cinema. A critical overview of the fragmentation of the South African film industry during apartheid is presented by Botha (1998b) in Schelfhout and Verstraeten's publication *De rol van de media in de multiculturele samenleving*, as well as in Botha (1997b, 2003a, 2004). The history of South African cinema is also chronicled in full-length documentaries and television series: Wayne Lines's *The Saga of the Silver Screen* (1987), Peter Davis's *In Darkest Hollywood: Cinema and Apartheid* (1993), Katinka Heyns's *Silwerdoekstories* (1994), Taryn da Canha's *Redefining the Griot: A history of South African documentary film* (2003), Neil Sandilands's *Impresario* (2010) and the kykNET TV series *Daar doer in die fliek* (2011).
2. Armes (2008) provides a list of all features shot in South Africa between 1909 and 2008. British directors such as Ken Annakin, Harry Watt, Cy Enfield, Val Guest, Don Chaffey, Peter Collinson, Peter Hunt and J. Lee Thompson made films in South Africa. Recent productions include Clint Eastwood's *Invictus* (2009).
3. A comprehensive biographical history of white Afrikaners has been written by Giliomee (2003).
4. See Giliomee (2003) for an in-depth discussion on Afrikaner nationalism.
5. Afrikaners refer to the Afrikaans-speaking white community in South Africa.
6. See Louw and Botha (1993).

Chapter 2

A few liberal voices in the 1950s

The reality of South African film-making was that in many ways black South Africans were excluded during the colonial and apartheid years. Black South Africans had no money to make films. They had no access to equipment. Opportunities were almost non-existent for black scriptwriters or directors to create their own images on the screen or to explore the socio-political realities of the country (Pichaske 2007; 2009). Though cinema was introduced to South Africa in 1896, films were not screened in 'black' townships or rural areas for decades. In fact, 40 years later, there remained only four 'black' cinema halls in the whole of South Africa. There were a small number of community film programmes, which were organized by missionaries and philanthropists in co-operation with the mining industry for the purpose of moralizing the leisure time of Africans (Balseiro & Masilela 2003). And apartheid policy led to a very fragmented film industry (Botha 2004). It was left to a very few white independent film-makers between 1948 and 1950 to examine the socio-political realities of South Africa under apartheid in a critical manner. A small number of individuals should be noted for their contributions to the local film industry. They attempted to move beyond an exclusive cinema for only white audiences.

Eric Rutherford, Donald Swanson and Tim Spring

Schlesinger's African Film Productions Ltd had secured a monopoly of the production of English language films till the late 1940s. Into this situation stepped Eric Rutherford and Donald Swanson, two Britons who had been working in southern Africa for the Rank Organisation of Britain. They were outsiders, people not brought up in the stifling racial atmosphere of South Africa. Their first film, *African Jim – Jim Comes to Jo'burg* (1949), became a landmark in South African cinema. Influenced by Italian neorealism and post-war British cinema it used ordinary black South Africans in everyday situations and in actual locations. It also celebrated the talent of black South Africans such as Dolly Rathebe on the screen, talents which had been ignored by local film-makers for decades up to the 1950s. Rathebe only returned to the South African screen in 1988 for her moving performance in *Mapantsula* (1988) (see Chapter 8).

Swanson's *The Magic Garden* (1950) is a classic chase story, a hunt for a thief and stolen money. The film involved the technical expertise of one of South African cinema's veteran film-makers, Tim Spring, who has enjoyed a professional career in the film industry for more than 50 years. A versatile craftsman Spring was born in Liverpool on 20 September 1932.

Come Back Africa. Michael Rogosin

He matriculated in Johannesburg and started to work in theatre and film, simultaneously, as camera assistant on set and lighting assistant on stage. He served as camera assistant and then editing assistant for the production of *The Magic Garden*, which was shot in Alexandra township with an all-black cast, starring Dolly Rathebe and Tommy Ramokgopa. Spring worked in a facilities house for 5 years, which involved everything from lab work, negative cutting, track laying and sound mixing to title shooting.

Spring photographed and edited about 20 episodes of the game series *The Michaels in Africa*, shown on US television in the 1950s and 1960s, becoming very wise in the ins and outs of animal photography. This knowledge came in handy when he directed the feature *Catch Me a Dream* (1974), about two 11-year-old children and a cheetah, and when doing the animal photography for *The Last Lion*, with Jack Hawkins, in 1969. To Spring, this meant working on foot with a pride of five lions for 6 months.

Spring started his own production company in Harare, Zimbabwe (then Rhodesia), in the sixties, working in a variety of areas from commercials to religious features via documentaries. In 1968 he joined Kavalier Films, a feature film production company, in South Africa as sound editor and then went on to become the editor and then one of the directors working for the company. Spring returned to television and joined SCY Productions when the company closed in 1979. Over the next 13 years, he directed about 16 television drama series with the occasional feature (e.g. *Reason to Die*, 1989), winning two best director awards[1] and receiving several nominations (Blignaut & Botha 1992).

Spring spent early to mid-nineties in Los Angeles, which for him was an intense learning period, during which he finally learnt the nuances of script writing. After returning to South Africa, he worked for M-Net New Directions, an initiative to discover new writing and directing talent in films all over Africa, and then finance the production of the best of these entries. He was part of a panel that judge new directors and writers. In 1999 he produced two New Directions short films in South Africa and over the next 4 years line-produced and mentored four 30-minute drama films in Nigeria. In addition to M-Net New Directions he has conducted writing and directing workshops throughout South Africa and other African countries (Nigeria, Ghana, Zimbabwe, Senegal and Zanzibar).

Concurrent with this, Spring has given feature directing courses at the community film school, Newtown Film school, as well as invitation lectures at Allenby Film School in South Africa and ITPAN (the training school of the Independent Television Producers Association of Nigeria). While in Johannesburg he was a judge for the Avanti awards, and after relocating to Cape Town he was appointed judge for the National Television and Video Association (NTVA) awards. In 2001 Spring was made part of an advisory panel appointed to assist the NFVF of South Africa in evaluating film-funding applications. (The NFVF is discussed in Chapter 10.) Currently he nurtures directing students at the CityVarsity School of Media and Creative Arts in Cape Town.

Zoltan Korda and Lionel Ngakane

Attempts at socio-political film-making, which would include black South Africans, were represented by Zoltan Korda's *Cry, the Beloved Country* (1951), which was based on the book by Alan Paton. The film depicts the social and moral degradation of black South Africans in a way never done before.[2] The film introduced the talents of one of the pioneers of African cinema, Lionel Ngakane (1920–2003), who rendered a superb performance in his first acting role. With no further prospects in South Africa after that film, Ngakane left for the United Kingdom and was in exile until he was able to return to his home country in 1993.

Ngakane was born on 17 July 1920 and educated at Fort Hare University College in the Eastern Cape of South Africa as well as at the University of the Witwatersrand. From 1948 to 1950 he worked for *Zonk* and *Drum* magazines. He entered the film industry in 1950 as director Zoltan Korda's assistant on *Cry, the Beloved Country*.

Between 1951 and 1980, while living in the United Kingdom, he acted in several films as well as theatre and television productions. He also participated in several radio dramas. He appeared, for example, in dramas such as *Mark the Hawk* (1957), *Two Gentlemen Sharing*

(1969) and *The Squeeze* (1977). At that point he earned his basic living by running an antique shop in London's Portobello Road.

Ngakane received international acclaim for his short film *Jemima and Johnny* (1966), which was inspired by riots in Notting Hill. It portrays the political tensions of the time in the story of a friendship between a white boy and a black girl. It received an award at the Venice Film Festival.

Ngakane travelled and lived in many African countries when he was in self-exile, during which time he made documentary films in Nigeria, Liberia and the Ivory Coast. In 1977 he took over as director of Golden Baobab Entertainment in Senegal, heading its film department. Ngakane later also directed documentaries about apartheid and African development. He was elected honorary president and regional secretary for southern Africa of the Pan-African Federation of Film-Makers (FEPACI), of which he was one of the founding members. He was a consultant on *A Dry White Season* (1989). He was also member of several international juries for recognized film festivals like Carthage in Tunisia, Leipzig, Edinburgh and Amsterdam.

Back in South Africa during the 1990s Ngakane advised on the development of township cinemas and was part of the working group of the Film Development Strategy of the DACST. The objective of the group was to formulate policy for a post-apartheid film industry. In 1997 Ngakane received an honorary doctorate from the University of Natal. He also served on the M-Net All African Awards film competition panels as well as in an advisory capacity for the M-Net New Direction series.

He finally served on the inaugural Council of the National Film and Video Foundation of South Africa between 1999 and 2003. The NFVF established a Dr. Lionel Ngakane Scholarship Fund with an annual pledge of R1 million. He was also a board member of the Film Resource Unit, a community-based distribution agency, and served in various other film industry bodies until the time of his death. In 2003 the Cape Town World Cinema Festival awarded the Lionel Ngakane Award to the most promising film-maker in the festival competition. Ngakane died on 26 November 2003. He was 76 years old.

Lionel Rogosin

By the end of the 1950s and the first decade of the National Party Government most of the worst laws of mandatory separation had been passed – regulating education, sexual relationships, work, living space and, in fact, virtually on every area of human activity – on the basis of race. The independent New York film-maker Lionel Rogosin's *Come Back, Africa* (1959), the first local film to be made covertly, tells the story of a black man, Zacharia, who gets trapped in the classic South African situation: A migrant worker without skills looking for a job where he has no right to work. The film is a seminal work on the conditions of blacks under apartheid.[3]

Rogosin was part of the so-called New American Cinema Group, which included Shirley Clarke, Emile de Antonio, Morris Engel and Adolfas Mekas. He was a pioneer of docudramas, which examined themes such as exploitation and racism. His work was socially conscious. He placed non-professional actors within their natural environments and requested them simply to perform their daily activities without trying to 'act' for the camera. Rogosin was hugely influenced by Italian neorealism.

Owing his concern about the inhumanity of the apartheid system, which reminded him of fascism, Rogosin decided to direct *Come Back, Africa* (Davis 2004). When he arrived in South Africa in May 1957 Rogosin was confronted with the high treason trials of 156 members of the African National Congress, including Nelson Mandela. Rogosin made contact with writers from *Drum* magazine, namely Can Themba, Bloke Modisane and Lewis Nkosi. Rogosin gained the respect of these writers because he was willing to listen. He wanted to tell a simple story from the perspective of a black South African: How did blacks experience life in the apartheid state, for example, memories of pain and humiliation. The film was born of the exchange of ideas between Rogosin, Nkosi and Modisane.

Rogosin shot the film in Sophiatown on the eve of the demolishment of the township by the apartheid's state machinery. In the process the film became the most detailed audio-visual document of daily life in Sophiatown. It was one of the first South African films to give a voice to the black majority. Though not strictly a documentary (the film blends a fictional narrative with improvized documentary footage), it is often cited as one of the first resistance documentaries to be produced in South Africa. Wanting to create an authentic, inside look at black South African existence, rather than a 'shallow Hollywood film', Rogosin spent a year in South Africa prior to filming and hired Nkosi and Modisane to write the script and act in the film (Balseiro & Masilelo 2003; Pichaske 2009; Tomaselli 1989).

This collaboration, along with the use of non-professional actors, improvized dialogue and documentary footage and helped create one of the first films ever to provide an authentic look at black South African life under apartheid. This is exemplified in the well-known shebeen scene in which a group of black intellectuals freely discuss their views on white South Africans and their denial of black intelligence. The language and acting in the scene bear a unique mark of authenticity – in part because the actors themselves are members of the black intellectual set and the heavily improvized dialogue is based on their own thoughts and experiences. Rogosin's attempt demonstrated that by democratizing the production process and collaborating with insiders, even an outsider like himself could make a groundbreaking authentic and important South African film (Pichaske 2009).

Come Back, Africa might have provided a useful model for future South African documentary film-makers to follow had it not been virtually impossible for them to do so. For whites and blacks to collaborate in creating anti-government films during the 1950s and 1960s would not only have been dangerous but also extremely difficult to fund because state subsidies (see Chapter 3) were the only readily available sources of funding. South Africa lacked the mechanisms for supporting independent film-makers that would have been found in other countries in the form of grant-making organizations, broadcaster support

or formal training (Pichaske 2009). Thus, documentary film-makers and their products remained bound by the restrictions of the apartheid state, and the opportunity for white directors to benefit from black input and collaboration remained limited.

Rogosin passed away in December 2000.

Notes

1. Spring won a Star Tonight Award for Best Youth Television programme for *Abafama Bezicathulo Ezinamasondo* (1984) and *Umhlobo Wenene* (1988).
2. Maingard (2007) and Davis (1996) provide an analysis of the film with regard to the representation of race and/or racial identity.
3. Peter Davis's publication (2004) on the making of *Come Back, Africa* is a brilliant documentation of the problems faced by Rogosin to shoot the film in apartheid South Africa.

Chapter 3

Pierre de Wet, Jamie Uys and Afrikaans cinema in the 1950S and 1960s

A total of 35 features were made during the 1950s. Two directors, Pierre de Wet and Jamie Uys, played a significant role, especially commercially, at the outset of an era of cinematic escapism for mainly white Afrikaans-speaking audiences. There were, however, Afrikaans-language films, which also explored the identity of Afrikaner whites and their socio-political realities in more depth than before. Pierre de Wet's *Geboortegrond* (1946) examined the reality of poverty and patriarchy in an Afrikaner family in the form of social melodrama. Once again Schlesinger's African Film Productions Ltd was the production company. The story is about a son who is treated almost like a slave by his father on their farm. Eventually he leaves, but his girlfriend convinces him to return to the farm, his place of birth.

Most of De Wet's oeuvre during the 1950s, however, served as a vehicle for the comic genius of actor Al Debbo and his acting partner Frederik Burgers. De Wet's work varies from the first South African musical *Kom Saam Vanaand* (1949) to local comedies such as *Altyd in My Drome* (1952), *Fratse in die Vloot* (1958) and *Piet se Tante* (1959). The white Afrikaans audience for this local cinema was relatively large and very stable, guaranteeing nearly every Afrikaans-language film a long enough run to break even as long as it provided light entertainment, basically escapism, and dealt with Afrikaner reality and beliefs in an idealist way. It meant that Afrikaners wanted their ideals visualized in these films. This idealistic conservatism was characterized by an attachment to the past, to ideals of linguistic and racial purity and to religious and moral norms. Many of the Afrikaans-language films of 1940s and 1950s, although sometimes melodramatic or comic, were also covertly nationalist, enhancing the culture of an increasingly dominant Afrikaans influence in filming (Fourie 1981; Greig 1980; Tomaselli 1989; Van Staden & Sevenhuysen 2009).

Afrikaans cinema during the late 1940s and 1950s was also a vehicle for many stage actors who were later to become known as some of the acting pioneers in South African cinema, for example, André Huguenet, Wena Naudé, Gert Van den Bergh, Siegfried Mynhardt, Anna Cloete and Patrick Mynhardt (Le Roux & Van Zyl 1982). A notable example of the influence of Afrikaans theatre on film production is *Hans die Skipper* (1953), which in a visually elegant manner explored the patriarchal nature of Afrikaner culture by telling the story of a conflict between father and son in a small fishing community. Based on a novel by D.F. Malherbe the film was directed by Bladon Peake for Schlesinger's African Film Productions Ltd. Like many Afrikaans-language films of 1930s and 1940s the film is characterized by a strong theatrical approach to the subject matter. Well-known actors from Afrikaans stage drama, including André Huguenet and Wena Naudé, played major roles in the film, which

Hans die Skipper. M-Net

added to the theatrical style of acting. Cinematically the film consisted of beautiful black and white compositions by cinematographer David Millin, an important innovator in the film industry of 1950s and 1960s, especially with regard to the use of cinemascope and other technological advances.

Millin's greatest achievement was *Majuba* (1968), an epic reconstruction of the Battle of Majuba, which took place between British and Boer forces in February 1881. On an artistic level the film is impressive. The cinemascope images of landscapes and various battles together with excellent art direction and costume design by Ruth St Moritz and Angela Berry did full justice to the epic grandeur. Millin's script, based on Stuart Cloete's novel *Hill of Doves*, chronicles the conflict between the two sides in a nuanced manner by providing different viewpoints. It enhanced empathy for both Boer and British soldiers. Unfortunately, like many Afrikaans features since 1931, the acting by several great names, including Siegfried Mynhardt, Patrick Mynhardt, Tromp Terre-Blanche and Anna Neethling-Pohl, still reflected the influence of Afrikaans theatre on local film-making. The approach is theatrical. Ultimately *Majuba* was a romanticized version of a historical event.

Majuba. M-Net

Jamie Uys

In the 1950s Jamie Uys began to make a name as an independent film-maker with *Daar doer in die Bosveld* (1951), the first South African feature shot in colour. Uys was basically producer, scriptwriter, director, photographer and lead actor in films such as *Fifty/Vyftig* (1953), *Daar doer in die Stad* (1954) and *Geld soos Bossies* (1955). In several productions he fulfilled the roles of lead actor, director, scriptwriter, cinematographer, art director, editor and sound editor (Tomaselli 1992). As an auteur he received international acclaim for his work, for example, the 1981 Grand Prix at the Festival International du Film de Comedy Vevey for *The Gods Must Be Crazy* (1980). In 1974 he became the first South African director to receive the Hollywood Foreign Press Association's Golden Globe Award for best documentary for *Beautiful People*.

Jacobus Johannes Uys (30 May 1921 to 29 January 1996), better known as Jamie Uys, directed 24 films in total. In 1964 he established Jamie Uys Film Productions, which later became Kavalier Films. He left the company in 1966 to make films for Mimosa Films till the end of his career.

Daar Doer in die Bosveld. M-Net

In *Daar doer in die Bosveld* (1951) Uys already created some of the characteristics of his later work: an ultra-shy, rural-based protagonist who is trying in a socially awkward way to impress an urban heroine; the evocative use of rural landscapes; and unlike previous Afrikaans features, the use of minimal dialogue to tell a story more visually. The shy protagonist featured in later works such as Emil Nofal's *Rip van Wyk* (1960), Uys's *Die Professor en die Prikkelpop/The Professor and the Beauty Queen* (1967) and *The Gods Must Be Crazy* (1980).

After marriage Jamie Uys moved to his father-in-law's farm on the Palala River in the former Northern Transvaal. His love of the wild had an important impact on his films, especially in *Daar doer in die Bosveld* (1951), *Dirkie* (1969), *Beautiful People* (1974) and *The Gods Must Be Crazy* (1980). In the last three features he used evocative images of the Namib and/or Kalahari deserts. *Dirkie/Lost in the Desert* tells the survival story of 8-year-old Dirkie in the desert after a plane crash, whilst his father is trying desperately to find him. Uys played the part of the father. His son Wynand was cast as Dirkie. The desert landscape is represented from the child's perspective; thus it is dangerous but also evocative. Pastoral beauty, which has been a part of Afrikaans cinema since the 1930s, is a strong element of *Beautiful People* (1974), a labour of love for Uys. For more than 4 years, travelling over 160,000 kilometres, he shot unusual images of wildlife in the Namib and Kalahari deserts and edited 80 hours of footage with the then linear technology of the era into a love letter to the region by combining classical music (e.g. Tchaikovsky's *Waltz of the Flowers*) with stunning landscape frescos. Clearly not intended as an in-depth documentary on wildlife in the region, *Beautiful People* succeeds more as an impressionistic kaleidoscope of images of animals and landscapes. It treats animals as stereotypes by drawing similarities between their behaviour and that of humans. Towards the end of the film Uys created an impressive montage of scenes of devastation to wildlife in the Kalahari Desert when he presents a lake that suddenly dries up and young pelicans, yet unable to fly, start a death march on the desolated plains to look for water. When relief finally comes in the form of a thunderstorm nature rejoices in quite a brilliant montage of animal movements and classical music (Carl Maria von Weber's *Invitation to the Dance*, orchestrated by Hector Berlioz).

Several of his earlier work have dealt in a satirical manner with 'conflicts' between Afrikaans- and English-speaking whites, between so-called 'Boers' and 'Britons': *Fifty/Vyftig* (1953), *Hans en die Rooinek* (1961) and *Lord Oom Piet* (1962). It became a comedic formula of Boer–Briton rivalry. These films based their humour on white ethnic difference, political rivalry and poked fun at English/Afrikaner intercultural taboos of the time (Tomaselli 1992).

Dingaka (1964) was Uys's first international breakthrough. Starring Stanley Baker as a lawyer and Juliet Prowse as his love interest the film attempts to be an examination of the conflict between tribal and colonial laws. When his child is murdered, Ntuku Makwena (played by Ken Gampu) avenges her death, following tribal laws. As a result Makwena himself is tried – but under the government's statutes. Once again the images of landscapes are quite impressive.

Hans en die Rooinek. M-Net

The Gods Must Be Crazy turned out to be Uys's biggest international success. Featuring a bushman called N!xau as the main protagonist, the slapstick comedy deals with a Coke bottle that was thrown out of an aeroplane. It fell in the Kalahari Desert and was found by a San tribe. Since the bottle was the only modern artefact in their world, they started to argue about whom should own the object. Finally it was decided that the bottle needs to be returned to the gods, who must have sent it there in the first place. N!xau was given the task to return it. The film enjoyed substantial commercial success in the United States, Japan, Europe as well as other regions. Initially the film rights were sold to 45 countries. A commercially less successful sequel, *The Gods Must Be Crazy II* followed in 1989. By the 1970s and 1980s Uys's work was either applauded nationally and internationally for the comic entertainment or condemned by many scholars on ideological grounds. Tomaselli (1992), for example, argued that Jamie Uys' films were 'used by Afrikaner intellectuals and Afrikaner-dominated capital to affirm cultural perspectives of the emerging Afrikaner petty bourgeoisie of the 1960s and '70s' (p. 193). According to Tomaselli the ethnic and political discourses of Uys's later films (1974–89) framed apartheid mythology.

Dingaka. M-Net

Funny People became another international and South African commercial success in 1976. It is a slapstick comedy in the same genre as *Candid Camera* in the United States. Uys creates humour by putting unsuspecting people in embarrassing situations. Its commercial success in South Africa led to many imitations by various film-makers including comedian Leon Schuster, for example, *You Must Be Joking!* (1986) and *Schuks Tshabalala's Survival Guide to South Africa 2010* (2010).

Jamie Uys died of a heart attack in 1996 at the age of 74.

The impact of the subsidy scheme

During the 1950s Hollywood's Twentieth Century Fox decided to become directly involved in South Africa. In 1956 they bought out the Schlesinger Empire. Between 1956 and 1969 Twentieth Century Fox controlled more than three-quarters of the South African film distribution network. One of the few independent film distributors outside the Twentieth

Century Fox network was the Pretoria-based Wonderboom Inry Beleggings (Wonderboom Drive-In Investments or WIB).[1] WIB developed into Ster Film Imports, which was financed by the insurance company Sanlam. During the 1960s Ster Films built three major film theatre complexes. By 1969 Sanlam bought out Twentieth Century Fox. This they merged with Ster Films to form Satbel (the Suid-Afrikaanse Teaterbelange Beperk or South African Theatre Interests Ltd). At that stage Satbel controlled 76% of South Africa's film distribution network. The other 24% was controlled by UIP-Warner. Afrikaner capital, thus, became a significant factor in the film industry when Sanlam acquired this major interest in Ster Films, a distribution company with the explicit intention to provide cinema predominantly for white Afrikaner patrons. By 1969 the financing, production and distribution of films in South Africa were now virtually in the hands of one large company.

It was the height of apartheid under Prime Minister Hendrik Verwoerd. In the early 1960s while the film industry was producing musicals, adventure stories, comedies, romantic war films and films about South African wildlife, the country was experiencing a stormy socio-political era. The large-scale opposition to apartheid legislation took on tragic dimensions on 21 March 1960 when at Sharpeville 69 people were shot dead, many in their backs, and 180 were wounded. A state of emergency was declared and over 11500 people were detained. On 8 April 1960 the African National Congress (ANC) was proclaimed a legally banned organization.

The run-up to a referendum to decide whether South Africa should become a republic was marked by internal political unrest and strong international criticism from abroad. On 31 May 1961 the Republic of South Africa was born. Black opposition became the order of the day; underground movements, including Umkonto We Sizwe, planned campaigns of sabotage. The main targets were petrol depots, power lines, government buildings, railway lines and communication networks. In 1963 the organizations were disbanded by the police and the leaders of Umkonto We Sizwe, including Nelson Mandela, were sentenced to life imprisonment. No example of a major film made locally reflects the traumatic events of this period.

It was the beginning of a highly fragmented South African industry with virtually no national film identity. The reason for this fragmentation and lack of identity is multifaceted, each facet interacting to produce a complicated set of associations and relationships (Botha & Van Aswegen 1992). Various academic scholars, such as Prof. Pieter Fourie of the University of South Africa (Fourie 1981), Prof. Keyan Tomaselli (Tomaselli 1989) and Prof. John Van Zyl (Van Zyl 1985), as well as research teams such as the Film and Allied Workers' Organisation's Film Commission (during the early 1990s) spent time in identifying and analyzing the ills of the South African film industry. Although their research suggests divergent reasons and although they would probably not offer a unified vision of the direction that the South African film industry should take in future, their work gives a significant and comprehensive picture of the predicament of the film industry. It is important, however, to note that the various theoretical and ideological methods and approaches of these researchers differ to a greater or lesser degree and thus influence their specific perception of South African cinema. Fourie (1981) approaches the subject from a structural and functional viewpoint, although he also stresses sociological factors. Tomaselli (1989) views the film medium as an ideological instrument to be used for social change, and his analysis is based on political economy. Van Zyl (1985) considers the film medium in a critical theoretical context and stresses the possible affiliation of the South African film industry with those in other African countries. Three books were published during the late 1980s and early 1990s which addressed the problems of the South African film industry (Blignaut & Botha 1992; Botha & Van Aswegen 1992; Tomaselli 1989).

In a nutshell, one could say that the apartheid policy, as well as ineffective state-subsidized film structures, contributed to the severe fragmentation of the South African film industry (Nathan 1991; Tomaselli 1989). Since the introduction of a regulated subsidy system in 1956, the Nationalist government and big business collaborated to manipulate local film-making. Ideology and capital came together to create a national cinema that would reflect South Africa during the Verwoerdian regime of the 1960s. However, it was initially a cinema for whites only and predominantly Afrikaans. Of the 60 films made between 1956 and 1962, 43 were in Afrikaans. Four were bilingual and the remaining thirteen were English (Botha & Van Aswegen 1992). The subsidy system only rewarded box-office success. Only when a film had earned a specific amount of money at the box office did it qualify for subsidy, which paid back a percentage of costs. This percentage was initially higher for Afrikaans-language films than for English productions. Evidently the Verwoerdian government realized the potential influence this Afrikaner-dominated industry would have on the growth and spread of the Afrikaans language and in strengthening the dominant culture.[2] Armes (2008) estimates that between 1930 and 2008 as many as 275 Afrikaans-language features were made and that the majority of these films were shot in the 1960s and 1970s thanks to the so-called Subsidy Scheme.

As in the 1950s the white Afrikaans audience for the Afrikaans-language cinema was relatively large and very stable, guaranteeing nearly every Afrikaans film a long enough run to break even as long as it provided light entertainment and dealt with Afrikaner reality and beliefs (Davies 1989).

With the exceptions of those by Jans Rautenbach and Manie Van Rensburg (who will be discussed in Chapters 4 and 5), many Afrikaans-language films of the 1960s and 1970s were unremarkable from an aesthetic viewpoint (Botha 1996). Fourie (1981) attributes this to the conservative attitude of Afrikaners towards the films during the 1950s and 1960s. Afrikaners wanted their ideals visualized in these films. This idealistic conservatism was characterized by an attachment to the (pastoral) past, to ideals of linguistic and racial purity and to religious and moral norms. The films had to subscribe to these conservative expectations in order to be successful at the box office. The films seldom attempted to explore a national cultural psyche. As such, they were a closed form, made by Afrikaners for Afrikaners, with little or no attention to their potential to say something important about their society to an international audience. The type of realism that could have analyzed Afrikaner culture in a critical manner was avoided. Instead use was made of folk stereotypes that showed the Afrikaner as chatty, heart-warming and lovable in a comedy tradition or as beset by emotional problems that had little to do with society but much to do with the mainsprings of western melodrama about mismatched couples overcoming obstacles on the path to true love (Botha & Van Aswegen 1992; Pretorius 1992). These films ignored the socio-political turmoil as well as the realities experienced by black South Africans (Botha 1996).

Fourie (1982) argued that most Afrikaans films communicated by means of obsolete symbols that had little multicultural communication value. They painted a one-sided and stereotypical portrait of the Afrikaner, leading to a misconception about who and what the Afrikaner was. Furthermore, the negative portrayal of blacks as a servant class in these films is a visual symbol of the deep-seated apartheid ideology. A few attempts, however, were made to address socially taboo subjects. Elmo de Witt's *Debbie* (1965), dealing with premarital sex and the difficult circumstances faced by a pregnant teenager, not only touched on a sensitive issue of the sixties but also emphasized the inadequacy of the outdated censorship system of the Publications Board, which initially restricted the film to audiences older than 21 years (Louw & Botha 1993: 165; Tomaselli 1989).

Another contributor to the fragmentation of the South African film industry was the creation of so-called *Bantu* film production during the 1970s. From 1974 to 1990 almost 250 features were produced under the so-called B scheme for black South African audiences (Armes 2008). This boost to 'black' films resulted in a large number of shoddy films in South African languages such as Zulu, Xhosa and Sotho that were screened in churches, schools and community beer halls. It was contrary to government policy to allow black cinemas in the urban 'white' areas, as this would concede the citizenship of urban blacks. The urbanization of blacks was portrayed as uniformly negative and homeland life as more fitting (Gavshon 1983; Van Zyl 1985).

From 1948 to 1980s black and white audiences were treated differently. They were separated, each with their own set of rules and operations, films and theatres. Any film that managed to be made that in any way reflected the South African society in turmoil was banned by the state, or received no distribution whatsoever, and thus did not qualify for any film subsidy. A true national film industry, therefore, did not develop through the *Bantu* attempt – only a few hundred inferior paternalistic films for blacks were made, chiefly by whites (see Chapter 7).

During the mid-1980s the South African film industry was further fragmented. By means of substantial tax concessions that made investing in films an attractive option, a boom occurred in the film industry (Accone 1990a; 1990b; Blignaut & Botha 1992; Powell 1990; Schoombie 1990; Silber 1990a; 1990b). Several hundreds of films were produced, mostly inferior imitations of American genre films (Armes 2008; Blignaut & Botha 1992; Tomaselli 1989). The majority of these tax shelter films did not reflect any recognizable socio-political reality or national film culture. At the end of the 1980s, the scheme collapsed. Chapter 8 deals with these developments.

Although a state subsidy for fiction feature films has been available between 1956 and 1995, no money was granted to documentary films other than propaganda films made by the National Film Board (NFB). Although the South African government of the 1950s consulted John Grierson of Canada's National Film Board regarding the establishment of a national film board for South Africa, his recommendations for experimentation within film to stimulate a truly national cinema and the democratic process were basically ignored. Ten years after he submitted his report in 1954, the NFB was established. It functioned primarily as a production and distribution facility for the apartheid government's National Party (NP) propaganda (Tomaselli 2006). The outfit was finally dismantled in 1979.

Documentaries such as *Anatomy of Apartheid* (1964) attempted to defend apartheid policy. Produced by the NFB in 1964, its goal was to paint a benevolent picture of apartheid by illustrating all the ways in which the state provided assistance to blacks with housing and social services. The film includes many images of black South Africans receiving such assistance; yet none of these subjects has a voice in the film. Rather, a white omniscient voice-over speaks for them. Another problematic characteristic illustrated by this film is the almost non-existent relationship between the film-maker and subject (Pichaske 2009). Antony Thomas, a young film-maker at the time, would later concede that he knew little of the realities of black South Africans when he made the film. Such was often the case when white film-makers documented black subjects in apartheid South Africa. The total disconnection between black and white worlds virtually ensured that no white film-maker would be qualified to accurately represent black subjects. And the didactic, propagandistic approaches that dominated the medium helped ensure that subjects would not have the opportunity to speak for themselves (Pichaske 2009: 113).

South African film production was dominated by male directors until 1962. A breakthrough came in 1962 with the neo-noir thriller *Man in die Donker* by director Truida Pohl. During the 113-year history of South African cinema only a few female directors managed to make features (Diana Ginsberg, Anna Neethling-Pohl, Marie du Toit, Louise Smit, Katinka Heyns, Elaine Proctor, Helena Noguiera, Jean Stewart, Stefanie Sycholt, Amanda Lane, Meg Rickards, Claire Angelique, Minky Schlesinger and Jann Turner), and only since the mid-1990s have black female directors been able to break into the feature and short film industry (Palesa Nkosi, Xoliswa Sithole, Meganthrie Pillay, Zulfah Otto-Sallies, Shamim Sharif, Rayda Jacobs, Joyti Mistry and Jayan Moodley).

Notes

1. Drive-ins became a reality in South Africa in the early 1950s.
2. See Tomaselli (1989) for an in-depth discussion of the subsidy scheme during apartheid.

Chapter 4

Jans Rautenbach

A few pioneers in the Afrikaans film industry of the sixties produced a number of films that could be labelled 'involved films'. The theme of these films was an examination of the cracks in apartheid ideology. They included Emil Nofal-Jans Rautenbach's films like *Die Kandidaat/The Candidate* (1968) and *Katrina* (1968).[1]

Several film historians regard Jans Rautenbach as the pioneer of modern, bold and South African film-making in the 1960s and 1970s.[2] Together with producer Emil Nofal he made groundbreaking films during a time when South African cinema hardly reflected the socio-political realities of the country.

Born in 1936 in Boksburg Jansen Delarosa Rautenbach grew up in a very poor household. His father worked on the mines. He started his school years at a primary school

Jans Rautenbach. M-Net

57

Jans Rautenbach.
Jans Rautenbach

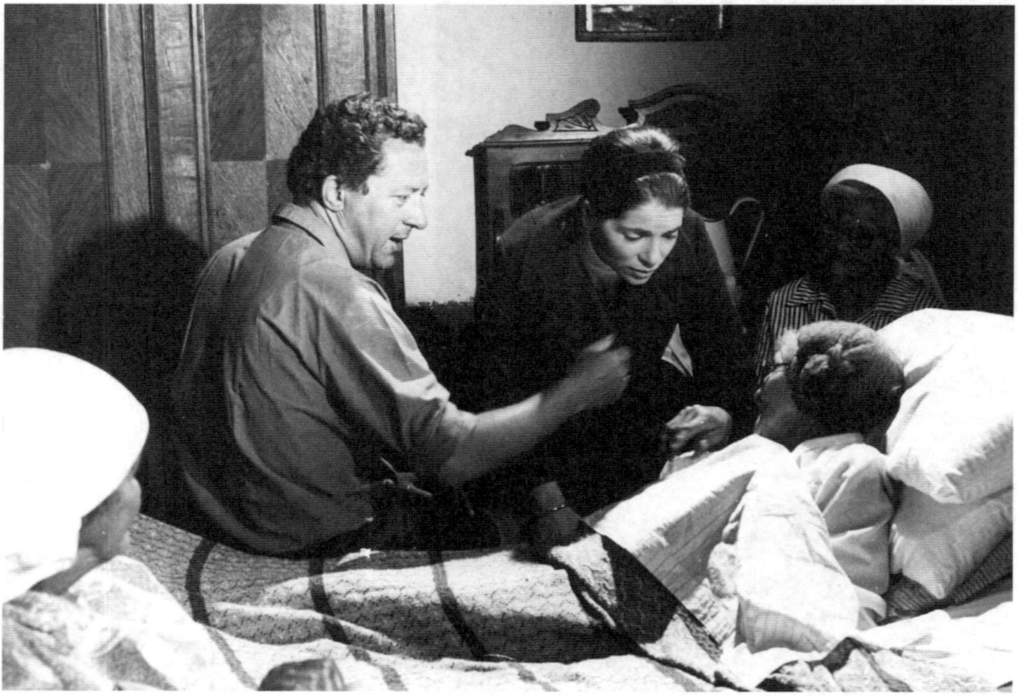

Jans Rautenbach. Jans Rautenbach

in Boksburg. Early influences in his life were literature, not cinema. After studying theology at the University of Stellenbosch for 3 years Rautenbach decided that it was not his calling, and he moved to Bloemfontein. While working as a clerk in a government department he studied criminology at the University of the Orange Free State. In January 1960 he accepted a position as criminologist in the Central Jail in Pretoria. But on 12 February 1963 he gave 24-hour notice to leave and work in the film industry.

He started his film career as a production manager for Jamie Uys Films but joined Emil Nofal later in 1963 to start a new company, Emil Nofal Films. Nofal's *King Hendrik* (1965) is a satire about relationships between Afrikaans- and English-speaking white South Africans and thus followed in the comedic tradition of Jamie Uys's *Hans en die Rooinek* (1961) and *Lord Oom Piet* (1962). The film included actors and crew members who later worked on the set of Rautenbach-directed features: actors Marié du Toit and Joe Stewardson, cinematographer Vincent Cox and editor Peter Henkel. The film was made during the time of very strict moral and political censorship in South Africa (Tomaselli 1989). The result was self-censorship by scriptwriters and directors, and two decades of film escapism. Comedies, musicals, adventure stories and tales about wildlife and nature dominated local film production during the 1960s (Botha & Van Aswegen 1992).

Nofal was one of the few English-language film-makers of the 1960s who made Afrikaans-language films. Born in 1926 in Johannesburg to ethnic Lebanese parents, Nofal started his career at the young age of 15 years at the Killarney Film Studios. He worked there for 13 years, first as assistant editor, then as cinematographer and finally as director of features such as *Song of Africa* (1951), a musical to showcase black talent including the African Inkspots.

Jim Reeves and Emil Nofal. Jans Rautenbach

Wild Season (1967)

Owing to the fact that the subsidy scheme provided no developmental money film-makers had to look for funding elsewhere. Joop Rijfkogel from Irene Film Laboratories became a major funder of Rautenbach's films. Nofal and Rautenbach combined their unique talents on *Wild Season* (1967), an acclaimed drama about the conflict between a father and his son, set against the backdrop of a fishing community along the west coast of South Africa. It was based on the song 'It Was a Very Good Year', which Nofal loved. The film depicts one season in the lives of a fishing community by focusing on personal conflicts, love and an early death. Dirk Maritz (an impressive performance by Gert Van den Bergh) has been a lonely and embittered man after the mysterious death of his older son at sea. He is a top fisherman and a symbol of perseverance of Afrikaners against the violence of nature as well as their own personal problems.

Maritz does not accept his younger son, the sensitive Michael (Antony Thomas). This leads to the dramatic conflict in the film, which in many ways examines Afrikaner patriarchy. Another strong theme is the short, single season of young love between Jess (Janis Reinhardt) and Michael. The approach to the subject matter is lyrical, an important characteristic of all Rautenbach's films.

Wild Season. M-Net

Wild Season. M-Net

    Wild Season featured many members of later Rautenbach films: Joe Stewardson, Marié du Toit, Vincent Cox, Peter Henkel and composer Roy Martin. Rautenbach built a professional relationship with a group of actors and crew members who shared his artistic vision and enabled him in using the film medium for personal expression as an auteur. Rautenbach developed a central theme around the identity of the Afrikaner in all his subsequent films, from *Die Kandidaat* to *Broer Matie* (1984). His films differ from the previous Afrikaans cinema in the sense that Rautenbach regarded film as an art form and thus a means for personal expression.

Die Kandidaat (1968)

The next three projects Rautenbach directed became milestones in South African cinema. In his directorial debut, Rautenbach examines various aspects of the urban (white) Afrikaner through the events surrounding the election of a new director for the Adriaan Delport Foundation in an acclaimed melodrama *Die Kandidaat* (1968). As the backgrounds of the potential candidates have been thoroughly checked the appointment should be a mere formality. Instead the meeting degenerates into a bitter dispute over which one of

Die Kandidaat. M-Net

the council members satisfy the requirements of genuine Afrikanerdom. *Die Kandidaat* explores the Afrikaner psyche critically and exposes the hypocrisy of those designated as 'super' Afrikaners. Drawing heavily on his own background in psychology Rautenbach presents the viewer with various Afrikaner types and in the process dissects the psyche of white Afrikanerdom.

Funding came from four Dutch-speaking individuals: Joop Rijfkogel, Boogertman, Ruijter and Klaver. The latter three funders were part of the building industry. Rautenbach received R150,000 for the production and wrote the screenplay before the start of production. He also conducted intense auditions for actors. He asked Gert Van den Berg to play a lead role. Actors were cast based on their ability to portray three-dimensional characters and not on their looks. In many ways this was a major departure from former Afrikaans cinema.

The Adriaan Delport Foundation in the film is a metaphor for the Akademie vir Wetenskap en Kuns (Academy for Science and Arts), an Afrikaner organization at the time committed to the promotion of the interests of the Afrikaner. In 1965 and 1966 two groups within Afrikanerdom debated Prime Minister Hendrik Verwoerd's apartheid ideology. A more enlightened group including Schalk Pienaar, the editor of the newspaper *Beeld*, who had serious doubts about Verwoerd's homelands-for-blacks policy, especially concerning its practicality. Pienaar questioned Afrikaner traditions and encouraged a more open approach to race relationships in South Africa (Botha 2006c). He raised questions about the multicultural realities of South Africa and the fact that these realities needed to be taken into account in the country's future political direction. Afrikaner conservatives, however, argued for an exclusive South African state for whites and especially white Afrikaners.

In *Die Kandidaat* the Delport Foundation is looking for a new director to replace one who had died. Based on the recommendations by the chair of the board, Lourens Niemand (Gert Van den Bergh), and a board member, Paula Neethling (Marié du Toit), one candidate – Dr. Jan le Roux – is proposed. He is known for his work at a centre for the rehabilitation of boys who had committed offences in society.

The selection process, however, turns out to be a dissection of the candidate's background, including his love relationships. The major catalyst in the process is a writer of the sixties, Anton du Toit (Cobus Rossouw). The bone of contention is that Le Roux is engaged to an English-speaking girl from a Catholic background.

The board members are representatives of the broader Afrikaner community, for example, a professor, a Dutch Reformed Church parson, a state bureaucrat, a truck driver and a woman, who rigidly protects the morals of the Afrikaner nation.

Most of the action is confined to the boardroom where the debate about Afrikaner identity is taking place. It is a claustrophobic setting, which has been brilliantly explored by means of Vincent Cox's camera set-ups and movements as well as an impressive use of *mise-en-scéne*. While the debate unfolds in the board room, the camera focuses on the artefacts of previous Afrikaner leaders in the form of statues and paintings in the background. They seem to observe the conflict as a silent but dominant collective presence.

Jannie Kruger, chief state censor of the 1960s, had major objections against the film, especially regarding conversations about whether the so-called Cape 'coloureds' (South Africans of mixed race who are Afrikaans speaking) could be considered Afrikaners. Rautenbach refused to make cuts and started a debate about the film's censorship problems in the Afrikaans print media with the assistance of enlightened media friends such as Schalk Pienaar and Tobie Boshoff. In a way Kruger received negative publicity.

Finally Rautenbach and Kruger reached a compromise regarding the dialogue, and the film was released to wide acclaim by both the Afrikaans and English press. It was regarded as a film equivalent to the literary work by a progressive group of Afrikaans writers, which included Etienne Leroux, André P. Brink, Breyten Breytenbach and Jan Rabie (Botha 2006c). In *Die Kandidaat* Rautenbach made the statement that the white Afrikaner is going to create a madhouse for himself with all his ideologies and dogmas.

From the Afrikaner political right Rautenbach was accused of humiliating the Afrikaner. The film introduced the major thematic concern in his oeuvre, namely who and what is the Afrikaner? Who could be regarded as a 'true' Afrikaner? In the process Rautenbach also examined class and ideological differences and viewpoints within Afrikanerdom.

Another important departure from previous Afrikaans cinema has been the clinical, modern and urban setting of *Die Kandidaat*. It is far removed from the pastoral landscapes of earlier Afrikaans features (see Chapter 3). The setting symbolized the material wealth of Afrikaners towards the end of the 1960s due to their privileged position in Verwoerd's apartheid state. The character of Paula Neethling is especially of significance: She is cold and manipulative. Paula is part of a new elite class, a new bourgeoisie. Du Toit's performance is simply perfect.

Three other Afrikaner types depicted are also important: The writer Anton du Toit (Cobus Rossouw), the woman who protects the morals of the nation (Hermien Dommisse) and the Dutch Reformed parson (Jacques Loots). Du Toit functions as a type of mouthpiece for Rautenbach, a liberal voice and the one who pulls off the mask of Afrikaner bias. He is symbolic of a more enlightened generation of Afrikaners. Du Toit is intellectual and brutally honest. The Dutch Reformed parson has a dignified presence but lacks a strong ability to lead. Hermien Dommisse's remarkable depiction of the *volksmoeder* (mother of the nation) displays her stubbornness and sad ignorance of the changing realities and values in Afrikaner society. She is still clinging to an era of outdated morality. In *Jannie Totsiens* (1970) this character will be confined to an asylum.

Katrina (1969)

After the critical acclaim for *Die Kandidaat* Rautenbach directed *Katrina* (1969), one of the most innovative films to come out of the apartheid years of the sixties. Based on a powerful play by D. Warner, *Try for White*, this is, for its time, a shocking exposé of the horrors of apartheid and the racial classification system. The film focuses on a 'coloured'

Katrina. M-Net

woman, Katrina, who 'tries for white'. She renounces her mother and father to make a better life possible for herself and her son in apartheid South Africa. Her son is unaware of his roots and is dating a white girl (played by Katinka Heyns). A white Anglican priest, Alex Trewellyn, falls in love with Katrina, and their lives are shattered when the secrets are revealed. The film showcases the talents of Rautenbach's regular team of actors and crew members: Joe Stewardson as the Anglican priest, Carl Trichardt as the father of the white girl and Regardt Van den Bergh as her racist brother. Cobus Rossouw is brilliant as a 'coloured' community leader who displays bitterness towards the white community. He serves as the catalyst of the story in the sense that he exposes Katrina and her son's real identity with tragic consequences. Don Leonard's portrayal of Katrina's 'coloured' husband is moving. Once again the crew included cinematographer Vincent Cox, Peter Henkel as editor and composer Roy Martin.

Rautenbach received death threats from the far right wing in South Africa and had to battle the censors in South Africa to make this film. Chief censor Jannie Kruger wanted to cut several scenes (Botha 2006c). Rautenbach once again involved media friends such as Schalk Pienaar to create a debate. Together with journalist Rykie Van Reenen and literary giant N.P. Van Wyk Louw,[3] Pienaar initiated a defence of the film and freedom of expression in the newspaper *Beeld*. The debate created an impression that a part of the Afrikaner nation was against Kruger's censorship demands. Kruger wanted to ban the film or destroy it by means of extensive cuts. At the end of the film Katrina commits suicide. Rautenbach makes the statement that the racial classification system created a cruel reality that drives South Africans to suicide.

Katrina continues Rautenbach's theme of cultural identity. In this case the impact of the apartheid state on the identities of South Africans has been examined, together with white racism and the biases of the white Afrikaner nation. After the production of *Katrina*, Rautenbach and Nofal decided to terminate their professional relationship. Rautenbach established his own production company, Sewentig. After the split Nofal co-directed one successful feature *The Winners* (1972), the story of a former Olympic athlete (Joe Stewardson) who puts enormous pressure on his four children to succeed at all cost in their sporting careers. Nofal died on 18 July 1986.

Jannie Totsiens (1970)

In *Jannie Totsiens* (1970), his next feature, Rautenbach uses a mental institution as an allegory of South African society under apartheid. This was South Africa's first avant-garde film, which caused a sensation, especially among the intellectuals of the time (Botha 2006c). Again using Afrikaner types Rautenbach examines the Afrikaner psyche. In *Katrina* and *Die Kandidaat* Rautenbach used the conventions of melodrama to reach a larger audience. In *Jannie Totsiens* his approach is avant-garde. There is no classical narrative structure to speak of. The situation in the film represents a microcosm of South Africa in 1970. The apartheid

Jannie Totsiens. M-Net

state has been represented as an asylum. The inmates are Afrikaner types such as a political right-winger (Don Leonard), a judge (Jacques Loots), a painter without arms, a girl with the mind of a child (Katinka Heyns) as well as an alienated English woman and one black person.

The institution is a private asylum that was created for Magda du Plessis (Hermien Dommisse). In *Die Kandidaat* she played the guardian of the nation's morals. Here she still practises this role by guarding over the other patients. With the assistance of her aggressive cats she ensures that nobody behaves in a manner that is morally unacceptable. Jannie (Cobus Rossouw) is a new patient. He does not even speak initially. The outspoken writer of *Die Kandidaat* has no voice in *Jannie Totsiens*. The character functions as a symbol of the state of critical voices in the arts during the apartheid system.

The brilliance of *Jannie Totsiens* can be attributed to Rautenbach's directing, the performance of the acting ensemble and the cinematography by David Dunn-Yarber and Koos Roets. The film has the feel of a psychological thriller and the experimentation with

Pappa Lap. Jans Rautenbach

colour, *mise-en-scéne* and sound was unrivalled in contemporary South African cinema. The film, however, was an isolated case in South African cinema during the 1970s. Escapism dominated the output of the film industry. The images of Afrikanerdom by Rautenbach in *Jannie Totsiens* certainly did not meet the expectations of audiences. They rejected these films and rather flocked to those who portrayed them as chatty, heart-warming and lovable. Their conception of socio-political reality was confined to the conventions of Afrikaans melodramas about mismatched couples who had to overcome obstacles on the path to true love! Sadly, severe moral censorship prevented South Africans from viewing the international landmarks such as Fellini's *Satyricon* (1969), Bertolucci's *Last Tango in Paris* (1972) and Pontecorvo's *The Battle of Algiers* (1966), which at that critical stage would have challenged our conceptions of sexuality, politics, race and aesthetics. *Jannie Totsiens* was part of political modernism in world cinema. Although South African audiences were not ready for this stimulating psychological drama, which has challenged Afrikanerdom's conservative culture, it remains even by today's standards a fascinating portrait of a nation's confused psyche and has anticipated developments in South African politics during the 1980s.

Rautenbach's next film, *Pappa Lap* (1971), deals with class divisions within Afrikanerdom and especially with the marginalized section of white Afrikaners, the very poor, who in the context of the film live as *bywoners*.[4] Class divisions within Afrikanerdom were also explored in *Eendag op 'n Reëndag* (1975). Both films benefited from brilliant cinematography by Koos Roets and outstanding performances by Katinka Heyns.

Rautenbach's second last feature, *Broer Matie* (1984), returned to the political discourse of *Katrina* and *Die Kandidaat*. *Broer Matie* is a gripping melodrama dealing with the unsettling political background of 1961 in South Africa. With happenings like the Sharpeville massacre still fresh in everyone's mind, the main character causes furore in a rural community when his last will and testament determines that a church minister of colour should conduct the sermon at his funeral. As in the case of *Die Kandidaat* Rautenbach exposes the hypocrisy of white Afrikaners and the importance for this part of the South African community to accept and face a multicultural society in which everyone should be treated as equal. The film was made a decade before the historical elections in 1994, which led to a government of national unity in South Africa.

Rautenbach never wanted to work for the South African Broadcasting Corporation (SABC) and thus stopped making features after 1984. He became instrumental in the establishment of the Klein Karoo National Arts Festival (KKNK) in 1994, which has developed into one of the largest national arts festivals in South Africa. He is currently living on a farm, Oulap, in the Little Karoo of South Africa.

Rautenbach's work featured in many international film festivals, including the 1989 Weekly Mail Film Festival, Kriterion's Focus on South Africa in Amsterdam, Utrecht and Den Haag in 1995 as well as the 14th Festival Cinema Africano d'Asia e America Latina in Milan (2004). A full retrospective was also devoted to his work on kykNET, the Afrikaans-language TV channel of M-Net, and he received several lifetime achievement awards for

Broer Matie. Jans Rautenbach

his oeuvre (Botha 2006c). During the 2006 Apollo Film Festival, an important platform for South African cinema, festival director Leon Van der Merwe organized a special tribute to Rautenbach, which included another lifetime achievement award.

Several outstanding South African film professionals owe their developed careers to their work in Rautenbach films: Actors Katinka Heyns and Regardt Van den Bergh became leading directors during the 1980s (see Chapter 8); Gordon Vorster, who played a main character in *Pappa Lap* (1971), directed amongst others one outstanding film of the 1970s, and Koos Roets, probably the greatest South African cinematographer of his generation, received an award and universal praise for his cinematography for *Somer* (1975). Based on a novel by C.M. Van den Heever the film focuses on a love triangle against the glorious pastoral beauty of the Eastern Free State highlands. Roets perfectly captures the lush landscapes during the magic hour and especially achieves brilliance in the sequence when the wheat fields are destroyed by a hailstorm. Editor Tim Spring's montages are impressive.

Gordon Voster's *Sarah* (1975) was shot in the Kalahari. It is the story of a Kalahari widow (brilliantly played by Trix Pienaar) into whose life comes an artist escaping from the law (Gordon Vorster), a man who has in his financially successful life lost all sense of values. By her strength Sarah rebuilds the man and renews him as a person and an artist. Vorster's own paintings became an important contribution to the text, which departs radically from a classical three-act narrative structure. It functions more like a combination of impressions of landscapes, characters and small events. Shooting in the Kalahari took a total of 10 weeks, and Vorster made use of several non-professional actors in this visually evocative film, including a Bushman couple, Karools and Rachel. Their relationship is movingly depicted and *Sarah* is one of the few Afrikaans films to avoid any paternalism in the representation of blacks.

The years 1959–1980 had been characterized by an artistic revival in film-making throughout the world, ranging from exciting political films in Africa and Latin America to examples of great art cinema in Europe and Asia. Unfortunately, because of moral and political censorship, a lack of audience development and inadequate film distribution South Africans and thus local film-makers were not exposed to these remarkable developments in world cinema.

Severe state censorship during the 1970s, for example, also prevented South African audiences to experience developments in world cinema. Many of the films by directors such as Pier Paolo Pasolini, Bertolucci and Fellini (in particular *Fellini Satyricon* and *Fellini's Casanova*) were banned. Cuts to remove violence, nudity, sex and/or 'foul' language in films such as *Midnight Express, Coming Home, The Omen, The Deer Hunter* and *Taxi Driver* left audiences with mutilated texts. The word 'fuck' was allowed for the first time uncut in 1979 in *And Justice for All*, but the 1980s and early 1990s were still characterized by moral and political censorship (see Chapters 8 and 9).

Opportunities to experience world cinema was provided by film societies, which had been in operation since the 1930s, film festivals and independent cinemas in major cities. Under the leadership of Freddy Ogterop from the Cape Provincial Library a successful 16mm film society network operated especially during the 1970s. The Bloemfontein branch, Fliekkliek, managed by Braam Muller, for example, offered audiences the opportunity to view a large selection of world cinema, such as the oeuvres of Fellini, Bergman, Fassbinder, Wajda and Werner Herzog.

In the late 1970s international film festivals in South Africa became crucial to break the sense of isolation felt by South African audiences. In some cases the censors of the 1980s were more lenient regarding film festival screenings and allowed some nudity and sex in films. The Cape Town International Film Festival started in 1977 – under the directorship of James Polley from the University of Cape Town's External Studies. It ran till 1999 when Polley passed away. The last edition was successfully directed by Trevor Steele Taylor, but the festival made way for the Southern African International Film and Television Market (Sithengi), which at that stage included a world cinema festival. Sithengi started in 1996 and unfortunately had its last edition in 2006.

The Durban International Film festival started in 1979. Under the directorship of Ros Sarkin the festival included screenings in the Umlazi township from the fourth edition onwards. The festival included a rich selection of world cinema as well as titles which South Africans would otherwise not have seen due to the cultural boycott and local censorship. In Johannesburg Len Davis staged the Johannesburg International Film Festival for most of the 1980s.

The Weekly Mail Film Festival, hosted under the umbrella of the independent newspaper *Weekly Mail* (later *Mail & Guardian*), offered an invaluable festival of independent, oppositional film-making in South Africa from 1987 to the early 1990s. Festival director Trevor Steele Taylor also included milestones from other African countries to break the isolation between South African film-makers and their colleagues elsewhere on the continent. At the Weekly Mail Film Festival of 1990, for example, co-hosted by *Weekly Mail* and FAWO, a collection of rare films on South Africa found in archives around the world, examples of resistance cinema never seen publicly in this country, and 20 films by independent South African film-makers and over 20 short films in a short-film competition were screened.

The Out in Africa Gay and Lesbian Film Festival, under the leadership of Nodi Murphy, started in 1994 and the first Encounters South African International Documentary Film Festival was held in 1999. The founders are Nodi Murphy and Steven Markovitz. The latest film festivals in South Africa are the Tricontinental Film Festival, which had its first edition in 2005,[5] as well as the Cape Winelands Film Festival (from 2008 onwards), which in many ways filled the void left by Sithengi's World Cinema Festival and the Cape Town International Film Festival.

Independent cinemas were also crucial throughout the history of South African cinema to provide alternative programmes to the Hollywood-dominated menu on big screens. The Vistarama (in Johannesburg), managed by Heinz Kallenbach, offered a rich selection of European masterpieces between 1979 and 1985, including *The Night of the Shooting Stars*, *Padre Padrone*, *Diva* and *The Tree of Wooden Clogs*. This programme was complemented by the Piccadilly in Cavendish Street, Bellevue/Yeoville (Johannesburg), the Labia in Cape Town, the Lyric in Fordsburg (Johannesburg), 7 Arts in Norwood, the Electric Cinema in Durban North as well as the Corlett Cinema complex in Bramley (Johannesburg). Sadly, by the mid-1990s of all these independent theatres only the Labia in Cape Town was still going strong. The mainstream distributor Ster-Kinekor started a Cinema Nouveau complex at the Rosebank Mall in December 1987, and for most of the 1990s, thanks to programmers Jan du Plessis and Ludwig Wagner, it provided an excellent selection of world cinema, including Kiarostami's *The Taste of Cherry*, Kaige's *Farewell My Concubine* and Kieslowski's *Three Colours Trilogy*. After the departure of Du Plessis and Wagner the so-called Cinema Nouveau circuit stagnated from 2000 to 2011, and mostly less commercial films from the United States and the United Kingdom were screened. The diverse selection from world cinema became a memory of the past (see Chapter 12).

The Moosa family's Avalon Group is one of the few independent cinema groups to survive. In October 2010 it celebrated 71 years of independence.[6] In Durban during the 1920s Aboobaker – or 'AB' – Moosa fell in love with films and longed to have a theatre of his own where he could watch the films he wanted for free. In 1939, at age 37, his dream was realized when he and Abdulla Kajee co-founded the Avalon Theatre in Durban's Victoria Street.

The theatre was a major success, catering largely to the South African Indian community. Moosa built on this success by becoming one of the first exhibitors to bring early Bollywood movies to South Africa and by establishing a distribution agreement with 20th Century Fox. The business boomed, and AB began opening theatres elsewhere in South Africa – in Johannesburg, Cape Town, Kimberley, Durban, East London, Port Elizabeth and Paarl.

In its heyday the Avalon Group operated 18 cinemas across South Africa, making up over 10% of the market share at the time. AB, however, soon fell foul of apartheid legislation and its Group Areas Act. In 1964, at the age of 21, Moosa Moosa witnessed his father's humiliation at their family's eviction from their home on the corner of Goble and Windmere Roads in Durban under the Group Areas Act. As Indians, they were no longer allowed to live in what had been declared a whites-only area. AB Moosa did not survive the eviction. The Group Areas Act and Reservation of Separate Amenities Act began to destroy AB's exhibition network. During this time, Moosa Moosa took on sole ownership of Avalon and ran only one cinema in Durban. In 1994 apartheid came to an end, and the Avalon Group's fortunes began to revive. Around that time Moosa was joined in the business by his only son, AB Junior, who was named after his grandfather. AB Junior had just left school and decided to work alongside his father.

With over 50 years in the industry, Moosa Moosa is the longest serving cinema exhibition executive in South Africa and among the longest serving in the world. In 1997 he appeared before the Truth and Reconciliation Commission (TRC) business hearings to give evidence on the abuses inflicted by the apartheid system on African, 'coloured' and Indian businesses, and in 1998 he was invited to appear before the portfolio committee in parliament to make representations in relation to the new Competition Bill. In 2007 Moosa was given a South African Film and Television Industry (SAFTA) lifetime achievement award. The Avalon Group is now the oldest and third-largest cinema operating company in South Africa, after Ster-Kinekor and Nu Metro, and a leader in distributing increasingly popular Bollywood movies in South Africa.

Notes

1. The work of Rautenbach is explored in-depth in a publication by Martin Botha, titled *Jans Rautenbach: Dromer, baanbreker en auteur* (2006c).
2. See Botha (2006c), Louw and Botha (1993) and Tomaselli (1989).
3. See Kannemeyer (1988) for a history of Afrikaans literature and biographies of literary figures such as N.P. Van Wyk Louw.
4. People who live on another's farm under certain conditions of services.
5. The 3 Continents Film Festival, which started in 2002, became the Tricontinental Film Festival.
6. This information is based on press releases by the Avalon Group in 2010.

Chapter 5

Manie Van Rensburg

Manie Van Rensburg. Grethe Fox

M ost Afrikaans-language films of the 1960s and 1970s ignored the socio-political realities of apartheid, especially the realities experienced by black South Africans (Botha 1996). The majority of Afrikaans-language films communicated by means of obsolete symbols that had little multicultural communication value (Fourie 1982). They painted a one-sided and stereotypical portrait of the Afrikaner, leading to a misconception about who and what the Afrikaner was. Furthermore, the negative portrayal of blacks as a servant class in these films is a visual symbol of the deep-seated apartheid ideology (Botha 1996). The exceptions were very few in the 1970s. Director Manie Van Rensburg entered the field of Afrikaner culture through political satire and became one of the leading film-makers in the 113-year history of South African cinema.

Career history

Hermanus Philippus (Manie) Janse Van Rensburg was born on 24 October 1945 in Krugersdorp, a town in the former Transvaal Province (Botha 2006b). He was part of a staunch, conservative Afrikaner family. Despite the restrictions imposed on him by this conservative upbringing, he tried to realize a dream to make motion pictures. The first step to this end was made when he bought his first movie camera at the age of 14 with his earnings as a church organist. Van Rensburg came from a strong musical background, which would later help him in creating lyrical images for the big screen (Botha 1997a; Botha & Dethier 1997).

Unable to further his education at an international film school due to financial and familial restrictions, he decided to go to the University of Potchefstroom where he obtained a degree majoring in English and psychology (Botha 2006b). Following this academic period, Van Rensburg began an intense practical learning period in the artistic drought of South African film-making of the 1960s. He tried to work for everybody who was somebody in motion picture production. In order to learn the trade thoroughly, he worked through all levels of film, from camera to editing to scriptwriting (Botha 2006b). He started as a darkroom assistant for a stills photographer in 1965. During 1966 he became an assistant cameraman. Van Rensburg continued his career as the cinematographer on *Hoor My Lied/Hear My Song* (1967), a soppy musical made with a large budget in the western Cape Province and in the USA. The film was an enormous success with white Afrikaans-speaking audiences and prompted the series of Afrikaans melodramas that appeared between 1967 and 1980 (Botha & Van Aswegen 1992).

Van Rensburg formed his independent film company, Visio Films, in 1969. He was only 22 years old. He directed and financed a film about loneliness in an urban environment, *Freddie's in Love* (1971). He started with R140 in the bank. He did not have any money for lights, so his production assistant who worked as a stage manager at Johannesburg's Civic Theatre would borrow what the film team needed. The film was eventually a moving character study of loneliness in cold, bleak Hillbrow, an area of high-rise blocks of flats (Botha 1997a). It was unique in that it did not conform to any of the social norms prevalent in South African film-making at the time – it was a film with avant-garde tendencies. Local audiences rejected it outright and stayed at home.

One year elapsed before he made the competent thriller *Die Bankrower/The Bank Robber* (1973). It received positive notices from the critics. After this feature, Kavalier Films (which was responsible for much of the escapism fare in Afrikaans film of the time) offered Van Rensburg a two-film contract. They would provide the finance for him to make one film of his own choice (provided it had commercial possibilities) on condition he made a feature for them based on a radio serial (Botha 2006b). The film he made for Kavalier, *Geluksdal* (1974), is his worst film and not at all different from the Afrikaans film escapism of the

Die Square. M-Net

period. The film was a financial success, but Van Rensburg admitted that this was not his finest hour (Botha & Dethier 1997).

The other film, his choice, *Die Square* (1975), was initially banned by the South African censors. Van Rensburg considered the film to be a fairy tale which revolved around a political party break-away (Botha 2006b). A politician's wife leaves him which spoils his image, and in order to save face he has to get her back, which means he has to conform to her standards and become less conservative. The film became a satire on Afrikaner hegemony in the political and moral life of the country. Years later, with *Taxi to Soweto* (1991), a similar plot was used by Van Rensburg to address Afrikaner fears regarding black South Africans.

Van Rensburg was initially not part of the movement of anti-apartheid film-making. He made TV drama series for the SABC from the mid-1970s to 1987 (Botha 1997a; 2006b). The advent of television in South Africa during 1976 gave many local film-makers artistic opportunities that had not been available because of the ineffective subsidy scheme. Although censorship regarding political material was very tight at the SABC, Van Rensburg could make artistically successful drama series and films. He started with a 10-part comedy

Manie in Dakar with ANC members. Grethe Fox

series, *Willem*, about the trials and tribulations of a private detective. This series earned Van Rensburg his first SABC Artes Award for directing (Botha 1997a; 2006b).

He decided to move from Johannesburg to Cape Town where he met Johan Van Jaarsveld, a writer who became his partner, and under the umbrella of Visio Films, his best television work followed. This relationship with the SABC, however, was cut after Van Rensburg decided to join 52 prominent South Africans in 1987 who travelled to Dakar, Senegal, in order to have discussions with members of the then banned ANC (Botha 1997a). The 52 South Africans mainly included Afrikaans-speaking people like Van Rensburg's friend Van Zyl Slabbert, a prominent oppositional political figure of the 1980s. The conference in Dakar was a joint undertaking between the Institute for Democratic Alternatives in South Africa (Idasa) and the ANC, with discussions about a liberated economy, the form of a liberated government and solutions to South Africa's conflict. When Van Rensburg returned to South Africa, he found himself out of work at the SABC. For 2 years he could not work. With the establishment of FAWO he hoped to find a sympathetic, progressive group to support him in his work (Botha 1997a; 2006b). *The Native Who Caused All the Trouble* (1989), a film about a black man's struggle to get the land back he lost because of racist colonial legislation, was his contribution to the new critical, anti-apartheid cinema of the 1980s, and it established him as part of the anti-apartheid movement.

Van Rensburg's short film *Country Lovers* (1982) also criticized apartheid policy and is based on the work by Nobel Prize winner Nadine Gordimer and forms one of seven short films, collectively titled *Six Feet of the Country*. To date this series has been seen by over 300 million people worldwide. It has been accepted by the New York Film Forum as well as being screened in Germany, the Netherlands, Belgium, Italy and Channel Four in Britain (Botha 1997a).

Ironically these films were banned from general release in South Africa, and special screenings were only permitted at South African film festivals in the 1980s, despite the fact that six of the seven films were made by South African casts and crews. *Country Lovers* revolves around a young white Afrikaans boy's affair with a black farm girl he grew up with. As a result of the 'immorality' of this situation, Van Rensburg's film was labelled as anti-South African propaganda by the South African censor board. *The New York Times* critic described the film in a review of 18 May 1983 as a delicate and ferocious tale about a love affair of a young Afrikaner and the pretty black girl who grows up with the boy on his father's prosperous farm (Botha 1997a; 2006b). The point of the story is the manner in which the innocence of the pair is ultimately destroyed by the Immorality Act. The tale is beautifully acted by Ryno Hattingh and Nomsa Nene as the lovers and is related in such a low key that the full horror of it is not apparent until it is almost over.

Thematic and stylistic concerns

Throughout his television and film dramas, director Manie Van Rensburg exhibits the same thematic pre-occupations, the same recurring motifs and incidents and basically the same visual style (Botha 1997a; 2006b; Botha & Dethier 1997). His work explores the psyche of the Afrikaner within a historical as well as a contemporary context. He is preoccupied with communication problems between people, especially within love relationships. The outsider is a dominant figure in his universe. By studying Van Rensburg's *oeuvre* over the past years, one realizes that together with Jans Rautenbach he could be regarded as South Africa's most prominent film auteur.

Themes that Van Rensburg tends to portray in his chronicles are the psyche of the Afrikaner in a contemporary or historic situation (especially the period from the 1920s to the 1940s); the way of life of, and motivation for, individuals living on the 'edge' of society; loneliness; and the exploration of the communication potential of film and television to convey contextual and experiential information to the viewer (Botha 1997a; 2006b; Botha & Dethier 1997). Within these themes Van Rensburg experiments with particular filmic codes not seen in the work of his contemporaries, Jan Scholtz, Daan Retief, Franz Marx, Bertrand Retief, Ivan Hall and Elmo de Witt. Van Rensburg's cinema can be divided into three periods: his Afrikaans films of 1971 to 1975, his television work from 1976 to 1987, and from 1988 onwards, his shift towards the international film scene with *The Native Who Caused All the Trouble* (1989), *The Fourth Reich* (1990) and *Taxi to Soweto* (1991).

The first period includes *Freddie's in Love* (1971), *Die Bankrower/The Bank Robber* (1973), *Geluksdal* (1974) and *Die Square/The Square* (1975).

The second period includes drama and comedy series made for the SABC after the introduction of television in this country in 1976. These television works include the 10-part comedy series *Willem* (1975), starring the brilliant comedian Tobie Cronjé;[1] another 10-part series *Sebastian Senior* (1976), which concerned the adventures of a Johannesburg taxi driver; *Mickey Cannis Caught My Eye* (1979); *Good News* (1980); the authentic folk stories of *Doktor Con Viljee se Overberg* (1981), which earned him the Star Tonight Award in 1982; *Anna* (1982); *Good News* (1982), about issues of female rights portrayed in a contemporary vein; *Verspeelde Lente/Wasted Springtime* (1983); *Die Perdesmous/The Horse Trader* (1982); *Sagmoedige Neelsie* (1983), a light-hearted comedy based on the works of C.J. Langenhoven; *Die Vuurtoring/The Lighthouse* (1984); *Heroes* (1985) and *The Mantiss Project* (1986).

Van Rensburg's *oeuvre* should be seen as chronicles of the Afrikaner psyche during three significant periods: firstly, the 1930s and the trauma of urbanization and struggle to retain the land; secondly, the revival of Afrikaner nationalism during South Africa's involvement in the Second World War; and thirdly, the modern, urban Afrikaner of the 1970s and 1980s (Botha 1997a; 2006b; Botha & Dethier 1997).

Van Rensburg's unique style; his treatment of location, time and place; as well as his thematic concerns of the political realities of South Africa during the previous century will be examined in the remainder of this chapter. His representation of race and class relations, as well as the outsiders to the 'normative society', is of importance to this discourse. The portrayal of communication problems between people and a unique historical documentation of the Afrikaner culture make Van Rensburg a chronicler of this part of South African society.

The 1930s: The trauma of urbanization and the struggle for land

Van Rensburg's major works are set in the 1930s. These years, up to 1948, marked two significant stages in the rise of Afrikaner nationalism as the dominant political and social force in South Africa and in the evolution of the country's segregationist race policies.[2] At the beginning of the thirties, however, Afrikaner farmers had a traumatic struggle to retain their land during the Great Depression. The severe drought of 1932, the worst in living memory, heightened the sense of disaster among farmers.[3]

General J.B.M. Hertzog's National Party was predominantly a rural party. However, it wished to promote the industrial development of South Africa rather than allow the country to remain economically a relatively underdeveloped colony of Britain (Botha 1997a). The party's programme for industrialization derived from the fear that gold mining was a wasting asset. Consequently, the party desired to expand the internal market for the products of South African agriculture. Allied to this was a determination to create employment opportunities for Afrikaners, who were often 'poor whites', moving from rural districts to the towns. A general concern with making the country more self-sufficient and with checking the drain on its reserves was another important aspect of the party's policy.

Verspeelde Lente (1983)

Verspeelde Lente/Wasted Springtime portrays these historic events, drawing in culture, class and rural–urban conflicts. Pop le Roux, the daughter of a poor white family, so-called bywoners[4] on a farm, experiences hard times in a severe drought. Due to moral pressure from her parents, she decides to jilt her young mineworker boyfriend, Hermaans, to marry a rich old widower, Jan Greyling, who is 51 years old. He has a son, Gert, of her own age.

The setting is not too far from the gold mines. Pop and Hermaans both come from poverty-stricken families who are no longer able to make a living from their small pieces of land. Hermaans goes to the city to find work on the mines in order to support Pop when they get married.

The wealthy landowner Jan Greyling, however, asks her to marry him. She is torn between her love for Hermaans and the security that a marriage to Jan Greyling will bring to both her and her parents. The 4-hour-long drama ends pessimistically, metaphorically admitting to the cultural trauma inherent in the Afrikaner's move to the city. This is symbolized in *Verspeelde Lente* by Hermaans who rends up as an embittered alcoholic, and, to a lesser degree, by his mother who still uses candles instead of electricity in their small urban household (Botha 1997a).

The first shots in the film are of poor whites in a drought-stricken landscape. There is nothing green, no crops only rocks. Van Rensburg's milieu is more than realistically depicted (Botha 1997a; Botha & Dethier 1997). It is, in fact, a metaphorically portrayed wasteland, the end of the Afrikaner's Eden, that is, the unspoiled rural paradise. In the portrayal of Pop and Hermaans' living conditions, one sees poverty: Pop's father, for example, hunts jumping hare for food. But the film has its lapses into folk humour: Pop's father tells absurd stories to his neighbour. These rich rural tellings are reminiscent of Van Rensburg's remarkable television series *Doktor Con Viljee se Overberg*, based on stories by C.G.S. de Villiers. These anti-rational folk stories portray aspects of the rural Afrikaner's psyche. Some of the dialogue in *Verspeelde Lente* also gets a rich cultural significance because of these stories. The film is thus not only a sombre, pessimistic look at Afrikaner urbanization and a struggle to retain the land (Botha 1997a).

The contrast between rich and poor is clearly visible in *Verspeelde Lente*: both Hermaans and Jan Greyling come to visit Pop to ask for her hand in marriage. The class distinction is made clear in shots of the two on their way to Pop: Greyling in his car, Hermaans on his bicycle, trying to stay on the road after Greyling has passed, leaving him in a cloud of dust.

When Pop arrives at Greyling's traditional Cape-Dutch-style house with gables, wooden louvre shutters and a garden (the first signs of green in the film), she is confronted with a different style of living, depicted by shots of the table and food. Greyling's son, Gert, demands that she should have asked for Greyling at the kitchen door, not at the front door, meaning that he sees her as low class and subordinate (Botha 1997a).

There are other images of class distinction and poverty: Some linger in the mind of the viewer, for example, a family on a donkey car travelling through the wasteland on their way to the gold mines and of Pop trying to plough the dusty, rocky earth – powerful images of despair and the loss of Eden.

Verspeelde Lente is dominated by long shots of lonely figures breaking the horizontal lines of barren landscapes. The use of this milieu and the social and political background in Johan Van Jaarsveld's complex script serve as motivation for Pop's decision to marry Oom Jan and to escape the hardship. Well-rounded characters are created, not the stereotypes of poor Afrikaners as is the case in Jean Delbeke's *The Schoolmaster* (1990). Van Rensburg has, in fact, created a 4-hour epic of social realism, stylistically characterized by the use of minimal music, long shots of lonely figures against barren Cape landscapes and simply edited (Botha 1997a; Botha & Dethier 1997). In many ways Van Rensburg was a realist in his approach to film-making. In an interview with Schalk Schoombie in the *Die Burger* newspaper (17 July 1990) he stated that editing and camera movement should support the filmic narrative. He admired the neorealism in European films, and this realistic approach became his style throughout his work. Sometimes he would complement his realism with real archival documentary footage and original recordings of popular music of a period to add authenticity to his work (Botha 1997a).

Verspeelde Lente characterizes his close collaboration with a team of actors, scriptwriters, editors and producers, who appear in the production teams of most of his dramas: actors Elize Cawood, Ian Roberts, Emile Aucamp, Jannie Gildenhuys, Wilma Stockenström, Limpie Basson, and later Mees Xteen, Grethe Fox and Ryno Hattingh; editor Nena Olwage; scriptwriter Johan Van Jaarsveld and producer Richard Green.

When Pop moves to Jan Greyling's house, she effectively changes her class position. She learns to drive a motor car instead of a donkey cart, has servants to do the chores she used to do and is able to enjoy the luxury of leisure. All these are indicators of a lifestyle particular to the bourgeoisie and petty bourgeoisie (Botha 1997a). Pop slips relatively easily into the role of 'madam', quickly leaving the drudgery of her past life behind. However, she retains her love for Hermaans, and their encounters on his occasional appearances in the district demonstrate the growing rift between them. These meetings take place within the ruins of a building, a symbol of their wasted love. Gert's initial antipathy towards Pop slowly turns from camaraderie into love, and when she falls pregnant, there is a hint of ambiguity about whose child it is. However, Gert is then free to go to the city to study medicine, as his father will have another heir to the farm. The film, however, re-emphasises the rural–urban clash, as Gert retains his link with the farm through his attraction to Pop.

After Jan Greyling's death on his birthday, Pop goes to find Hermaans in the city but realizes that their relationship is irreconcilable. She returns alone to her son and the farm. Her class position has changed at this stage, and she is now the rural landowner in contrast to an urbanized working-class wage earner. It is apparent from their brief meeting that Pop and Hermaans have nothing left in common except the memory of their relationship and their backgrounds. This illustrates another important Van Rensburg thematic concern: the lack of communication between people (Botha 1997a; Botha & Dethier 1997).

In their conversation it is clear that communication is strained:

Hermaans:	Sit down.
Pop:	Aunt Hessie is getting old now.
Hermaans:	Yes.
Pop:	You have a beautiful little place here.
Hermaans:	Yes.
Pop:	You did not become a blaster?
Hermaans:	No.
Pop:	Is dynamite dangerous?
Hermaans:	It depends.

(Silence)

Pop:	I see ...

(Silence)

Hermaans:	Yes.
Hermaans:	Would you like to listen to music?
Pop:	No, we are talking so nicely.

(Silence)

Hermaans: Would you like a drink?

(He stands up, fixes the drink and gives her one.)

Hermaans: To your health.

(Silence)

Hermaans: I like a drink when I arrive home.

Money is the solution to the hardship depicted in *Verspeelde Lente*, either by moving to cities to get work in the factories or in the gold mines, or by marrying a wealthy landowner. But the film is much more than just a portrayal of class distinctions and the traumatic urbanization of the Afrikaner. It is also an authentic chronicle of the Afrikaner of the 1930s, as well as a sensitive portrayal of the female psyche, and human longings (Botha 1997a; Botha & Dethier 1997). Jan Greyling's loneliness after the death of his wife after a marriage of 28 years is prominent. It also ends with signs of loneliness in Hermaans, his life reduced to one-night stands and booze.

The Afrikaner wedding is an example of the authenticity of Van Rensburg's film, and it shows the flaws in the depiction of similar social gatherings in Delbeke's *The Schoolmaster*. The speech by Pop's father about the loss of a daughter, in fact, the gaining of a bourgeois lifestyle, beautifully symbolized by the new shoes of Pop's mother, exemplifies Van Rensburg's knowledge of a specific culture and characterization. The remarks of the guests are typical of the great rituals of Afrikanerdom. The jokes, Boer music and dances are also authentic, perhaps one of the best portrayals of Afrikanerdom on the screen. Similarly brilliant scenes of Afrikaner rituals are to be found in *The Fourth Reich*. In this sequence, the moral dilemma of Pop (beautifully portrayed by Elize Cawood) regarding her marriage is handled with great sensitivity. She goes to her bedroom. She tries to smile while watching children play outside the house on a bicycle. This reminds her of Hermaans and possibly their children. She remarks to her mother, 'I want to stay here … I don't want to go away.'

Van Rensburg's depiction of her anxiety on her wedding night is also remarkable. His detail of her initial class position is admirable, for example, her reaction when she gets coffee in bed the next morning. She is not accustomed to such a lifestyle. At the breakfast table, she says, 'I don't want to eat porridge ever in my life again.' Her table manners and use of language also betray her class position. Van Rensburg shows her naivety in several memorable scenes: When Jan Greyling asks her what she wants from town, she says, 'Sweets!' When he arrives from town, she jumps through the window and runs to him, not as a wife but as a child. When Jan tries to show her the vastness of his 'kingdom', she remarks, 'Are we going to stay here the whole day like baboons?' But everything changes and Pop changes: Towards the end of the film, Jan brings her pearls, not sweets, and she has lost her naivety (Botha 1997a).

In another sequence, Van Rensburg touches upon the issue of Afrikaner nationalism, which is a major theme in his later *Heroes* and *The Fourth Reich*. Hermaans and Pop meet in the ruins, and Hermaans mentions to her that he is joining a union at the mines. He says,

The workers are the bosses of the mine. We are many. Without us they can't do the work. If Hermaans Cronjé complains to the mine bosses, they only laugh. But we have a union, an organisation that exists for the workers. And if the union speaks, then the bosses listen. The days of exploitation, of treating the workers as slaves, are gone. It is not a scandal to be a worker. There is money. And if everyone stands together, we have power.

Van Rensburg probably refers here to attempts by the Afrikaner Broederbond[5] in the 1930s to promote both Afrikaner unity and Afrikaner economic power within the so-called 'economic movement'. For the Broederbond, class cleavages as well as political divisions threatened the prospects of Afrikaner unity, with the most glaring manifestation of class cleavage among Afrikaners being provided by the persisting 'poor white' problem. The purpose of the economic movement was consequently both to mobilize Afrikaner capital and to alleviate Afrikaner poverty (Botha 1997a).

At the same time, Christian National trade unions were promoted in opposition to existing unions in order to wean Afrikaans-speaking workers away from organizations based on class, to improve their position in the white labour force, and capture their support for nationalism. Hermaans probably refers in *Verspeelde Lente* to the Afrikanerbond Van Mynwerkers,[6] a union that was formed in 1937 in opposition to the Mine Workers' Union.

Van Rensburg refers in the series to the Fusion Government of General Hertzog and General Jan Smuts, and ultimately its break-up in September 1939 over the question of South Africa's neutrality or participation with Great Britain in Second World War. This is also the theme of *Heroes* and to a large extent of *The Fourth Reich*. But let us move first to two other films that portray the struggle for land in the 1930s: *Die Perdesmous* and *The Native Who Caused All the Trouble*.

After the realistic style and linear structure of *Verspeelde Lente*, Van Rensburg used a complex narrative structure in both *Die Perdesmous* and *The Native Who Caused All the Trouble*. To some extent it is similar to the structure that he and scriptwriter Johan Van Jaarsveld used in *Doktor Con Viljee se Overberg*. The structure consists of more than one character's perspective. There is also an element of a journalistic approach in terms of hand-held shots of quasi-interviews with characters giving their subjective opinion of an incident (Botha 1997a).

Die Perdesmous (1982)

Die Perdesmous/The Horse Trader depicts the true story of an Afrikaner farmer, Sias Johannes Christopher Vlok, born on 17 December 1898 at Wolmaranstad. The film depicts his struggle for his land during the 1930s as a 39-year-old outcast. He has been convicted for several offences: assault (19 April 1918), burglary (7 November 1918 and 23 October 1919), rape, assault with the intention to cause bodily harm and so on. These facts about the character are given by a voice-over commentator in typical documentary fashion at the beginning of the film. Van Rensburg uses this device throughout *Die Perdesmous* to give a context to the social and political meaning of the film (Botha 1997a).

The structure consists further of numerous flashbacks that serve as an explanation of Vlok's eventual killing of nine people. The reasons for this bloodbath are given step by step within the non-linear narrative structure, but Van Rensburg also makes use of hand-held shots of witnesses, people in Vlok's life, who tell their side of the story. Some are lying, others not. These characters include Vlok's employee, Willie Krause; Vlok's wife, Mabel; and his niece and lover, Ester Cronjé. The scenes depicting the attempts of the police to arrest Vlok in his farmhouse are similar to those of the Native's arrest in *The Native Who Caused All the Trouble*, a film which has the same kind of narrative structure and also shows witnesses at a court hearing (Botha 1997a).

Vlok is a wealthy farmer in 1932. He and another farmer, Gericke, become involved in a court case about the price of cattle. Vlok loses the case twice with great cost and as a result starts to hate and mistrust the South African judicial system. He also becomes paranoid regarding the motives of the people nearest to him.

Greed plays an important part in Vlok's story. Several of his family members are involved in schemes to get his land. The scenes depicting their plotting take place in the dark interiors of farmhouses, symbolising a world of betrayal and intrigue. Similarly sinister scenes are found in *The Fourth Reich* and *Heroes*.

Die Perdesmous is Van Rensburg's most complex film. The absence of a linear structure, the multi-layered levels of narration and the several flashbacks within flashbacks lead to a mosaic of levels of meaning motivating Vlok's behaviour. Vlok, for example, is also a narrator (Botha 1997a; Botha & Dethier 1997).

Several reasons are given for Vlok's bloodbath at the end of the film, especially his childless marriage with his wife (played by a Van Rensburg regular, Wilma Stockenström, a great name in Afrikaans literature and film[7]) and her involvement with Muisen, the husband of her daughter by her previous marriage. Muisen antagonises Vlok from the start of their interaction by insulting him at his wedding by draping a Union Jack over the wedding car. Within the Fusion Government of Hertzog and Smuts, Muisen supports the British elements of the government. Vlok is probably an Afrikaner Nationalist, a supporter of D.F. Malan's Purified National Party. At the wedding the hatred between the two men is visually manifested. (It is also one of the rare moments in a Manie Van Rensburg movie that classical music is used, in this case Gounod. Another example is Schubert in *The Fourth Reich*. Van

Rensburg usually relies more on indigenous music from South Africa and other African countries than European influences.)

Vlok assaults Muisen after he throws the Union Jack over Vlok's head. It is clear that the strife between the two men also has ideological origins, an aspect that is fully developed in *Heroes*. This incident between Vlok and Muisen leads to a court case regarding assault and an 18-month sentence of hard labour for Vlok. After the court case, his wife divorces him. She sells some of his belongings, which lead to more hatred and paranoia (Botha 1997a).

Vlok's relationship with Ester is troublesome since she is a blood relative. A police captain, Willie Krause, and 11 policemen try to arrest Vlok, and his relationship with the naive Ester is suddenly doomed. This relationship is to some extent similar to the initial relationship between Pop and Jan Greyling in *Verspeelde Lente*: He is the father and she the daughter. Ester's naivety is characterized by her words: 'Let's flee to Angola. I have heard that there are people who speak Afrikaans. Nobody will know us there. There are even Afrikaners in Argentina.'

After killing and wounding the policemen and Ester, Vlok becomes the typical outcast in Van Rensburg's films. He now lives on the edge of Afrikaner society, existing only to avenge the past. He tells another character in the film: 'I have just shot a few policemen on my farm. I am going into town to shoot a few more people. Then my accounts will be paid.'

The Native Who Caused All the Trouble (1989)

In *The Native Who Caused All the Trouble* the outcast, Tselilo, in contrast to Vlok, is not a violent person. He only wants to build a church for his God on a piece of land he had bought previously. The land now belongs to an Indian family. He drives them off the property and is confronted by the police. This leads, after several attempts to remove him, to his arrest and a court case. As with Vlok in *Die Perdesmous*, Tselilo loses the case and is sentenced to several years' hard labour. Both films can be considered critical of the South African judicial system during colonial times (Botha 1997a; Botha & Van Aswegen 1992).

But *The Native Who Caused All the Trouble* should be seen in a broader context, which is the Fusion Government's development of South Africa's segregationist race policies. In 1935 Hertzog proposed the creation of an advisory Natives Representative Council of 22 members, presided over by the Secretary for Native Affairs. This Native Representation Bill provided for four African representatives in the Senate and for a Natives Representative Council. The Native and Land Bill allocated a further 7.2 million *morgen* (5.8 million ha) to be added to the 10.4 million *morgen* (8.3 million ha) already reserved for Africans under the 1913 Land Act. The Natives Representation Bill which Hertzog presented to the joint sitting of both Houses of Parliament in early February 1936 excluded any form of African representation in the House of Assembly and placed the required two-thirds majority in jeopardy. Hertzog submitted a final version of the Native Representation Bill to parliament on 17 February 1936 and proceeded to obtain the required two-thirds majority. The Native Trust and Land Bill, which did not need a two-thirds majority, was then passed.

The policy of segregation, both political and territorial, had been greatly advanced. Cape Africans had not only been removed from the common voters roll, but they had also been deprived of their right to purchase land outside of the reserved areas. In 1937 the Native Laws Amendment Act followed, extending and strengthening the system of urban segregation and influx control (Botha 1997a).

In *The Native Who Caused All the Trouble* this dilemma faces the outcast, Tselilo (brilliantly played by actor John Kani). The conflict of value systems (western colonial versus African traditional) is explored superbly in the movie. The laws of whites are the norm of the day.

This was the first film made by Van Rensburg's Film Theatre Institute to promote local progressive culture in contrast to *Doktor Con Viljee se Overberg, Die Perdesmous* and *Verspeelde Lente,* which were made for the SABC TV1 Afrikaans Drama Department.

Owing to criticism by Afrikaans viewers about the portrayal of themselves as poor whites, Van Rensburg turned to English-language features, thus broadening his audience for his exploration of Afrikanerdom (Botha 1997a).

The Native Who Caused All the Trouble. Grethe Fox

Structurally *The Native Who Caused All the Trouble* resembles *Die Perdesmous* and *Doktor Con Viljee se Overberg*. Although a filmed play, the film consists of a non-linear narrative structure. The story begins with an establishing shot of a female narrator giving background to Tselilo in a monologue. This is followed by a sequence which indicates the beginning of the court case. Tselilo is led into the courtroom, which we see through his eyes. Behind him is a portrait of General Jan Smuts. By means of close-ups the most important characters of the film are introduced to the viewer. The court case is interrupted by flashbacks of Tselilo's arrest and discussions with his Jewish lawyer. The film ends with the narrator giving a pessimistic account of Tselilo's sentence and a bourgeois lifestyle being adopted by even the more socially conscious characters in the film. Bruce, the liberal white policeman who supported Tselilo, becomes more interested in buying a big car than in the struggle of the oppressed (Botha 1997a; Botha & Van Aswegen 1992).

The film's criticism of the segregationist race policies takes the form of Tselilo's statements during the court case. He says,

From the little I understand, the law is a way of judging under which all men are equal, a way of judging that all men must respect, a way of judging that started with the commandments from God. Every law that does not see the black man the same as the white man is a sin against God. Because of these things it is my duty to demand dignity for my God, my people and myself. Therefore, I cannot allow myself to accept your authority; I cannot accept the authority of this court; I do not accept your judgement; I do not accept your sentence. Do what you will.

In stark contrast to the Africans in *Verspeelde Lente* and *Die Perdesmous*, who are farm workers, the African as outsider gets a voice, and a strong one, in *The Native*. His attack on racial laws reaches its peak with the words: 'If the people of this place cannot be taught of how much bloodshed there will be, if they do not find a way to become one people under God then they must fear for the lives of their children.'

These words are prophetic: The eighties and early nineties had been characterized by an unsurpassed amount of violence in South Africa, leading to the scrapping of apartheid laws including the Land Acts and a call by President F.W. de Klerk to build one nation within a new South Africa. But strong right-wing elements existed in South Africa during the nineties which threatened the peace process (Botha 1997a). This is the warning in two of Van Rensburg's greatest historical dramas, *Heroes* and *The Fourth Reich*.

1939–1948: The rise of Afrikaner nationalism

Fusion, and the consequent split between General Hertzog and D.F. Malan, was of the greatest significance in the history of Afrikaner nationalism (Botha 1998a). Although Malan's Purified National Party was numerically exceptionally weak, confined largely to the

Cape Province and with only 19 seats in the House of Assembly, within 15 years it had established itself as a dominant force in Afrikaner political life and as the new governing party in South Africa. In its ideology and institutional grounding in Afrikaner life, the party represented a fundamental departure from the Hertzog traditions of Afrikaner nationalism (Botha 1998a; Botha & Dethier 1997).

The focus of Hertzog's nationalism was the legal status of Afrikaners. As such, his principal objectives had been the securing of language equality for Afrikaners, the civil rights of Afrikaans speakers and the constitutional independence of South Africa. His definition of an Afrikaner was not narrowly exclusive and embraced not only Afrikaans speakers but also English-speaking whites who were loyal to South Africa and accepted language equality. A powerful sense of 'South Africa first' distinguished his nationalism, and this helped to shape his foreign and economic policies (Botha 1998a).

Malan's new party was formulating a far more aggressive nationalist ideology. Strongly republican, and ethnically exclusive, it stressed the distinctiveness of Afrikaner culture and saw as a priority not merely the legal parity of Afrikaners but their social and material predicament. These objectives were given institutional form in a range of political, cultural and economic agencies with and through which the party worked to articulate Afrikaner aspirations and to develop and entrench its hold on Afrikaner voters (Botha 1998a).

When the British Prime Minister Neville Chamberlain announced on Sunday 3 September 1939 that Britain was at war with Germany, Hertzog presented his colleagues with his decision that South Africa should adopt neutrality, a decision which he had reached in the knowledge that Malan's Purified National Party would support him. The Cabinet was irrevocably split by the decision. Smuts, however, proposed an amendment that the Union sever its relations with the Third Reich and refuse to adopt a position of neutrality. Hertzog, however, compared Hitler's behaviour with his own struggles in the cause of Afrikaner freedom. Smuts replied that it was impossible to reconcile neutrality with South Africa's obligations towards Britain and the Commonwealth. Hertzog's motion was defeated. He resigned, and Smuts was invited to form a government. On 6 September the new government issued a proclamation to sever relations with Germany. More than 2 million South Africans volunteered for service in Second World War, including 120,000 blacks (Botha 1998a).

In *The Fourth Reich* this split between Smuts and Hertzog is portrayed in a long sequence. Relationships between supporters of Smuts and those of Malan worsened, as depicted in *Heroes*. Under the leadership of Hans Van Rensburg, the Ossewabrandwag,[8] a right-wing organization, had initially enjoyed cordial relations with Malan and Hertzog's newly formed National Party, and many prominent party members had joined the movement. The Ossewabrandwag grew massively during the early war years; by 1941, its membership had reached between 300,000 and 400,000. It also became increasingly militaristic in style. A crack elite corps, the Stormjaers (storm troopers, similar to the Nazi *Sturmabteilung*) was established. Acts of sabotage carried out by members of the movement embarrassed the National Party, which, as Malan primly pointed out, relied on constitutional methods to achieve its objectives (Botha 1998a; Botha & Dethier 1997).

It is within this context that both *Heroes* and *The Fourth Reich* must be understood. During these stormy times of the Second World War the hatred between Smuts and Malan supporters was blatantly obvious.

Heroes (1985)

Heroes portrays an Orwellian world during the beginning of the forties in a linear narrative structure and a realistic style. Van Rensburg returned to the format of *Verspeelde Lente*. The viewer sees figures, faces and farmhouses in dark spaces, while paranoia and corruption reign everywhere. The complexity of the socio-political situation of this period was remarkably well-portrayed for a local television production (Botha 1998a; Botha & Dethier 1998).

The friendship between an Afrikaner, Hendrik (played by Ian Roberts, one of the regulars in Van Rensburg's work), and an Englishman, Patrick Joseph (played by Neil McCarthy), is the central focus of the narrative. Both are in love with an English-speaking nurse, Isadora Collins. Hendrik works in a garage for an elderly Jew, Mr Hymie Galgut. Isadora becomes a lodger with the Galgut family whose son, Ira, wants to join up in the war to fight Hitler and fascism. His father replies by identifying the enemy as a product of anti-Semitism, telling his son: 'We don't have a country. We have only ourselves.' Mr Galgut tends to exploit his employees, a practice to which Ira strongly objects (Botha 1998a).

The tension between those South Africans who have joined the war effort and those who have not is visible from the first sequence in the movie when Hendrik accidentally bumps into soldiers at the station. The soldiers demand an apology. The initial feelings of anti-Semitism are also visible in a sequence in which Isadora buys food in a shop and some Afrikaners make rude remarks about Jews.

Patrick remarks: 'We are not all alike. I am English.'
Isadora replies: 'One can be rude in any language.'

The scene changes to the Stormjaers trying to sabotage the railway line. General Fourie of the Ossewabrandwag arrives on the scene and is seriously hurt after an explosion. Hendrik, on his way home in his car, is asked by a member of the Stormjaers, Uncle Willem (Mees Xteen, who played Vlok in *Die Perdesmous*), to help him tow his car to a farmhouse (Botha 1998a).

He tells Hendrik, 'We Afrikaners must stand together, Hendrik.' The wounded body of General Fourie is in the car but being hidden from Hendrik. Unconsciously Hendrik, who is not politically polarised towards the right, becomes involved in Stormjaer activities.

Patrick is also not politically polarised, although his father, an English doctor, tries to persuade him to join the armed forces in the war. Patrick remarks that he will only join up if the Germans attack Jamestown. The change in the characters of these two men, initially friends, makes up the narrative of *Heroes*, a development in character that is no less remarkable than that of Pop in *Verspeelde Lente*.

Van Rensburg also portrays the tension in the relationships between the Afrikaner nationalists in the town and the Jewish family. In order to get medicine for the seriously injured General Fourie, some Stormjaer members kill Patrick's father and flee with the medicine. Hendrik meets with members of the Stormjaers, including Gerhard Lombaard (played by Ryno Hattingh, who also portrays Robey Leibbrandt in *The Fourth Reich*). They try to persuade him to join the ranks of the Stormjaers.

The episode has a brilliant sequence when the three friends, Patrick, Hendrik and Isadora, got to the local cinema to watch a movie titled *Singapore Woman*. On the screen a propaganda newsreel film with Wagnerian music flickers full of images of heroic young men joining the war. When 'God Save the Queen' is played on the soundtrack, some Stormjaer members refuse to stand, and they are attacked by soldiers. Later, the Afrikaner Nationalists tell Isadora, Patrick and Ira,

> We would like to show you English that we don't have grudges against individuals. We just don't accept the English king and the English flag and the English country … It is time you people realized that you're not living in an extension of England. You people came here to try to take this country away from us and now you are standing with one leg here and the other in England.

When Patrick's father dies in hospital, the scene intercuts with the death of General Andries Fourie. The ideological polarization now begins in the lives of Hendrik and Patrick. The latter is embittered and changes from a womanizer into a determined volunteer for the war. He objects to Hendrik's involvement with the Stormjaers at Stutterheim. Now, *Heroes* becomes a vivid exploration of growing fascism in South Africa with uncomfortable parallels with similar right-wing sentiments in South Africa of the early 1990s (Botha 1998a).

Patrick tells Hendrik, 'It is impossible to stay neutral in this war.' When he tries to make love to Isadora, he suffers from impotence. In a moving scene the friends have a farewell party in the fields, and nothing is the same after that.

Patrick joins the armed forces and his mother collapses, but finds emotional strength in Isadora, while Hendrik becomes a member of the Stormjaers after a quarrel with Mr Galgut, who becomes more and more isolated in the community. The growing polarization mirrors the same tendencies in South Africa during the P.W. Botha regime of the 1980s. The extreme of this polarization in the film is portrayed in a gruesome physical assault on the young Jew, Ira, forcing the Jewish family finally to leave the community.

Van Rensburg's major achievement in the film is in giving every side a human perspective: the Jewish family, the Afrikaner Nationalists and Patrick's family. People are caught up in a spiral of violence (Botha 1998a). One of the most remarkable scenes in the film is when Hendrik is sworn in as a member of the Stormjaers. Van Rensburg repeats this ritual several times in *The Fourth Reich*. He touches here at the heart of Afrikaner extremists, in an emotional ceremony that frightens the viewer because of its emotional intensity. Hendrik is now part of 'the war within South Africa' (as opposed to the war outside the country) and the ideology of Afrikaner nationalism. He begins to cut ties with Isadora and the communication between them suffers.

Hendrik is arrested after he tries to sabotage the railway line and realizes later he has been set up by his new friends who are not prepared to perform the act themselves because of the danger involved. In his discussions with the police, explaining his motives, he refers to the traumas of urbanization, the drought on the farms and the absence of capital to save Afrikaner farmers. In the concentration camp, Hendrik's humiliating physical check-up and his detention again show clear parallels with the state of emergency during the 1980s in South Africa and the thousands of detentions without trial (Botha 1998a).

Both Hendrik and Patrick betray their friends, returning home with physical and emotional scars. This makes the title of the film highly ironic. Neither the volunteers in the war nor the Stormjaers fighting their own war inside the country can be regarded as heroes in Van Rensburg's filmic world (Botha 1998a; Botha & Dethier 1997).

Hendrik, disillusioned by the Stormjaers, informs on them to the security personnel in the camp. (This incident is reminiscent of a similar act in *The Fourth Reich* when Jan Taillard betrays Robey Leibbrandt at the end of the movie.) Patrick too acts in a cowardly fashion when he tries to run away from a hand grenade that falls between him and his buddies on the battlefield, instead of throwing himself on it, giving up his life in order to save theirs. He is, however, wounded in the back. Hendrik becomes the Van Rensburg outcast, living in paranoia on the edge of society. At the end of the film he is shot by the fascist, Gerhard.

The Fourth Reich (1990)

The director's cut of *The Fourth Reich*, also linear in structure and realistic in style, is Van Rensburg's greatest achievement. The film is basically structured as a thriller, a hunt by a dedicated Afrikaner policeman, Jan Taillard (Marius Weyers), working undercover to expose and capture the fascist Robey Leibbrandt (Ryno Hattingh) before he carries out his plan to assassinate General Smuts. Van Rensburg's themes of betrayal, the outcast, communication problems in relationships (in this case between Taillard and his wife) and Afrikaner nationalism are all present and brilliantly developed in the director's cut which runs for over 3 hours (Botha 1998a; Botha & Dethier 1997).

The controversy surrounding the production has suggested that the shorter theatrical version is perhaps not fully the film Van Rensburg made, and to see his concept at its best one should watch the 3-hour television version (Botha & Dethier 1997). But even the shorter version is still an impressive achievement: It depicts, as does *Heroes*, a time when the country was divided, as thousands of Afrikaner patriots, instead of joining the war effort, flocked to an ultra-right-wing organization violently opposed to the British (Botha 1998a).

The Fourth Reich. Grethe Fox, David Selvan

Right-wing extremist sentiments are personified in the Leibbrandt character. He objects to his parents' friendship with a Jewish family. According to him, they are exploiting the Afrikaner nation. Later in the film, he and members of the Stormjaers blow up the shop of this Jewish family. During the recruiting of members, he remarks, 'The Afrikaner grew up with his Bible in his one hand and his gun in the other. This is why we are still here.' After this sequence, he starts a sabotage campaign.

The film is well structured and edited. Its linear structure involves two parallel narrative lines of Leibbrandt and Taillard, respectively, starting their missions, receiving instructions and making contact with crucial people. These storylines become one in both characters' involvement with a German woman (brilliantly played by Grethe Fox). Taillard cannot tell his wife about his mission. His obsessive involvement in his work contributes to the separation between them. It is never resolved (Botha 1998a).

The Fourth Reich is one of the few South African films to make the great landscapes of South Africa (in particular the Cape Province, a recurring landscape within Van Rensburg's oeuvre) an integral part of the narrative structure.

Visually the film is hauntingly beautiful, photographed by Dewald Aukema. It fully deserved the 1990 AA Life/M-Net Vita Award for best cinematography.[9] The film's authentic images consist mostly of long shots of figures against the landscapes of a rural South Africa in contrast to medium and close-up shots of characters within darkly lit indoor settings.

Louis Van Rensburg composed a remarkably authentic score for the film, developing specific musical themes for the key characters. Concertinas and violins were used throughout, as well as the Second Movement of Franz Schubert's Piano Trio in E-Flat Op 100, for the characterization of the German woman, Frau Dorfman.

The failure of the film at the box office, however, was a shock for the industry. It cost some R16 million to make, raised mostly through the tax incentive scheme of the 1980s. The film opened with 20 prints, a saturated media and highly favourable reviews. Van Rensburg took best director at the Vita Awards. It featured great acting talent: Elize Cawood, Grethe Fox, Ryno Hattingh, Marius Weyers, Tertius Meintjies and Ian Roberts. Mark Wilby's art direction is brilliant.

The Fourth Reich. Grethe Fox, David Selvan

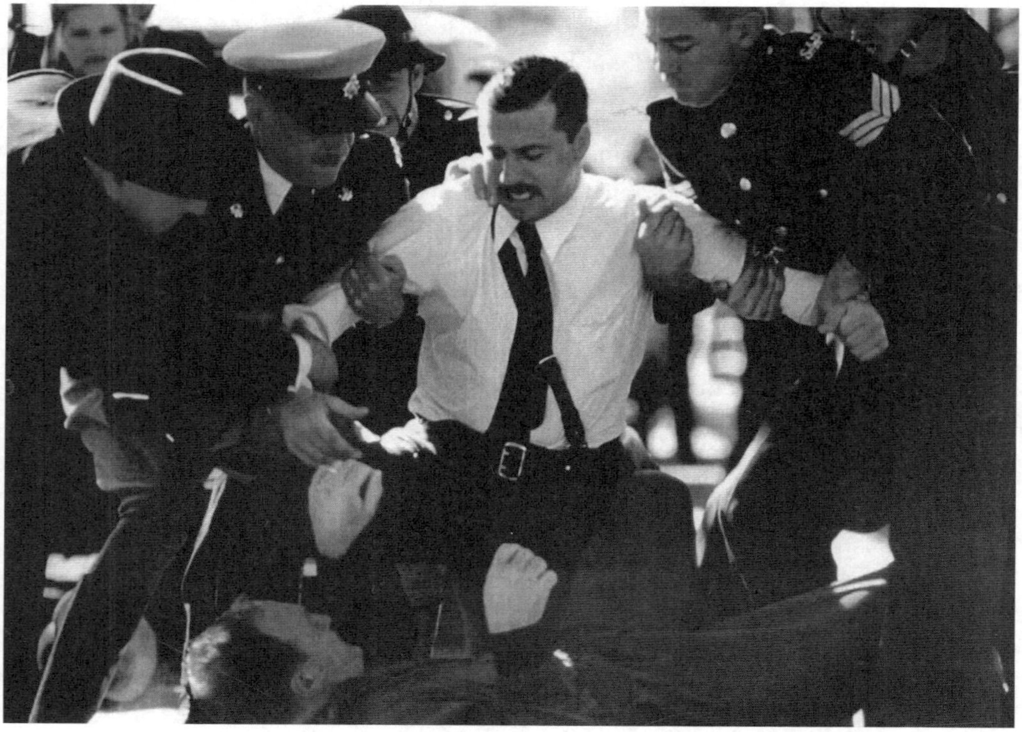

The 1970s and 1980s: The urban Afrikaner

Van Rensburg's best work is set in the past. His work about the psyche of the contemporary urban Afrikaner is placed within the conventions of light comedies like *Die Square*, suspense dramas such as *Die Vuurtoring* and *Die Bankrower*, or adaptations of radio stories like *Geluksdal*. Subsidy based on box-office income, censorship of local political films and the lack of audience demand for risky, experimental work during the seventies might have inhibited Van Rensburg in fully exploring contemporary issues. Although some of these films do not attain the same standard as his period dramas, they are still examples of Van Rensburg's thematic concerns, and *Die Vuurtoring* especially is a major achievement (Botha 1998a).

Country Lovers (1982)

Country Lovers is a short fiction film based on the work of the South African writer, Nadine Gordimer. It depicts a contemporary love story across the racial barrier. The children of a white farmer and of the black farm labourers play together. Then comes the time when the white children leave to go to school and the black children begin to call their former playmates 'Miss' and 'Master'. The film deals with the story of Paulus and Thebedi, former playmates who become lovers. Thebedi is courted and married by another of the farm labourers. She gives birth to a light-skinned child. The tragedy is inevitable (Botha 1998a).

The film was never screened on SABC TV and had a limited local festival and video release. Van Rensburg never had the freedom in his theatrical films of the 1970s as in the case of this short film, but these films do reflect some of his themes.

Freddie's in Love (1971)

Freddie's in Love, a financial failure, portrayed life in Johannesburg's metropolitan Hillbrow. In the depiction of a relationship between two lonely young people, Van Rensburg portrayed individual loneliness and communication problems between people within a contemporary urban context. The film's opening montage of Freddie's mundane lifestyle, brilliantly shot by Koos Roets, vividly captures the main character's solitude and alienation. The melancholic mood is further enhanced by the use of the Andante from Mozart's Piano Concerto No. 21 in C (K 467). Freddie's alienation is further explored in a sequence of a social function at his workplace. Van Rensburg is using images of characters involved in small talk, and thus seemingly meaningless conversations, while Freddie is merely observing, in silence, from a distance. Franz Marx's performance as Freddie is understated and ultimately very moving. Van Rensburg introduces some of his most

Freddie's in Love. M-Net

important themes in this first feature: loneliness, communication problems and a world of possible betrayal, in which happiness is short-lived. These themes would later be more fully explored in the made-for-SABC drama *Die Vuurtoring* as well as his masterpiece *The Fourth Reich*.

Die Bankrower (1973)

Die Bankrower/The Bank Robber, a suspense story, depicts the strategy of a burglar in a corrupt world. The burglar is Anton, the son of a wealthy bank owner. He has many risky ideas to make and invest money. His father, however, wants nothing to do with these plans. Anton, therefore, decides to demonstrate one of his plans. In order to do so, he needs money, which he steals from his father's bank. The film becomes quite intriguing when a real burglar steals the money from Anton. *Die Bankrower* is a well-made film, technically advanced for its time and an indication that an Afrikaans director can handle suspense successfully within this genre (Botha 1998a).

Die Vuurtoring (1984)

Van Rensburg's experimentation with film reached a peak in *Die Vuurtoring/The Lighthouse*. The hero, Wim Kleynhans (played by scriptwriter Johan Van Jaarsveld), lives an anti-social existence on the 'edge' of a modern, urban society. Obsessed with his work, he communicates more with his computer than with his wife, even addressing the computer as 'Darling'! The patience he shows the computer is absent in his relationship with his wife. Their sterile marriage is symbolized by the clinical setting of their modern household, which Van Rensburg makes white throughout. The characters wear black clothes in sharp contrast to their surroundings and hide their emotional insecurity behind health-conscious practices (Botha 1998a; Botha & Dethier 1997).

The lighthouse becomes the symbol of a dissection of the inner worlds of these characters, their betrayal and personal conflicts. Wim becomes involved with a sinister organization that contracts him to break a computer code to obtain information about 'female fashions'. In trying to find the right code, the right language, he feeds the computer an impressive alphabet of terms, but in his communication with his wife, he uses only the most basic of sentences such as 'I am working tonight' and 'Goodbye'.

As with Taillard in *The Fourth Reich*, the hero cannot tell his wife about the nature of his work. He also cannot find the time to talk to her, like Horace in *Taxi to Soweto*. His wife, Helena, becomes involved in a relationship with another man, Leon Wessels.

At the end of the film, Wim does break the computer code and realizes that the database consists of detailed information about missiles. He also finds secret video recordings of his wife's infidelity as well as their conversations at home. During this sequence he realizes the sterility of their marriage. Like the main character in *Die Perdesmous*, he turns to violence (Botha 1998a).

This drama allows a free interpretation by means of an open structure. The contrast between the disintegration of human communication and the artificial, sophisticated world of technical communications (accentuated by shots of the interior of a telephone exchange and switchboard, a video camera, the use of an answering machine and a television) is portrayed by means of alternating black and white with colour shots in a structurally fragmented way. The world of this ambitious television drama is an Orwellian one, full of paranoia and corruption within the ranks of a sinister organization, not much different from the historical settings of Van Rensburg's period work (Botha 1998a; Botha & Dethier 1997).

Taxi to Soweto (1991)

In this Ster-Kinekor released film, Van Rensburg sets himself the tricky task of balancing sentiment and humour. *Taxi to Soweto* principally concerns a bored, middle-of-the-road, middle-aged, over-pampered, rich, urban Afrikaans woman, Jessica du Toit (played by Van Rensburg's regular, Elize Cawood), her workaholic husband, Horace (Marius Weyers), and a snappy street-sharp taxi driver, Richard (Patrick Shai), whose lives become entwined despite the chasm known as the great South African racial divide (Botha 1998a).

Horace and Jessica's marriage has settled into stagnation in the 'wastefully wonderful white-washed world of the old South Africa' (Botha 1998a). But a series of unexpected events signal a swift reversal. On her way to fetch Horace from the airport, Jessica's car breaks down. She is 'rescued' by Richard, who in turn is hijacked at gunpoint, and Jessica is thrown headlong into 'the black experience' of Soweto. Her restricted perspective of South African life is about to change forever.

Van Rensburg explores communication problems within many spheres of South African society: between people of different race groups and especially within the urban rat race of wealthy whites. He does not flinch from showing class differences between people living in poverty in sectors of Soweto and the rich whites of the northern urban areas of Johannesburg (Botha 1998a; Botha & Dethier 1997).

Horace and Jessica's life is characterized by a lack of communication due to Horace's obsession with his work. As is the case in *Die Vuurtoring*, communication takes place within the restrictions of telephone answering machines and short telephone calls. Horace and his employer simply do not have the time for personal phone calls from their wives. Horace and Jessica's house looks like a fortress, with a sophisticated security system, a vicious dog and high security fences. The purpose is to keep the 'enemy' out. In a very funny moment in the film, this security system literally backfires on Horace when he is attacked by his own dog, and the security agency considers him to be a burglar (Botha 1998a).

When Horace arrives home after a business trip his world crumbles on finding a message from a black man on the answering machine, referring to Jessica as 'Baby'. He starts a long quest to find her. Suddenly his work loses its meaning. The quest resembles a similar process in *Die Square*, a comedy about a so-called pure Afrikaner who loses his wife and sets out to look for her in the 'strange' urban world of Hillbrow, in many ways alien to pure Afrikanerdom.

Similar to *Die Vuurtoring*, the hero in *Taxi to Soweto* is confronted with his failed marriage by means of an audio-visual recording. Horace sees the break-up of his relationship with Jessica in the form of a television soapie. In a way this sequence becomes a critical comment on the portrayal of relationships in the Afrikaans film 'soapies' of the local industry during the seventies (Botha 1998a).

The people who bring Jessica and Horace together again are, in fact, the 'enemy', the blacks from Soweto. Jessica and Horace do get a new perspective on their lives and marriage, and on a changing South Africa. Unlike the pessimistic ending of *Die Vuurtoring*, their marriage is saved.

In *Taxi to Soweto* there are no outcasts, nor liberal whites who fight for the rights of blacks such as in *A Dry White Season* (1989), nor the ultra-right-wing Afrikaner stereotypes of Roodt's *A Place of Weeping* (1986). A human face, although critical, is given to both the activists and the rich whites (Botha 1998a; Botha & Dethier 1997).

The film was shot in Soweto and Johannesburg. Several languages have been used: Afrikaans, English, Zulu, Xhosa and Sotho. This reflects the rich cultural diversity Van Rensburg is portraying. In many ways this is the first filmic presentation of the dawn of a post-apartheid South Africa. The award-winning performances by Patrick Shai, Ramalao Makhene and Mary Twala were highlights of Van Rensburg's last feature.

Conclusion

Manie Van Rensburg's chronicles of Afrikanerdom are noted for their humane treatment of the characters, including outcasts and the political right wing. These films and television dramas are more than mere profiles of the politics of the time. Most of his work addresses communication problems between people in a universe that is characterized by distrust, paranoia and eventually betrayal (Botha 1998a; Botha & Dethier 1997). Even comedies such as *Die Square* and *Taxi to Soweto* address the issue of mistrust between humans. Van Rensburg's work as a whole gives a portrait of the strange, complex and divided creature who is the Afrikaner. This portrait is an important alternative to the oversimplified images of Afrikaners as mere racist villains usually depicted in anti-apartheid images of this society.

Van Rensburg placed himself within the Afrikaans lager and, with films such as *Die Square* and *Verspeelde Lente*, managed to upset the establishment. *Die Square* caused a stir by depicting Afrikaners as hypocrites. *Verspeelde Lente* upset Afrikanerdom with its images of poor, lower class Afrikaners. Being Afrikaans was a source of tension, but also creativity, in his work. He was not interested in portraying Afrikaner history but in exploring Afrikaners against the larger history of the country. Later, examinations of racism and anti-Semitism became important themes in his work such as *The Native Who Caused All the Trouble*, *Heroes* and especially *The Fourth Reich*. The latter examined the destruction caused by power, racism and anti-Semitism (Botha 1998a).

If his work has a common theme, it is the conflict between the outsider and communal acceptance, an aspect he experienced in real life. His trip to Dakar during the repressive days of State President P.W. Botha got wide, somewhat hysterical publicity in Afrikaans newspapers and meant an effective end to his career in the local mainstream film industry and unofficial blacklisting by the SABC.

He divided his career into his pre- and post-Dakar periods. Before Dakar he had work. After Dakar he found himself out of business. He was suddenly a film-maker in search of a spiritual home; after being a sought-after, popular director, he struggled to make films. And the Left also held pitfalls. One remembers an interview with him where he stated his dissatisfaction with FAWO. Someone there phoned him and asked why he had not yet submitted his script on *Taxi to Soweto* for approval. His answer was unprintable. He did not need anyone's seal of approval, from the Right or the Left. He was too honest to take an approved political point of view and too independent to leave artistic and political judgment to others. At the time of his suicide on 3 December 1993, he was only 48 years old (Botha 1998a).

His last film *Taxi to Soweto* dealt with racial reconciliation as far back as 1991, years before the historic democratic elections of 1994, and other South African film-makers produced numerous 'Rainbow Nation' comedies such as *The Angel, the Bicycle and the Chinaman's Finger* (1992), *There's a Zulu on My Stoep* (1993), *Soweto Green* (1994), *Inside Out* (1999), *Mr Bones* (2001), *Mama Jack* (2005) and *White Wedding* (2009).

Ironically, the first retrospective of Van Rensburg's oeuvre was held in Brussels in 1996, *not* South Africa, where he still needs to be fully acknowledged by academics. The retrospective formed part of a launch of a book on Van Rensburg co-authored by myself and Prof. Hubert Dethier (1997) from the Free University of Brussels.

In South Africa Van Rensburg was considered to be a 'director with the talent and skill that could eventually put him with the ranks of the world's best' (Tony Jackman in the *Cape Argus* newspaper of 14 March 1983). He received an Honorary Prize from the South African Academy of Science and Art for cultural achievements in cinema. The *Star* newspaper's Tonight Award was given to him four times. The South African Broadcasting Corporation's Artes Award was presented to him twice, and the Afrikaanse Taal-en Kultuurvereniging (Afrikaans Language and Culture Society, ATKV) bestowed awards on him. He also received the AA Life/M-Net Vita Award for Best Director for *The Fourth Reich*, and the Idem Award for direction for *Die Vuurtoring/The Lighthouse*.

In the 1990s the Award for Lifetime Achievement in African Cinema by the pay-TV channel M-Net was named after Van Rensburg. At the 2007 edition of the KKNK the first ever South African retrospective of Van Rensburg's oeuvre was organized by the director of the Cape Winelands Film Festival, Leon Van der Merwe.

Notes

1. Tobie Cronjé is one of South Africa's most celebrated and iconic actors. His career includes more than 100 stage roles, numerous television performances and an impressive display of his acting abilities in films such **as** *Inside Out* (1999) and *Promised Land* (2002).
2. A prominent source, apart from Giliomee (2003), used in this chapter regarding the history of South Africa is Cameron and Spies (1986).
3. See Giliomee (2003).
4. People who live on another's farm under certain conditions of service.
5. Since 1918, this highly organized clique of so-called super-Afrikaners has by sophisticated political intrigue waged a remarkable campaign to harness political, social and economic forces within

South Africa to its cause of Afrikaner nationalism. See Wilkins and Strydom (1978) for an in-depth study of the subject.

6. Afrikaner Union of Mineworkers.
7. See Kannemeyer (1988).
8. The Brigade of Oxwagon Sentinels, a paramilitary, ultra-nationalist mass movement, was formed in 1939 following the Voortrekker centenary celebrations. It sought to arm the Afrikaner nation for the coming struggle to conquer the English-dominated urban centres.
9. See Blignaut and Botha (1992) for full lists of South African award-winning productions between 1978 and 1992.

Chapter 6

Ross Devenish

part from Rautenbach and Van Rensburg another outstanding South African film-maker of the 1970s was Ross Devenish, who made three internationally praised South African films, *Boesman and Lena* (1973), *The Guest* (1977) and *Marigolds in August* (1979).

Devenish, one of the most internationally acclaimed South African directors, was born in Polokwane (Pietersburg) in 1939. During his childhood years in Brits, a town outside Pretoria, he dreamt about becoming an engine driver. His father served in the South African air force during the Second World War. When his dad returned from the front he brought with him a roll of 16mm film, which had been taken from the camera filming engagements over enemy territory. Devenish became fascinated with these film rolls, and he decided to make films (Botha 2006b).

At 19 he went to study film in London at the London School of Film Technique. He made several documentaries during the 1960s in war zones such as the Civil War in Yemen, Borneo, Malaysia, Congo and Vietnam. He worked for Associated Rediffusion, which was the precursor of Thames Television when he filmed conflict in Congo during the sixties. His last war experiences were in Vietnam just before and during the Tet Offensive. At that stage he worked for ITV – Thames Television. The Vietnamese war had a huge impact on Devenish, and he realized that the very same thing could happen in apartheid South Africa.

Before working in South Africa Devenish received international acclaim for two documentaries: *Now that the Buffalo's Gone* (1968), a moving account of Native Americans, and *Goal!*, a film about the Soccer World Cup competition held in England in 1966. *Now that the Buffalo's Gone* won the American Blue Ribbon Award. *Goal!* received the Robert Flaherty Award from the British Academy of Film and Television Arts (BAFTA).

Boesman and Lena (1973)

In the 1970s Devenish and playwright Athol Fugard created three highly acclaimed films, *Boesman and Lena*, *The Guest* and *Marigolds in August*. *Boesman and Lena* (1973), based on Fugard's play, was the first local feature to portray the poverty and enforced removals of South Africans classified as 'black' under apartheid. The film won a gold and silver medal at the 6th Atlanta Film Festival in the United States. Fugard himself played the part of bitter Boesman, with Yvonne Bryceland as Lena, his common-law wife, who complains constantly of his ill-treatment of her. The opening sequence of *Boesman and Lena* is haunting: Boesman taunts the driver of a bulldozer that is levelling their makeshift house. In helpless rage he and Lena take their belongings and take to the road in search of a new home. By the end of the film they are still homeless. They became the marginal characters, who would dominate post-apartheid cinema (see Chapter 12). The film is a searing portrait of marginality.

The Guest (1977)

In *The Guest* (1977) director Ross Devenish examines Afrikaner intellectual, poet, writer and opium addict Eugene Marais's fight against drug dependence during an incident at the end of his life. In stark contrast to several Afrikaans-language films of the sixties and seventies, with their idealized depiction of white Afrikaners, Devenish provided a critical portrait of this part of South African society. Morphine addiction changes Marais's life completely and transforms his promising future into an existence of terrible pain and loneliness, which finds expression in the sombre vision informing his poems and other literature.

In a sequence, while Marais is preparing an injection, one hears his voice-over:

The supreme danger which lies in the use of intoxicants as a cure for mental suffering and which often renders the remedies worse than the disease is of course the morbid organic changes resulting from habitual use. Cessation of use causes what are known as symptoms of abstinence, of a severity and painfulness proportionate to the usual dose

The Guest. M-Net

The Guest. M-Net

and the duration of the habit. These symptoms are always painful and a dose of the poison invariably affords relief from their immediate effects. Long-continued usage therefore sets up in time the so-called 'double pull' – the craving for the characteristic euphoria and a dread of the painful symptoms of abstinence. There is a continual alternation between the deepest gloom of abstinence and a mental state … which through continuous use of the drug resembles sluggish mental anaesthesia rather than positive happiness. But for the individual concerned this temporary respite is preferable to the normal condition of suffering. (Fugard & Devenish 1992: 76)

Morphine became the catalyst in the life of this respected Afrikaner; his dark vision emerges from the euphoria and the pain; it is this knowledge that dictates his ideas and actions. Devenish focuses on a small period in the life of Marais, going 'cold turkey' on a farm, called Steenkampskraal. Athol Fugard plays Marais as he staggers inevitable towards suicide. Devenish cuts incisively through the mythical stereotype of Marais, who believed that the existence of life is founded on pain and sorrow. This pain is the subject of a graceful, austere and controlled film, which handles its themes almost with musical skill. It is passed on and explored with almost fugue-like pattern, from person to person, from voice to voice, until Marais' point seems irrefutable (Ronge 1977). The mood is brilliantly enhanced by the use of music by Johann Sebastian Bach on the soundtrack.

Devenish also brilliantly depicts two contrasting worldviews. The Meyer family, who hosts Marais, is a simple, conservative Afrikaner group. The father (Gordon Voster) and mother (brilliantly played by Wilma Stockenström) are initially unaware of Marais's addiction. Although alienated by his social aloofness the family still tries to be friendly and supportive hosts. Marais, however, is experiencing an existential crisis and he is withdrawing more and more from society. Only his friend, A.G. Visser (Marius Weyers), provides some form of comfort, especially when they engage in literary and philosophical discussions.

While most South African films of the 1970s approached their subjects by means of social melodrama *The Guest* is influenced by Italian neorealism as well as the style of the Indian master Satyajit Ray. It is an austere film, which was not popular with South African audiences but received ecstatic international acclaim (Tomaselli 1989). This masterful film won numerous national and international awards, including a Bronze Leopard Award at the Locarno Film Festival.

Marigolds in August (1979)

Marigolds in August (1979) portrays the tension between a poor, black man, Daan (Winston Ntshona), and an unemployed black man, Melton (John Kani), who is struggling to support a family in a township near Port Elizabeth. The film was made at Schoenmakerskop, a 'white' beach resort on the outskirts of Port Elizabeth. Some 10 kilometres from Schoenmakerskop is Walmer, a 'black' township where servants who work in the resort live. The township is a place where malnutrition is rife and where unemployed blacks and squatters gather. It is from this

Marigolds in August.
M-Net

place that Daan walks in early morning light to work in the 'white' beach resort as a gardener. His security, however, is threatened by the presence of Melton (movingly played by Kani), who is looking for work. One of Melton's children has died recently, and his wife and a second child suffer from malnutrition. He has no money or food and is desperate (Botha 2006b).

Melton's presence in the town means danger to Daan since his own passbook is not in order in apartheid South Africa, and Melton's presence could attract the attention of the South African police. A fierce conflict develops between Daan and Melton, and this becomes a struggle for self-preservation, one in which Paulus (played by Fugard), a man who ekes out a meagre living by catching snakes for the snake park, serves as a catalyst. Gradually Daan grows to understand his dilemma. He realizes that the apartheid system divides blacks and plays them against each other. Solidarity and compassion towards each other is the only solution.

The third of director Ross Devenish's collaborations with playwright Athol Fugard, the film was one of the few local features in the 1970s which examined the conditions of blacks in South Africa. While most of local film-making created an idealized South Africa in which blacks did not exist in the 1970s Devenish confronted the dilemma of black unemployment in a universe where whites are only seen behind glass, in their houses or cars, separated from the socio-political realities of apartheid South Africa. It is shot in the style of Italian neorealism and the fifties work by Satyajit Ray, and the film consists mostly of exteriors, shot in natural light.

The film, shunned by South African audience during its release in 1980, became an international award winner at various film festivals, including the Berlin International Film Festival, where it won two awards, including the Silver Bear. Despite the international acclaim Devenish found it impossible to work under apartheid and went into exile. *Marigolds in August* was his last South African feature.

Devenish left for the United Kingdom in the 1980s, where he directed several acclaimed television dramas such as an eight-part series of *Bleak House* and features such as *Happy Valley* (shot in Kenya), *Death of a Son* (1987) and *Asinamali* (1987), a BBC adaptation of Mbongoni Ngema's stage play about the state of emergency in apartheid South Africa. *Bleak House* won three BAFTAs.

Devenish returned to South Africa in 2002. Unfortunately once again he was faced by a funding climate, which thus far has not been supportive of his film projects. His screenplay, *Ways of Living*, an adaptation of Zakes Mda's novel *Ways of Dying*, has been rejected by the NFVF due to the fact that the screenplay structure deviates from a three-act structure and embraces oral aesthetics in storytelling. Devenish also removed his directing credits from a screen adaptation of John Kani's successful stage play, *Nothing but the Truth*, after filming finished in December 2006. He resumed his professional relationship with Fugard and co-directed the playwright's *The Train Driver* at the new Fugard Theatre in Cape Town in 2010.

Film-makers such as Devenish and Rautenbach found it difficult to make the kind of film which deals critically with socio-political issues. They have encountered problems with the subsidy, censors, distributors and the predominant white audiences of the 1970s. During the 1970s black and white audiences were still treated differently. The audiences were separated, each with their own set of rules and operations, films and cinemas. Only by 1985 were cinemas in South Africa desegregated.

Chapter 7

B Scheme films

In the 1970s, attempts were made to cultivate a cinema dealing with black themes and geared for black audiences, but with dismal results. The motivation driving this development was a new government subsidy system, the B Scheme, which enabled white film-makers with little or no experience to produce low-budget films in ethnic languages with government support.

The makers of these films demonstrated little knowledge of black culture. Many did not even speak the ethnic languages in which their films were shot and had to rely on actors to translate their own dialogue. Corruption under this system was rife, the quality of films abysmal and documentaries generally non-existent (Pichaske 2009). The result was a large number of shoddy films in ethnic languages that were screened in churches, schools and community and beer halls. It was contrary to the Nationalist government's apartheid policy to allow black cinemas in the urban white areas, as this would concede the citizenship of urban blacks (Murray 1992; Tomaselli 1989). The urbanization of blacks was portrayed in these films as uniformly negative and homeland life as more fitting. Armes (2008) estimated that approximately 250 films were made under the B Subsidy Scheme from 1974 to 1990. Originally a maximum of R70,000 was payable, based on the number of tickets sold for 18 cents or less. The majority of these films were made by white directors with black actors. They were shot in Zulu, Xhosa, Sotho and other South African languages. Armes (2008) lists 206 films which were shot in Zulu and/or Xhosa and 35 in Sotho.

The films were made with low budgets, sometimes as little as R10,000 (Gavshon 1983). Van Zyl (1985) distinguishes between the different types of B Scheme films:

> The first is the 'return to tribal life' in which a black person rejects the urban experience and returns to the kraal where he or she eventually finds happiness. These films are generally crudely conceived and executed and black filmgoers view them with some suspicion. The second type of film is set in an urban township. Sometimes these films are made by black directors (Simon Sabela being a notable example) with white finance. These films involve plots about township life – feuding taxi-owners, unfaithful wives, and so on – but still ignore political realities. Other films involve boxing encounters, in which action is the main theme. Another type is the 'disco' film, made mainly by Ronnie Isaacs, with a great deal of music and the rags-to-riches theme in its plot. (p. 106)

Makgabutlane (1989) criticises the poor artistic quality of the B Scheme films. In many of these films the actors and actresses were literally taken off the street and had not had any formal training in film techniques or acting. Some of these films had no script and were made in the record time of 12 days. These films contrast sharply to the work by Ross Devenish in the 1970s.

On the political front the Soweto uprising of June 1976 claimed the lives of almost 700 people and provoked responses worldwide. Enforced removals of black South Africans continued as part of apartheid policy. Any film that managed to be made which in any way reflected the South African society in turmoil was banned by the state, such as *How Long* (1976) by Gibson Kente or Nana Mahomo's *Last Grave at Dimbaza*, (1974), or received no distribution whatsoever, and thus did not qualify for any film subsidy. In 1976, for example, more than half of the 698 films examined by the Directorate of Publications for screening in South Africa were either partly censored by means of cuts or banned outright (Friedberg 1978). Only 249 films were approved unconditionally, 341 were cut and 61 were totally banned. *The Omen* was so brutalized by the censors' scissors – the final sequence in the film having been completely eliminated – that some newspaper critics refused to review it (Friedberg 1978).

Directors such as Simon Sabela (*U-Deliwe*, 1975), tried to make more meaningful work within this system, but they were severely constrained by censorship and white dominance in the film industry. Sabela played a role in Ashley Lazarus' *e'Lollipop* (1975), one of the few films made during apartheid, which imagined some type of friendship between blacks and whites. The setting, however, is not apartheid South Africa but a Catholic mission in Lesotho. A white boy (Norman Knox) and a black boy (Muntu Ben Ndebele) spent their childhood in the idealized pastoral beauty of the mountains. The film did not challenge apartheid ideology and thus enjoyed a general theatrical release in South Africa.

Sabela's own work as director included *Isivumelwano* (1978) and *Ngaka* (1978). Produced by Heyns Productions the first title is based on a radio serial and tells the story of a dedicated clergyman whose wife cannot reconcile with giving up the bright lights of her modelling career for a life of austerity. She runs away with a charming gangster. Leading parts are played by Congress Majola and Cynthia Shange. *Ngaka* is a comedy about the clash between western and tribal medicine. Significantly both films' crew members included several black technicians. Thematically, however, these films avoided addressing the socio-political realities of the seventies.

One of the seminal documentaries of the 1970s on the horrors of apartheid is Nana Mahomo's *Last Grave at Dimbaza* (1974). It gives an insight into the lives of people living under apartheid during the 1970s. So powerful was the indictment provided by *Last Grave at Dimbaza* that the South African government produced a film during the 1970s to counter its effects, entitled *To Act a Lie* (1978). The South African Embassy in London tried to stop Mahomo's film being broadcast on the BBC, and in the controversy that followed, the BBC allowed the South African government to screen their own film alongside *Last Grave at Dimbaza*. This film led to an international media war over South Africa's image (Unwin & Belton 1992). *Last Grave at Dimbaza* won the Grand Prix at the Melbourne Film Festival. When Mahomo made *Last Grave at Dimbaza* in 1974 he was a member of the Pan Africanist

Congress (PAC) and wanted to use the film medium to educate people about the horrors of apartheid and the conditions in South Africa. His films are characterized by a direct and simple approach to shooting (much of the camera is hand held and shots are repeated) and edited with the intention of maximizing understanding. Unfortunately Mahomo was forced to live a large part of his life outside South Africa, amongst others in Botswana. He and Simon Sabela were among the few black film directors in South Africa during the 1970s.

Chapter 8

The voices of the 1980s

In the early 1980s film attendance dropped to its lowest level as a result of the popularity of television, which was introduced in 1976, and a scarcity of good South African films. The A subsidy scheme still undermined the possibility of producing local films, which would have been critical of apartheid or simply experimented with narrative structures and/or film form. The subsidy system did not make provision for developmental funding. It only rewarded box-office success. Only when a South African film had earned a specific minimum gross sum (which was altered from time to time) could it be considered for a subsidy, which covered a percentage of the production costs.

Self-censorship played an important role since few financiers were prepared to back a local film that risked being banned or could be a commercial disaster. Adjustments to the subsidy system during the late 1970s did little to provide better solutions. The 1979 formula required that a film should earn at the box office a minimum of R100,000 within the first 2 years of its release before qualifying for a state subsidy. If an Afrikaans-language film earned R200,000 at the box office it qualified for a 70% subsidy; for R300,000 the subsidy was 80% and for R400,000 the subsidy amounted to 50% (Botha & Van Aswegen 1992). A box-office income of R500,000 received a 40% subsidy, and one exceeding R500,000, a 30% subsidy. A maximum of R300,000 could be earned by subsidy. Local films in English were subsidized in a similar way, except that the maximum was 60% and the minimum subsidy granted was 20%. The A scheme was intended for films dealing with 'white' subjects and themes. Needless to say the system promoted escapism and discouraged any form of formal experimentation or the exploration of political themes. Consequently a box-office success was rewarded with greater profits, and this in turn led to the making of safe-formula films under the A subsidy scheme throughout the 1960s, 1970s and 1980s. In March 1995 this system ceased to exist.

Although very restrictive in terms of political censorship the SABC became a significant outlet for Afrikaans-language drama series, such as the work of Manie van Rensburg (Chapter 5), Danie Odendaal's impressive *Veldslag* (1990), dealing with women's experiences in wartime, as well as Dirk de Villiers's *Arende* (1988–91), a reconstruction of the experiences of prisoners of war on the island of St Helena during the Anglo-Boer War. In fact, De Villiers (born 26 July 1924) experienced his most creative period in the 1980s after a series of unremarkable genre films during the 1970s, with the exception of his psychological thriller *My Broer se Bril* (1972) starring Cobus Rossouw and featuring fascinating cinematography and *mise-en-scène*. The SABC provided De Villiers with the opportunity to display his great talent as a director and chronicler of South African history. The 10-part television series

Arende/Eagles was a moving portrait of the Anglo-Boer War and British concentration camps. It was edited into a full-length feature in 1992. De Villiers continued his chronicles of the Anglo-Boer War in *Arende II* (1991) and the feature *That Englishwoman* (1989), about Emily Hobhouse, the British welfare campaigner, who is primarily remembered for bringing to the attention of the British public, and working to change, the appalling conditions inside the British concentration camps in South Africa built for Boer women and children during the Anglo-Boer War.[1] Dirk Gysbert De Villiers made 25 full-length films and 13 documentaries including *Kango* (1984), a visually spectacular account of the remotest parts of the Cango Caves in the Little Karoo. A lung infection ended his life on 28 December 2009.

Outside of the A Subsidy scheme or the SABC it was difficult for an independent film director or producer to obtain local finance and distribution. The discouragement of active participation by black film-makers was also one of the most significant restrictions in the film industry under apartheid.

Several South African film-makers won international acclaim for their work on wildlife, the environment and nature conservation. They include Neill Curry[2] (*A Stitch in Time, African Ark, A Fragile Harmony, Bring Back the Red-Billed Oxpecker, Touchstones, Eagles and Farmers*) and Trevor de Kock (*Springbok of the Kalahari, City Slickers*).

Film production boomed during the mid-1980s owing to an additional funding system whereby films were tax deductible (Botha & Van Aswegen 1992; Silber 1992). During the period 1984–86 film producers could rely on tax benefits to cover production costs and show a profit. The loopholes in the tax concession system encouraged certain producers to exploit it for greater gain. It was especially Section 11 (bis) of the Income Tax Act that allowed this, although it was originally introduced to promote the export of films. It soon became apparent that the more one spent to export one's product the greater the amount that could be written off against tax. The result was that some people saved up to 250% on taxation. Between 1985 and 1989, for example, this system made possible 150 productions costing about R400 million. During August 1988 local and overseas producers shot 22 features in South Africa (Botha & Van Aswegen 1992). It is claimed that the abuse of tax benefits occurred when a number of films were produced solely to be written off against tax and never released. Sadly the system led to dozens of imitations of American genre films, which were chiefly released on video abroad. Several of these genre films merely used South African landscapes to depict another country or region, for example, Vietnam, South America, east or central Africa or an island in a vast ocean (Botha & Van Aswegen 1992). A small percentage of the work was distributed by the South African distributors Ster-Kinekor and Nu Metro. Because of the cultural boycott of South African products many tax-benefit films were released abroad as productions of the film industries of southern Africa such as Botswana or Zimbabwe. By 1987 a substantial number of local and international producers had joined in the South African film boom not to create 'authentic' local stories but rather to exploit the benefits accruing from the tax concession system.

According to film historians 1986/87 can be regarded as the turning point in the South African film industry. Only then did several feature films begin to critically examine the

South African milieu as well as apartheid and colonial history. The film academic Keyan Tomaselli calls this the new wave in the South African film industry. Martin Botha and Adri Van Aswegen labelled it an 'alternative film revival', a cinema that gave a voice to those who were previously marginalized by apartheid. The films touched on issues of black-white conflict during colonial times (*Jock of the Bushveld, Fiela se Kind*), the poor treatment of black farm workers by certain farmers (*A Place of Weeping*), the effects of the South African Border War (*The Stick*) as well as the trauma of racial conflict (*Saturday Night at the Palace*).

Johan Blignaut estimated that 944 features were made during the 1980s as well as nearly 998 documentaries and hundreds of short films and videos.[3] Although most of the features were of mediocre value thanks to the restrictions of the A and B subsidy schemes, a few remarkable local feature films were made. They included *Mapantsula* (1988), a vivid portrayal of the state of emergency in the late eighties; *On the Wire* (1990), about the psychological scars left by the war in Namibia and Angola;[4] *The Road to Mecca* (1991), a film on the life of artist Helen Martins (featuring a brilliant, final performance by Yvonne Bryceland, who passed away in January 1992); Andrew Worsdale's *Shotdown* (1987), a political satire about

the alienation of young white liberals in South Africa during the eighties; Francis Gerard's *A Private Life* (1988), a moving account of the destructive effects of apartheid on a family unit depicted over several decades after the mother (brilliantly played by Jana Cilliers) had been classified as 'coloured'; John Smallcombe's *An African Dream* (1988), which deals with the friendship of an emancipated Englishwoman and a black intellectual (John Kani) in Cradock in the beginning of the previous century; the evocative Afrikaans dramas by director Katinka Heyns, with strong female characters, *Fiela se Kind* (1987), *Die Storie van Klara Viljee* (1991) and *Paljas* (1997); Darrell Roodt's *Jobman* (1989), a strong anti-apartheid drama set in the years after the Sharpeville massacre; David Wicht's *Windprints* (1989), the story of a young liberal Afrikaner trying to come to terms with his role in a society at war with itself; as

The Stick. Anant Singh, Videovision International

The Stick. Anant Singh, Videovision International

well as Manie Van Rensburg's critical portrayal of Afrikaner nationalism during the 1940s in *The Fourth Reich* (1990).

Unfortunately many of these films were not viewed by the majority of South Africans at the time. Some were severely censored like *The Stick* (1987) and *Shotdown* (Burns 1990; Ozynski 1989). *Jobman* and *Shotdown* were never released commercially. In fact, by the end of the 1980s and early 1990s it was easier to view these films in London, Amsterdam and Paris than in South Africa (Botha & Van Aswegen 1992). Worsdale's *Shotdown* remained banned until the early 1990s. Cedric Sundström's *The Shadowed Mind* (1988), a psychological thriller (with strong gay male content), was banned for screening at the Weekly Mail Film Festival of 1990. South Africans were only allowed to view Bertolucci's *Last Tango in Paris* for the first time on the general circuit in 1991. Since April 1992 South African audiences may attend commercial film screenings in cinemas on Sundays! During 1992, a mere 2 years before the final collapse of the apartheid state, censorship was still a significant reality: Of the 1312 feature films submitted to the censors 83 were banned as 'undesirable'.

One should also note that cinemas were only desegregated in South Africa by 1985. SABC channels in the 1980s fragmented audiences across race and language. Despite the lack of audience support, directors like Jans Rautenbach, Manie Van Rensburg, Ross Devenish, Darrell Roodt, Katinka Heyns and Oliver Schmitz are evidence that there was indeed great talent in the local film industry of the 1960s, 1970s and 1980s. Van Rensburg's *The Native Who Caused All the Trouble* and *The Fourth Reich* are films that were built on the foundation of post-1987 new wave (Botha & Dethier 1997). Despite the restrictive climate of the 1980s several directors made significant contributions to the development of South African cinema. These voices are discussed in the rest of this chapter.

My Country My Hat (1983)

After having studied film in London, director David Bensusan tried to make films in South Africa under apartheid. *My Country My Hat* (1983) was his first, independently financed feature, made against all odds by even taking a mortgage on his house. Bensusan wrote, directed and produced the film. He wanted to show the complexities of the South African society and not just one dimension of the South African socio-political scene.

This very powerful film examines the paranoia of a white working-class couple and their relationship with a black man, who is struggling to get a passbook under apartheid laws. They illegally employ the man as a gardener. The theme is not so much the accidental killing of a man who may or may not be a housebreaker but the plight of a man who simply does not exist because he has no reference book in apartheid South Africa. The film stars Peter Se-Puma as James Fingo, the pass-less Sowetan who desperately tries to work for a living and to get a pass to officially exist. Regardt Van den Bergh takes the role of Piet, a menacing municipal refuse truck driver, and Aletta Bezuidenhout is Sara, his fear-stricken wife who is deeply suspicious of James.

Bensusan highlights the basic, paranoid fear of whites for blacks in apartheid South Africa. Just through his presence in so-called white areas the black person becomes a threat to the white community.

At a time in South African cinema when the majority of local films portrayed a South African society consisting of white principal characters and a few blacks as servants in the backdrop, *My Country My Hat* features a black principal character that interacts with white principal actors on screen. As in the case of *Saturday Night at the Palace* (1987), the film openly deals with racial conflict in an apartheid society, an aspect which was only explored previously by very few South African directors such as Jans Rautenbach in *Katrina* (1969).

The film was passed by the South African Publications Control Board but was turned down by the major South African film distributors for general theatrical release in South Africa. It was shown in an independently run cinema in Johannesburg in 1983 and on the festival circuit in Cape Town and Durban from where British film critic Derek Malcolm took a 16mm print to Britain. From there it moved to the Netherlands and Australia, where it was screened in Sydney and Melbourne.

Saturday Night at the Palace (1987)

Born in Cape Town, director Robert Davies has been actively involved in the film industry since 1975 as a film producer, director, writer and cinematographer. In the early 1970s, after studying at Rai Television, he based himself in Rome and was active in the Italian film industry. He then established his production company in 1977 through which he has produced and directed various series, documentaries and features for television. *Saturday Night at the Palace* (1987), based on a play by Paul Slabolepszy, was one of these features.

The film is a powerful portrayal of racial conflict within South Africa during apartheid. The story deals with an incident one night at an isolated roadhouse in South Africa in which two white men terrorise a black waiter.

The play was basically a political statement, and director Davies had not toned it down or made it more palatable. He also opened up the play without detracting from its overall emotional impact. The contrasting lifestyles of the principal characters are introduced at the beginning of the film. Paul Slabolepszy plays Vince, the frustrated white working-class psychopath. Bill Flynn is the overweight Forsie, his mate and the catalyst for most of the unfolding drama of the film. John Kani is the unfortunate waiter, September, a character imbued with enormous dignity despite his humiliation at the hands of the two whites.

The film was passed with an age restriction by the South African Publications Control Board and did get a general theatrical release by major distributors. Nationally and internationally it was hailed by critics as a landmark in South African cinema due to its important social message and as a powerful portrait of the emotional roots of apartheid (Botha & Van Aswegen 1992).

Johan Blignaut

After matriculating from the Dr. E.G. Jansen High School in Boksburg, Johan Blignaut took part in amateur theatre and in 1977 and 1978 won prizes from the ATKV for best actor and director. From 1975 he was associated with the Corsair Drama Group, which concentrated on community theatre in so-called coloured communities. He became a prominent writer, director and producer in theatre, television and film till his untimely death on 17 December 1997. Blignaut worked tirelessly towards establishing communication channels not only amongst South African communities but also within the film industry itself. In 1989 he founded Showdata, which was an invaluable database on the South African film industry of the 1980s and early 1990s.

Blignaut's major contribution to film directing is *Mamza* (1985), a portrait of searing bitterness, poverty and desperation among the 'coloured' community. It is the story of a mother's struggle (brilliantly played by the late Lulu Strachan) to beat the odds of racial injustice and poverty, which throw her family into the derelict squalor of second-class citizenship in the country of her birth. The film is a watershed in Afrikaans cinema. Blignaut uses the melodrama to look socio-critically at the lives of 'coloureds', from the viewpoint of 'coloureds' and not from a white perspective. The film is also a milestone in that criticism of apartheid is voiced in the Afrikaans language. The picture-postcard shots of idyllic surroundings as seen in Afrikaans cinema of the 1970s are also missing, and in their place are urban images of stark reality. Actors Jennifer Abdul, William Abdul, Schalk Jacobsz, Edward Soudien and Anthony Wilson[5] complemented Strachan's unforgettable performance.

Gray Hofmeyr

Gray Hofmeyr began his career in television in the 1970s in the United Kingdom where he was a floor manager at the BBC. He began directing for television in 1975 and in 1992 began an award-winning scriptwriting career. He was a key figure in the early days of television in South Africa, having directed the hit series *The Villagers* and popular comedy series *People Like Us*, *The Big Time* and *Suburban Bliss*.

Hofmeyr's early film career is characterized by his made-for-TV films for the SABC during the 1980s (e.g. *The Outcast* [1983] and *Thicker Than Water* [1985]) as well as features such as *Jock of the Bushveld* (1986), *Lambarane* (1989) and *Sweet 'n Short* (1991). The latter started a highly successful professional relationship with comedian Leon Schuster, which resulted in a series of slapstick comedies, which triumphed at the South African box office: *There's a Zulu on My Stoep* (1993), *Mr Bones* (2001), *Mama Jack* (2005) and *Mr Bones 2* (2008). Hofmeyr also created and produced the popular South African drama series *Isidingo*, which has become the flagship series for SABC 3 and has captured audiences across the cultural spectrum.

To date Hofmeyr's finest film has been *Jock of the Bushveld* (1986). He was invited by producer Duncan MacNeillie to join the project as director, which led to his co-writing the script with John Cundill. The story was taken from Sir Percy Fitzpatrick's literary classic about a transport driver and his dog, who criss-crossed the Transvaal of the eighteenth century. The visual impact of the South African landscape is captured exceptionally well. Cinematographer Michael Buckley's pastoral images are drenched in soft pastel colours. Director Hofmeyr also uses the tale of the legendary dog and his owner to give a subtle view of the miners of Pilgrim's Rest as well as to portray the racial attitudes of the time. The film takes a critical stance on racism, for example, by regarding a character that beats his black workers when he is dissatisfied with them (Tomaselli 1989).

In *Lambarene* (1989) Hofmeyr examines the life of Nobel Peace Prize winner Albert Schweitzer in the jungles of Congo in Africa. The main character (played by Malcolm

McDowell) tries, on the one hand, to eliminate the self-destructive practices arising from certain traditions while, on the other, fighting against western 'progress' in Africa during the 1950s that is promoted at the expense of the Africans. By creating a milieu familiar to patients, Schweitzer tries to adapt his hospital to African values. He allows families of the inhabitants to stay on the hospital grounds, cook their own meals and keep their own domestic animals. Similarly his techniques as a doctor are adjusted to the African context. As a result visiting American sponsors disapprove and are prepared to build a modern hospital with all the latest equipment. Schweitzer rejects their offer and is rewarded by the positive psychological effect of his decision on his patients.

Muller (1992) regarded the film as a simplistic approach to historic themes which could have been reworked to make them more valid for contemporary South Africa, at the time of the film's release on the verge of tumultuous political change. From an artistic viewpoint the film is visually stunning, and Zane Cronjé's soundtrack is pervaded with musical variations on Bach, accentuating Schweitzer's love of that composer's music. From *Sweet 'n Short* (1991) onwards Hofmeyr's features changed to slapstick comedies in collaboration with Leon Schuster.

Darrell Roodt

Darrell Roodt was born in Johannesburg in 1962 and attended the King Edward School. He enroled at the University of the Witwatersrand to study drama but left after one week to make films. He is one of the most dominant and prolific figures in the South African film industry (Armes 2008: 112; Botha 2011), having already made 25 feature films and three television series.

Roodt's *A Place of Weeping* (1986), made at the age of 23, was produced and marketed internationally by Anant Singh, who became one of South Africa's most prominent film producers. The film deals with racial conflict. A black farm worker is beaten to death by his employer after complaining about his poor wages. The murder goes unreported since other labourers fear for their future. A news reporter, however, becomes involved when a housemaid on the farm attempts to report the incident. Although seriously flawed because of poor performances from the actors the film featured striking cinematography by Paul Witte (Botha 2011).

Roodt's *The Stick* (1987) was the first South African film to examine the deployment of South African troops in cross-border raids during the South African Border War. The war is also commonly referred to as the Angolan Bush War in South Africa and is also known as the Namibian War of Independence. It refers to the conflict that took place from 1966 to 1989 in south-west Africa (now Namibia) and Angola between South Africa and its allied forces (mainly UNITA) on the one side and the Angolan government, South-West Africa People's Organisation (SWAPO) and their allies – mainly the Soviet Union and Cuba – on the other. It was closely intertwined with the Angolan Civil War (Botha 2011).

Darrell Roodt and Heinrich Dahms. Cape Winelands Film Festival

The film begins with an introductory sequence filmed in one long take in black and white: One of the white heroes of the film (Greg Latter) is shown in his school uniform and his voice-over on the soundtrack states, 'My father sent me to war to make a man of me. He was wrong'. The character is part of a 'stick' of men. Seven soldiers and a black tracker enter presumably Angola on a mission to exterminate a traditional healer, whose advice to rebel forces is regarded as destructive to South African security force efforts. Roodt's personal vision of the South African Border War between South Africa and SWAPO is one that is linked to the genre of the American war films of the 1970s, films praised for their critical examination of the psychological scars left on soldiers by the Vietnam War. These films (e.g. *The Deer Hunter*, *Apocalypse Now*, *Platoon* and *Born on the Fourth of July*) are characterized by their graphic, detailed depiction of war. Roodt's film is no exception to this. By portraying war vividly and emphasising fear and confusion through the use of first-person narration on the soundtrack Roodt aligns himself with the anti-war genre (Botha 2011; Botha & Van Aswegen 1992).

What fascinates Roodt is the physical and mental disintegration of the white protagonists after they have destroyed African lifestyles by wiping out a village of women and children as well as the traditional healer. The film becomes a surreal and nihilistic work – that which is incomprehensible to the white protagonists, namely Africa is portrayed as sinister and irrational. They are clearly not equipped to combat this 'supernatural' force. The film becomes an allegory of South Africa's political and military failure in Angola and Namibia to defeat SWAPO. This sentiment is made clear by the young hero's words to a senior military officer at the end of the film. When the soldier returns to South Africa he is confronted by the traditional healer in the shape of an ordinary black man. In other words, Africa still surrounds him – he cannot destroy it. To fight against it means self-destruction (Botha 2011; Botha & Van Aswegen 1992).

The film was initially banned in South Africa, and the ban was upheld through various applications for screenings at film festivals until it was finally allowed to be screened at the

Weekly Mail Film festival in 1989. The censors ordered 48 cuts before they would consider re-appraising the film (Ozynski 1989).

Stylistically *The Stick* is a remarkable film and forms part of auteur Roodt's trilogy on racial conflict in a rural milieu (*A Place of Weeping, The Stick* and *Jobman*). In the rural 'wastelands' of animal carcasses (*The Stick*) or wrecked cars (*Jobman*), over which the camera of Paul Witte slowly pans in long takes from left to right, Roodt envisages a disintegrating white middle class (magnificently conveyed in the party scene in *Jobman*). The pastoral Eden of the earlier Afrikaans cinema of the 1970s has given way to an inhospitable symbolic 'wasteland' in which people eventually would die (e.g. the final shoot-out in *Jobman* or battle in *The Stick*). David Barkham's art direction contributes significantly to the representation of this wasteland (Botha 2011).

Jobman (1989) tells the story of a 25-year-old deaf and mute 'coloured' man (Kevin Smith) who has been messed around and misunderstood all his life. When the film opens he is in Kimberley. The setting is Christmas 1960. Jobman is picked up by the police and stripped of his humanity. A parallel story moves the setting to a Karoo farm, where Jobman was born. The farmer dies and the farm is reluctantly inherited by his son, Carel (Tertius Meintjies in an award-winning performance). Jobman returns to the farm to fetch his wife and child but is rejected by his own community as a social outcast. He also provokes fear in the white community. The only person who sides with him is the young farmer. As the situation finally ends in violence, a confrontation arises between Jobman and the farming community. Roodt's film vividly analyses the tragic paradox and practice of Christian brotherly love during the first years of the Verwoerdian regime. The images depict a disintegrating white middle class trapped in its laager in an arid landscape strewn with wrecked cars and the carcasses of animals. David Barkman's art direction is excellent. The film was the last one shot by Paul Witte, who was tragically killed in a car accident in 1990.

Roodt's *Sarafina!* (1991), based on Mbongeni Ngema's stage musical about the school boycotts of 1976 and their brutal suppression by the police, resulted in international recognition for the director. It received a 10-minute standing ovation at the 1992 Cannes Film Festival where it was shown in the official selection. It stars Whoopi Goldberg, Leleti Khumalo and Miriam Makeba. *Sarafina!* characterizes Roodt's use of genre (the musical) in combination with strong socio-political content (the Soweto youth uprising of 1976). *Jobman* is a western which features a marginalized character in South African society of the early 1960s. *The Stick* fits into the Vietnam War genre but also explores South Africa's military involvement in Angola and Namibia.

It was therefore no surprise that Roodt would also explore the period drama. In the early 1990s Ronald Harwood adapted Alan Paton's novel *Cry the Beloved Country* (1994) for Roodt and producer Anant Singh. Set in the 1940s it follows the journey of a Zulu pastor, Stephen Kumalo (James Earl Jones), from rural Zululand to Johannesburg to look for his son. Kumalo's journey brings him into direct conflict with a white man, James Jarvis (Richard Harris), who has lost his son in a violent crime – he was killed by Kumalo's son. Through various tragic events, both men are forced to learn the lesson of forgiveness with dignity, a theme relevant to post-apartheid cinema. Visually the film is exquisite and John Barry's musical score enhances the deep-felt sadness of the events in the film (Botha 2011).

Anant Singh has been an important partner for Roodt over the years. They met as anti-apartheid film-makers, felt a connection and have been making films together ever since (Treffry-Goatley 2010). Singh has worked as a producer on many of these films, and the distribution arm of his company, Videovision, has also been responsible for certain international and local sales. Videovision, as the production company for many of these films, has also been an important source of finance for Roodt, who noted in the director's commentary for *Yesterday* (2004) that he is very lucky to have Singh's support because he has sometimes financed entire productions such as *Faith's Corner* (2005).

Although Roodt has made many politically and socially conscious films, he has also shot numerous genre-orientated films for the foreign market. These include *City of Blood* (1986), *To the Death* (1991), *Father Hood* (1993), *The Second Skin* (2000), *Pavement* (2003), *Dracula 3000* (2003) and *Prey* (2006). During the past decade Roodt moved away from his genre work to a series of remarkable films about South African women on the margin of South African society (see Chapter 12).

Oliver Schmitz

Oliver Schmitz was born in 1961. After school he studied at the Michaelis Art School at the University of Cape Town. He directed *Mapantsula* when he was only 27 years old. The film received international acclaim. During the late 1980s he worked for an underground left-wing documentary unit in South Africa and has subsequently directed several feature documentaries, including seminal films about the struggle against apartheid such as *Fruits of Defiance* (1990), as well as the award-winning *Joburg Stories* (1997). *Hijack Stories* (2000) is his second South African feature. The film is an innovative gangster comedy about a young middle-class black actor living in traditionally white suburbs who has to audition for a role as a hijacker in a film. He knows nothing about the lifestyle, so he travels to Soweto where he undergoes some kind of method training with a real-life gangster. Funding came from Germany, France and the United Kingdom. Schmitz currently lives in Berlin. His latest feature is *Life, Above All* (2010), based on Allan Stratton's novel *Chanda's Secrets*. The film, which received a standing ovation at the 2010 Cannes Film festival, is a moving drama about a young girl (played by first-time actress Khomotso Manyaka) who opposes the fear and shame that have poisoned her community. The film vividly captures the enduring strength of loyalty and courage. Its characters on the margin of society fit into the cinema of marginality, which characterizes post-apartheid cinema (see Chapter 12).

Marginal lives are also a major theme of *Mapantsula*, a multi-award winning film, which depicts the story of Panic, a small-time crook, who stays out of South African politics but discovers that he can not stay apolitical after he is picked up by the cops for questioning and dumped in a cell with township militants. Panic is slowly drawn into the machinations of

Mapantsula. Oliver Schmitz, M-Net

the political struggle. The police see him as a potential informer who can be used to spy on the unionists in his cell. He is also tortured until he is forced to take a stand.

Mapantsula was shot in 1988 and should be seen against the background of that time in South Africa – the state of emergency, insurrection, municipal elections and detention without trial. The theme of the film is a black man's growing awareness of the link between apartheid and the economic exploitation of the black working class, not only by whites but also by a group of blacks who are seen to be part of the apartheid system (Botha & Van Aswegen 1992). Arising from this socio-political situation, the film sketches the dilemma of a socially crippled milieu. The complexity of the situation in which the black majority find themselves is critically examined and laid bare through the attention paid to a range of social challenges. For example, unemployment and poverty related to an ever-rising cost of living (including the raising of rentals) lead to crime and malpractices such as the formation of gangs and pickpocketing. These issues are all pertinently depicted in the film.

In addition disrupted family life and concomitant instability of interpersonal relationships and strained communication between people are portrayed. These situations provoke different kinds of resistance that are directed towards and manifest themselves in school boycotts, trade union activity, collective resistance in jails (in the form of hunger strikes and intimidation) and finally also in protest action in which physical violence occurs (Botha & Van Aswegen 1992).

The themes examined in *Mapantsula* are embodied in the situations experienced by the main protagonist, Panic. He almost acts as a spokesperson by giving perspective to the conditions of the black majority under the apartheid system of the 1980s. The story was co-scripted by Schmitz and actor Thomas Mogotlane, and can be regarded as a pioneering work because it has been one of the first truly South African films made from a black African point of view (Botha & Van Aswegen 1992). It was the first South African feature to compete in the Un Certain Regard section of the Cannes Film Festival, indeed a great achievement.

Panic is a complex character. He is not only a product of the apartheid system but also the result of other social factors and personal flaws (self-centredness, impulsiveness, conformity to the system for his own advantage and at the cost of the community interests of blacks). He has a criminal record which includes theft. His record cannot be blamed exclusively on the apartheid system since he has made no attempt to find work and is reliant on the goodwill of his girlfriend for accommodation. He robs whites on the streets and is also guilty of shoplifting.

Schmitz and cinematographer Rod Stewart brilliantly examine the class inequalities between black and white South Africans, for example, the sharp contrast between the luxurious world of white suburbs and the poverty-stricken way of life in the townships.

Mapantsula. Oliver Schmitz, M-Net

Contact between black and white South Africans mainly features economic exploitation, intimidation, conflict, verbal and physical aggression, racism, lack of concern and labelling on the part of the whites. It is a bleak universe which vividly captures the mood of the late 1980s under the state of emergency in South Africa (Botha & Van Aswegen 1992). At the time there was no possibility of state dialogue with groups such as the ANC, and detention without trial under the countrywide state of emergency was the order of the day.

Many whites are represented in *Mapantsula* as being in a dominant position of power manifested in behaviours such as intimidation, racist jokes (for instance, referring to blacks as monkeys), exploitation, assault, threats, bravado and arrogance. Existing labels such as 'kaffir' are replaced with empty concepts such as 'terrorist', 'communist' and 'tsotsi', all of which have exceptionally negative and condescending connotations (Botha & Van Aswegen 1992).

The structure of the film is non-linear. Panic's gradually evolving political consciousness during his detention alternates with flashbacks to incidents from his past that depict experiences of his environment. Through the technique of the flashback the viewer is drawn into Panic's self-discovery and the presentation of his social reality. The development of Panic's character is delineated in exceptionally filmic terms. The first shots of Panic depict him as a hunter, observing his prey, half-shadowed in a doorway. He resembles a gangster. Effective cross-cutting reveals Panic and his prey in the busy streets of Johannesburg. Close-ups underline Panic's appearance: his swanky shoes and hat and so forth. The further the story develops and Panic starts on his painful journey of self-discovery, the more he is stripped of his original finery until, finally, he sits naked in the office of his interrogators. This progression distinguishes the mood of the film – the happy gathering in a 'discotheque' (*shebeen*) during the early part of the film finally gives way to turmoil: empty classrooms, protest marches and clashes with the security police (Botha & Van Aswegen 1992).

Mapantsula remains a milestone in South African cinema and received substantial attention from academics (Balseiro & Masilela 2003; Botha & Van Aswegen 1992; Davis 1996; Maingard 2007; Marx 1996; Tomaselli & Prinsloo 1992). It won several AA Life/M-Net Vita Film Awards, including Dolly Rathebe (Best Supporting Actress), Thomas Mogotlane (Best Actor), Schmitz (Best Director) as well as for the musical score by Thapelo Khomo, Lloyd Lolosa, Nana Motijoane and Ian Osrin.

Regardt Van den Bergh

Regardt Van den Bergh was born in Johannesburg. He attended school at Louw Geldenhuys Primary and matriculated at Linden High. Regardt grew up in an acting family. His father, Gert Van den Bergh (who starred in *Wild Season* [1967] and Jans Rautenbach's *Die Kandidaat* [1968]), and mother, Dulsie Van den Bergh (who is well-known for her role as Aunt Stienie in the SABC television series *Agter Elke Man* [1984–86]), were well-known in the acting fraternity and popular with audiences. During Van den Bergh's school career he acted in several films, most notably *Die Kandidaat* (1968). His performance as a juvenile delinquent won him recognition as an actor, and it led to several roles as a troubled young man (*Katrina* 1969; *Eendag op 'n Reëndag* 1975; *Die Eensame Vlug* 1979; *Blink Stefaans* 1981). His performances in *My Country My Hat* (1983) as well as *Die Storie van Klara Viljee* (1991) received widespread acclaim.

After school Van den Bergh worked as a trenching foreman for the South African Railways to earn money for his studies. In 1972 he went to the University of Cape Town to obtain a BA degree and a Performers Diploma in Speech and Drama. Before the end of his second year, Van den Bergh received a part in *Ongewenste Vreemdeling* (1974). He decided to do the film and left the university. He joined director Jans Rautenbach's crew as a general gofer, assistant editor and actor. Van den Bergh worked and acted for 2 years after which he landed a lead in the first Afrikaans television series, *Dokter, Dokter*. For 4 years Van den Bergh acted in many television dramas and several films until he made his directing debut

Van der Merwe PI. M-Net

135

in 1980. *Vyfster*, an eight part mini-series about prison inmates, won Van den Bergh many awards and great acclaim in the industry (Blignaut & Botha 1992). Since then he spent most of his time directing television programmes during the 1980s for South African companies on a freelance basis.

In 1983 Van den Bergh became the resident film director for Philo Pieterse Productions. His first feature film, *Boetie Gaan Border Toe* (1984), a satire about military recruits, broke all box-office records in South Africa. Subsequent films ensured his status as one of South Africa's foremost film directors. *Vyfster* and *Boetie Gaan Border Toe* featured the type of troubled, even anti-social male characters which Van den Bergh played in the 1960s and 1970s. The films of the 1980s were also characterized by exploring generic and narrative possibilities in South African cinema, for example, the prison drama (*Vyfster*), military comedy (*Boetie Gaan Border Toe*), crime comedy (*Van der Merwe, P.I.*, 1985), literary adaptation (*Circles in the Forest*, 1988) and historical drama (*The Sheltering Desert*, 1991).

In the process he won several nominations and awards (Blignaut & Botha 1992). Most notable of these are *Circles in a Forest*, nominated as best picture, as well as *The Sheltering Desert* for which Van den Bergh received the AA Life/M-Net Vita award for best director in 1991. It is his greatest achievement to date. The film is based on the novel by Henno Martin and chronicles the experiences of two German geologists who tried to escape internment during Second World War by living 2.5 years in the Namib Desert. Starring Jason Connery as Henno Martin and Rupert Graves as Hermann Korn the film is a stunning historical reconstruction (like Manie Van Rensburg's *The Fourth Reich*) of the period in southern Africa owing to spectacular cinematography of Namibian towns and desert landscapes by George Jiri Tirl and the production design by Francis Darvall. An ensemble of fine actors such as Joss Ackland, Kate Normington, Franz Dobrowsky, Gavin Hood and Patrick Shai complements Van den Bergh's excellent directing. Thematically the film also indicated a change in the director's auteurist concerns. In his novel Henno Martin focused on the indescribable physical and mental hardship the geologists had to suffer, the challenge to survive in the vastness of the Namib desert, the constant threat of detection and their gradual adaptation to live life as bushmen, while being confronted on the radio with the horrible clash of civilizations in Europe and the terrible loss of lives. Van den Bergh's film is highly successful as an elegant visual equivalent to the novel, but it also examines the men's attempt to remain human and compassionate against inhuman conditions. At the end of the film Van den Bergh embraces a strong spirituality, which would characterize his future oeuvre.

After *The Sheltering Desert* Van den Bergh's films focused overwhelmingly on faith and personal healing. In 1993 he directed a docudrama called *The Gospel According to Matthew*. This 4-hour word-for-word biblical series soon became the top-selling Christian video in the United States and is still selling thousands, eighteen years later. This project led to a so-called Faith Trilogy, based on the lives of real-life characters and their personal struggles with spiritual issues. The first *Faith Like Potatoes* (2006) focuses on the true story of Angus Buchan, a Zambian farmer of Scottish heritage, who left his farm in the midst of political turmoil to seek a better life in South Africa. The film deals with issues such as cultural identity, racial reconciliation, faith and perseverance against all odds. The second part of the trilogy *Hansie* (2008) chronicles the downfall of South Africa's cricket captain Hansie Cronjé after his confession to having taken money from bookmakers in exchange for information to fix cricket matches. After the public confession where Cronjé is shamed before the entire world and banned from cricket for life, he begins the long and difficult road back from despair to forgiveness and restoration, the central theme of the film. The third film in the trilogy, the poetic *Tornado and the Kalahari Horse Whisperer* (2009), tells the story of Pierre (Quintin Krog), a depressed and damaged young man, and Tornado, an emotionally tormented horse. Sensing Tornado's potential, Pierre travels to Noenieput, in the Green Kalahari, to find Barrie Burger (Danny Keogh), a horse whisperer. With Barrie's advice, Pierre and Tornado embark on a journey of healing and self-discovery. All three films also featured troubled young male characters, which Van den Bergh portrayed as an actor in the 1960s and 1970s.

In July 2009 Regardt Van den Bergh received international recognition for his lifetime contribution to South African cinema. He was awarded a Global Film Award at the 7th Ischia Global Film and Music Festival. His latest film, *Die Ongelooflike Avonture van Hanna Hoekom/The Incredible Adventures of Hanna Why* (2010) is a departure from the thematic

Tornado and the Kalahari Horse Whisperer. Zaria and Peter Lamberti

Die Ongelooflike Avonture van Hanna Hoekom. M-Net, Tertius Meintjies

concerns in his recent work. The film tells the tale of Hanna (Anneke Weidemann), a teenager with a wild imagination, and her unconventional family. Actress Anna-Mart Van der Merwe brilliantly portrays Hanna's artistic mother, while Gys de Villers plays her would-be actor step-father. Based on Marita Van der Vyver's youth novel Van den Bergh's film is a refreshing portrait of an extended Afrikaner family, which in many ways deconstruct the images of conservative Afrikaners in the cinema of the 1970s. Hanna's biological father, for example, is a flamboyant queer (a fine performance by Tertius Meintjies), and the children embrace hip hop and are very much part of a post-apartheid South Africa.

Katinka Heyns

Katinka Heyns has emerged as one of the outstanding multi-award winning film actresses and directors in South African cinema (Botha 2006b). She was born in 1947. Heyns graduated at the University of Pretoria with a BA degree in Drama (cum laude). Her involvement in the film industry started in 1969 in Jans Rautenbach's *Katrina*, in which she played a white girl who unknowingly falls in love with a 'coloured' boy. She then played demanding character roles in other Rautenbach features like *Jannie Totsiens* (1970), *Pappa Lap* (1971) and *Eendag op 'n Reëndag* (1975), for which she won a Rapport Oscar for Best Actress.[6] She became a well-known television actress in the comedy series *Willem* by director Manie Van Rensburg. She also appeared in many theatrical productions staged by the former Performing Arts Councils in the Transvaal and Cape provinces.

In 1974 Heyns founded her own production company, Sonneblom Films. After the introduction of television in South Africa Heyns also directed quality documentary programmes about famous literary figures such as D.J. Opperman and N.P. Van Wyk Louw, for which she won the award for Best Director by the ATKV. Since the 1980s television dramas and series followed: *Piet-My-Vrou* (1981), *Tekwan* (1984), *Die Avonture van Joachim Verwey* (1981), *Die Dood van Elmien Adler* (1983), *Simon en Sandra* (1989) and for M-Net, *Amalia* (2005). Numerous educational and children's television programmes also followed. She has twice been the recipient of the prestigious Medal of Honour from the South African Academy of Arts and Science, and has also received the Legendary Award for Woman in Film and Television International Crystal Awards (Botha 2006b).

Heyns has been acclaimed in South Africa and abroad for three outstanding award-winning features that deal with the female psyche in a very sensitive way: *Fiela se Kind* (1987), *Die Storie van Klara Viljee* (1991) and *Paljas* (1997).

Fiela se Kind (1987)

Fiela se kind was co-produced by Heyns and Edgar Bold, and is based on a popular novel by Dalene Matthee, about the fortunes of Benjamin, a white boy brought up by Fiela Komoetie, a 'coloured' woman of the Lange Kloof in the Cape. The boy, spotted by a census official, is brought before a magistrate's court and claimed by a white woman as the child she had lost some 9 years earlier. The heartbroken Fiela tries to retrieve the boy now named Lukas but is blocked by an implacable colonial legal system with strong racist overtones. Lukas is also ill-treated by his new father. The film is a powerful portrayal of social injustice in colonial South Africa. Although set between 1874 and 1886 the film exposes the roots of apartheid. In it the colonial rulers claim the right to make life-splintering decisions purely on the basis of race.

Ironically, Heyns did not consider the story in terms of colour. She stated that it is not a story about a coloured woman raising a white child but the story of a mother and a child, and the child being taken away from her. She described the story as a fairy tale, as the severe struggle of the hero against all odds. Heyns's husband, Chris Barnard, a well-known South African novelist, wrote the screenplay over a period of 6 months. Matthee gave them free reign. The screenplay follows the novel closely, both in terms of the development of the action and the dialogue.

South African critics praised the film in terms of its exposé of crucial socio-political issues in a sophisticated yet in a warmly human, non-melodramatic way. In the principal part of Fiela actress Shaleen Surtie-Richards gave a riveting marrow-and-bone portrayal. It won her

Fiela se Kind. M-Net

an AA Life/M-Net Vita Film Award as Best Actress in 1988. The film was also applauded for the visual evocation of novelist Matthee's three symbolic landscapes – the plains of the Lange Kloof, the forest of Kom-se-Bos and the sea around the Knysna Heads. Further praise came from critics with regard to the excellent use of music, including haunting pan pipes. The images of womanhood are also deeply moving, and issues around the oppression of women are subtly raised. The film won numerous AA Life/M-Net Vita Awards in 1988, including Best South African Film and Best Director (Katinka Heyns). The contribution by James Robb (cinematographer) and Avril Beukes (editing) was also praised. The film, which was released abroad, was also a huge success at the South African box office.

Die Storie van Klara Viljee (1991)

The story of director Katinka Heyns's second feature takes place in a small coastal town in the 1950s and deals with the self-imposed exile of a woman due to mysterious events. Like in Heyns's previous film, *Fiela se Kind*, the film is a sensitive and moving portrayal of women. It was considered by many critics to be a profound feminist statement (Botha 2006b).

Die Storie van Klara Viljee. M-Net

The principal character, Klara, sets in motion a process of almost magical transformation of patriarchy-shattering proportion in a small southern Cape village. Robbed by the ocean of her dad, as well as her boyfriend, she decides to deny the sea's presence by building her house on the landward side of a dune. When she learns that her boyfriend has actually never died and has in fact betrayed her, she begins to move the dune, using only a donkey and a plough. It seems to be an impossible task, but it is a strong metaphor for Klara's embracing of life after her denial of reality. The notion that men are in control of white Afrikaner society is subverted with subtlety. In the process of taking control of her life, Klara also influenced the lives of other women in the village and in some ways acts as the catalyst for their own emancipation from patriarchy (Marx 2003).

The film became a highly acclaimed, box-office success during the early 1990s in South Africa and a showpiece for the talents of a formidable team of actors and crew members: Anna-Mart Van der Merwe, Trix Pienaar, Lida Botha, Wilma Stockenström, Sandra Kotze and Regardt Van den Bergh as actors, Ronelle Loots as editor and Heyns as director and co-producer. Cinematographer Koos Roets does wonders with the South African light in his hauntingly beautiful pastoral images of the coastal milieu (Botha 2006b).

Paljas (1987)

One of the greatest features to emerge out of South Africa since 1994 is Katinka Heyns's *Paljas* (1997). The narrative occurs in the 1960s, when poverty amongst Afrikaners was a reality and the South African Railways a key mechanism in Afrikaner affirmative action (Shepperson & Tomaselli 2000). Director Heyns's third feature deals with the deterioration of an Afrikaner family isolated and shunned in the small community of Toorwater. Nothing seems to happen. Then a circus train loses its way and comes to rest in Toorwater, and

Paljas. Katinka Heyns, Videovision International

a mysterious clown brings fresh magic to the stagnating family, but to the rest of the community he poses a threat.

Screenwriter Chris Barnard and Heyns brilliantly succeed in creating a metaphor for the Afrikaner family's turbulent emotional, cultural and ideological journey from the darkness of apartheid back to the light of post-apartheid reconciliation (familial, cultural and political). (A fine analysis of this film is provided by Marx, 2003). The word *paljas* means to use magic, and in the context of the film it means to magically transform, to rid a community of its fears and uncertainties. *Paljas* won the Medal of Honour from the South African Academy for Science and Arts, after being accepted as the first official entry from South Africa for the Oscar in the category of Best Foreign Film. An important professional relationship in Heyns's success is that with her husband, Chris Barnard, who wrote most of the screenplays for her films, dramas and television series.[7] *Paljas* featured excellent ensemble acting by Marius Weyers, Aletta Bezuidenhout, Gerard Rudolf and Ian Roberts. The editing by one of South Africa's best editors, Ronelle Loots, also contributed to the quality of Heyns's best feature to date. Her impressive mini-series *The Feast of the Uninvited* (2008) will be discussed in Chapter 12.

Notes

1. See Le Roux (2009) for a discussion on the historical context of *Arende*.
2. See Blignaut and Botha (1992).
3. Some of these films were made due to tax breaks.
4. Aletta Bezuidenhout and Gys de Villiers's acting in the film received international acclaim.
5. Anthony Wilson was the first 'coloured' film-maker to direct a feature titled *Die Posman* (1987).
6. Various newspapers such as *Rapport* and *The Star* introduced awards during the 1970s and 1980s to stimulate South African film-making and talent.
7. See published scripts by Chris Barnard (1998).

Chapter 9

Oppositional film-making in the 1980s

It was not until the late 1970s that several key events came together to create the conditions for an independent documentary film industry to develop. The introduction of television in 1976 necessitated a lifting of the ban on video technology, thereby making more affordable small-format video cameras available to South African film-makers and broadening the national skills base. While news programming on SABC1 was tightly controlled, producers of drama series and other programmes were afforded a surprising bit of leeway with regard to making social statements that challenged the state (e.g. the work by Manie Van Rensburg, which was discussed in Chapter 5).[1] In 1982, the introduction of SABC2 and SABC3, two new networks aimed at black audiences, further opened the door. In some cases the national broadcaster even unwittingly provided tools and training that would be used to produce anti-apartheid films (Pichaske 2009).

Around the same time, a few South African universities began teaching film and video studies, which facilitated the emergence of a new generation of critical viewers and liberal film-makers. Less restricted than their professional counterparts, South African university students began to explore documentary topics that were critical of the state and/or exposed some of the hardships endured by black South Africans at the time (Steenveld 1992). Since the late 1970s and early 1980s a group of film and video producers and directors who were not affiliated to the established film companies in the mainstream film industry made films and videos about the socio-political realities of the majority of South Africans (Botha 1996). Some of these films were shown at local film festivals such as the Durban and Cape Town International Film Festivals and, from 1987 to 1994, the Weekly Mail Film Festival. Other venues included universities, church halls, trade union offices and the private homes of interested parties. Most of the films experienced censorship problems during the state of emergency during the 1980s, and many were banned (Botha 1996; Botha & Van Aswegen 1992).

The films had small budgets and were financed by the producers themselves; by progressive organizations such as the International Defence and Aid Fund for South Africa (IDAF) which strived for a united, democratic, non-racial South Africa, the National Union of South African Students (as in the case of *Wits Protest* [1970–74]), the South African Council of Churches; private investors such as the Maggie Magaba Trust; as well as European and British television stations (Botha 1996; Botha & Van Aswegen 1992). These films were chiefly the product of two groups that emerged jointly: a group of white university students opposed to apartheid and black workers who yearned for a film or video form using indigenous imagery that would portray their reality in South Africa and would give them a voice and space in local films (Botha 1996). Together with numerous documentaries, community videos and full-length films such as *Mapantsula*, as well as short films (which is discussed in Chapter 11), these productions marked the beginning of a new, critical South African cinema.

The IDAF was founded in the early 1950s by the chairman of Christian Action, Canon John Collins of St Paul's Cathedral, Britain, when money was collected to support the families of those charged and imprisoned in South Africa for their opposition to apartheid and to provide legal defence for those accused in political trials (Botha 1996). The fund ran a comprehensive information service on affairs in South Africa over the past decades, which included visual documentation. It also produced films on all aspects of repression and resistance against apartheid in South Africa. The best-known films included those by director Barry Feinberg, for example, a film about the life and work of Archbishop Trevor Huddlestone and his continuing commitment to the destruction of apartheid. The film *Makhalipile – The Dauntless One* (1989) includes interviews with Oliver Tambo, Desmond Tutu and Helen Joseph. The suffering of children under apartheid was examined in Feinberg's *Any Child Is My Child* (1988).

Song of the Spear (1986) portrayed the role of culture in the struggle for national liberation. By intercutting performances of the Amandla Cultural Ensemble while on tour in Britain, with mass singing of resistance songs on the streets of South Africa, this 16mm film dramatically depicted the emerging culture of liberation, which respects the humanity of all people without regard to race while reflecting the diversity of the South African population (Botha 1996).

Isitwalandwe: The Story of the South African Freedom Charter was made by Feinberg in 1980 on video and 16mm and made it clear that as a people's blueprint for democracy the Freedom Charter remained relevant for political change in South Africa (Botha 1996).

The major audiences for IDAF productions, however, were the international anti-apartheid movements. The work was intended to play a campaigning role for the liberation movement in South Africa and unfortunately offered an uncritical account of its policies. IDAF productions keep to *cinéma verité* techniques by avoiding voice-over commentary and by using live sound and letting political spokespersons speak for themselves. These productions unambiguously presented an ANC viewpoint (Botha 1996).

IDAF was instrumental in establishing an alternative news distribution office in London, namely Afravision, by providing financial and logistical assistance. Barry Feinberg's concern for the preservation of South Africa's anti-apartheid films resulted in the largest single collection of material at IDAF. With the changing political dispensation IDAF has placed this film archive at the University of the Western Cape (Botha 1996).

Many South African documentaries were made with an international audience in mind in order to get support for the anti-apartheid movement and to educate an international audience on the horrors of apartheid (Botha 2006b). Notable earlier work included Anthony Thomas's *The South African Experience* (1977), Peter Davis's *White Laager* (1977) and Chris Austin's *Rhythms of Resistance* (1979). In 1980 two major productions on the history of the South African liberation struggle against apartheid were released internationally: Peter Davis's *Generations of Resistance* (1979) and Barry Feinberg's *Isitwalandwe* for IDAF. The latter was the first in a long line of films and videos in the 1980s to keep the conscience of the world alive to the issues at stake in South Africa under apartheid. IDAF was instrumental in establishing an alternative news distribution office in London by providing financial and logistical assistance to anti-apartheid documentary film-makers.

Some of the most seminal political documentaries of the 1980s came from Video News Services (VNS), which included film-makers such as Brian Tilley, Laurence Dworkin, Nyana Molete, Seipati Bulane Hopa and Tony Bensusan (Botha 2006b). Collective film work by Tilley, Dworkin, Molete, Bensusan and Elaine Proctor led to the 25-minute anti-apartheid film *Forward to a People's Republic* (1991), which was completed with assistance from IDAF. This film portrayed the dynamics of the conflict in the country in the early 1980s by juxtaposing the people's militancy with white militarisation. In April 1985 VNS was formed with the assistance of the liberation movement and overseas financial support. VNS became the trade union COSATU's unofficial film unit. The film-makers saw themselves first and foremost as political activists. For VNS to achieve this aim and avoid being shutdown under the state of emergency, Afravision was established in London to interface with international anti-apartheid movements, and locally VNS crews made themselves indistinguishable from the foreign news media operating in South Africa (Botha 1996). At first VNS made television documentaries for international television companies but later started to make the so-called video pamphlets to distribute news about a wide range of issues from township to township. These videos were a type of news network and were aimed at South Africans. Most of the videos were 15- to 30-minute productions and ranged from vigilante killings to the white election process in 1988. The VNS Collective made various compelling short documentaries: *Tribute to David Webster* (1989), about the human rights activist, and *Fruits of Defiance* (1990), which portrayed resistance to apartheid in September 1989 in Cape Town.

Apart from VNS other documentary film-makers have also made important work on political issues during the apartheid regime, including the following themes (Botha 2006b; Pichaske 2009; Steenveld 1992):

- The forced removal of people from urban and rural communities under the Group Areas Acts and the Homelands policy: *Crossroads* (1976), *Mayfair* (1984), *Last Supper at Horstley Street* (1983) and *Katriver: End of Hope* (1984)
- Labour problems and organisation: *Passing the Message* (1981) and *Freedom Square and Back of the Moon* (1987)
- Different forms of community struggle, such as the development of literacy and health projects in rural and urban communities: *Ithuseng: Out of Despair* (1987) and *Robben Island: Our University* (1988)
- The role of women in the anti-apartheid struggle: *You Have Struck a Rock* (1981) and *The Ribbon* (1986)

- General political situation: *No Middle Road to Freedom* (1984), *The Struggle from Within* (1984), *Witness to Apartheid* (1986) and *The Two Rivers* (1985)
- The role of the church in the anti-apartheid struggle: *The Cry of Reason* (1987)
- The destruction of indigenous cultures: *The People of the Great Sandface* (1985) and *Have You Seen Drum Recently?* (1988)

Kevin Harris is one of the most significant as well as prolific documentary and community film-makers in South Africa. His work has already received much international praise[2] as well as several Oscar nominations. Kevin Harris was born in Pietermaritzburg in 1950 and qualified as an electrical engineer in 1973. From 1974 to 1979 he worked at the SABC. Since 1979, because of his political convictions, he practised as an independent documentary film-maker (Botha 2006b). Best known internationally for *Witness to Apartheid* (1986) this documentary was shot clandestinely during the state of the emergency of the 1980s and subsequently banned. It is a dramatic exposure of the extent of apartheid's violence and brutality. The narrative consists of testimonies of victims as well as eyewitnesses to police repression and torture, including children as young as 14 who were beaten in detention.

With the unbanning of political organization such as the ANC and the release of political prisoners in 1990, the immediate direct goal of anti-apartheid films had begun to be achieved (Botha 2006b). Political film-makers, however, continued to focus on the process of transition itself, to which a large number of films on CODESA (the negotiation process leading up to the 1994 democratic elections) and on the TRC attest. One significant film from the time is Liz Fish's *The Long Journey of Clement Zulu* (1992), which follows three political activists after their release from imprisonment on Robben Island and subsequent attempts to rebuild their lives as free men. The film is plot driven and foregrounds its characters' individual perspectives. The film vividly provides a truly intimate portrayal of the characters over the course of nearly a year (Pichaske 2009). The extended length of the narrative and the intimacy of content enable the audience to gain a true affinity for each character, empathy for Clement Zulu's views, and a desire to know what will happen in his life. The means by which Fish – an outsider with regard to race, class and personal experience – was able to create such an intimate and personal portrait are worthy of further examination. Of utmost importance, her racial outsider status was tempered by her status as a political insider. A long-time struggle activist and director of the Community Video Education Trust (CVET), she had close ties to black communities and had done considerable work with other Robben Island prisoners. She knew the cultures of her characters, and she knew their issues. In addition, Fish developed a personal relationship with her subjects that far exceeded the standards of apartheid-era film-making (Pichaske 2009).

This personal relationship served not only to deepen understanding between film-maker and subject but also paved the way towards a more collaborative approach to film-making. *The Long Journey of Clement Zulu* lets its subjects speak for themselves. Each of the three characters interrogates 'the struggle' on his own terms and through his own experience of being released back into a democratic South Africa only to wonder what has been gained. The message is subtle, the answers open ended and the views subjective and varied (Pichaske 2009).

Unprecedented freedom of access also allowed new forms of purely observational film-making: Harriet Gavshon and Cliff Bestall's series *Ordinary People* (1993), a groundbreaking product in terms of South African television at the time, followed ordinary South Africans as they dealt with newfound freedom and in the process documents the transitions in South African society. The *Ordinary People* series was shot in a *vérité* style and was entirely character and plot driven – creative choices that were entirely new for the SABC. By examining events from a variety of perspectives, the series actively challenged the very notion of fixed truths, encouraging the viewer to understand and respect multiple perspectives on the same issue (Pichaske 2009). This was a perfect message for a newly democratic South Africa and a positive sign of the new SABC fulfilling its social service mandate. For the field of documentary, it represented a critical first step away from the old conventions of presenting fixed, unified (pro- or anti-apartheid) arguments and binary (black/white, good/ evil) representations, in favour of open-ended narratives, multiple viewpoints and hybrid identities.

Film-makers were also now finally allowed to probe and reveal what actually happened under apartheid, with the result that many films were now concerned with the past. Various films about the TRC process were made, including Lindy Wilson's *The Gugulethu Seven* (2000), which depicts the uncovering by TRC investigators of security police duplicity in the murder of seven Cape Town activists. Many of the older generation of political film-makers have felt the weight of responsibility for making sense of a hitherto-concealed and painful past. Documentary film-making during the 1980s was based on audio-visual material that reflected the realities of the black majority of South Africa in their aspirations and struggle for a democratic society, but since the beginning of the 1990s other marginalized voices were added to these documentaries and short films, for example, those of women, gays and lesbians, and even the homeless. Most of these documentaries can be described as progressive film texts in the sense that the majority of them are consciously critical of racism, sexism or oppression (Botha 1996; 2006b). They dealt with the lives and struggle of the people in a developing country and were mostly allied with the liberation movements for a non-racial, non-sexist South Africa.

Some of these documentaries also dealt with events which were conveniently left out in official South African history books or in a contemporary context in actuality programmes on national television under control of the Nationalist regime (Botha 1996; 2006b). Therefore, they became guardians of popular memory within the socio-political process in South Africa.[3] Examples are *Between Joyce and Remembrance* (2003), *The Gugulethu Seven* (2000), *The Life and Times of Sara Baartman* (1998), *Ulibambe Lingashoni: Hold Up the Sun* (1993), *What Happened to Mbuyisa?* (1998) and *The Cradock Four* (2010). Developments in documentaries after 1994 will be discussed in Chapters 11 and 12.

Film reviewers

The 1980s was characterized by a generation of fine film reviewers for various South African newspapers. Individuals such as Barrie Hough, Andrea Vinassa, Barry Ronge, Paul Boekkooi, Roger Dean, Peter Feldman, Schalk Schoombie, Eben Meiring, Raeford Daniel, Leon van Nierop, Johan Bruwer, Braam Muller, Robert Greig, Jeanne Coetzer, Stephan Bouwer, Darryl Accone, Wilhelm Grütter, Owen Williams, Derek Wilson and George Claassen made a significant contribution to the understanding of world cinema. From the 1990s a new generation, which included Gabriël Botma, Wilhelm Snyman, Shaun de Waal, Andrew Worsdale, Laetitia Pople, Theresa Smith and John Matshikiza, continued in their footsteps.

The significant contribution to the critical discourse on South African cinema by academics such as Hannes Van Zyl, Pieter J. Fourie, Keyan Tomaselli, John Van Zyl and Harriet Gavshon during the 1980s was complemented by film critic William Pretorius (born on 9 June 1941). Pretorius had been writing on film, theatre, books and general entertainment since 1976. He began with regular film reviews and a book column concentrating on South African literature in the Afrikaans newspaper *Rapport*, where he worked until 1993. He also worked as freelancer for the *Weekly Mail*, now *Mail & Guardian*, writing on film under his own name and as Fabius Burger, from 1985 to 1995. His critical articles on South African cinema stimulated debates about the state of the film industry as well as its future (e.g. Pretorius 1992).

He has written on film for the local edition of *Penthouse*, the Afrikaans magazine *Insig* as well as for *The Sunday Times Metro*, Multichoices' television magazine *Edge*, a Technikon magazine on educational issues, and Media 24, among other publications. He was one of the founder writers for the magazine *De Kat* and was book editor for the progressive Afrikaans newspaper *Vrye Weekblad* for the period when it appeared in magazine form.[4]

He also wrote on film for the Afrikaans newspapers *Beeld* and *Die Burger*, and had a regular column on books in the *Northcliff Melville Times*. He was an experienced script reader and had acted as a judge for various film competitions, including Vierspel, Entshe Talente and Dramatic Encounters for the SABC and New Directions for M-Net. He also partly taught film and scriptwriting at the Actors Centre in Johannesburg. He studied Practical

William Pretorius. Tobie Cronjé

Criticism at the University of South Africa. Throughout his life Pretorius was very critical of censorship. He wrote outspoken articles about the apartheid censors during the 1970s and 1980s. Pretorius passed away on 26 June 2007.

The isolation from Africa

Apartheid led to an isolation of South African film-makers from their colleagues elsewhere on the African continent. Since the 1920s in Egypt, and especially after independence in sub-Saharan Africa, several hundreds of full-length films were made by African film directors (Armes 2008; Botha 1994; Convents 2003). The advent of sub-Saharan African cinemas coincided with the independence of many African countries after years of colonial subordination. The African film practitioners were deeply concerned with the issue of culture and national identity (Bakari & Cham 1996; Botha 1994). In both documents of the 1975 Algiers Charter on African Cinema and the Niamey Manifesto of 1982, the need was stressed to express the cultural legacy of the African peoples through films as well as the need to use films in the development of African nations.

Since independence feature and short films have been produced in Africa with a voice, content and aesthetic, which are rich, historical and creatively responsive to African social reality. The films also used oral storytelling traditions, and where the films reached their audiences, they were immensely popular (Botha 1994). Since the 1960s certain African countries have produced world-famous film directors: Ousmane Sembene and Djibril Diop Mambety from Senegal, Youssef Chahine from Egypt, Med Hondo from Mauritania, Idrissa Ouedraogo and Gaston Kabore from Burkina Faso and Souleymane Cisse from Mali.

Already in 1973 African films were prominent at the Cannes Film Festival when the Senegalese film of Djibril Diop Mambety, *Touki Bouki*, was screened in the Quinzaine des Realisateurs section. In 1975 *Chronicle of the Burning Years*, a 3-hour epic directed by the Algerian film director Mohamed Lakhdar-Hamina, won the much sought after Golden Palm Award at the Cannes Film Festival. In 1986, the Tunisian film *Man of Ashes* was screened in the official selection round for the Cannes Film Festival. With the upsurge of film art in especially western Africa, Cisse's *Yeelen* won the Jury Prize at Cannes in 1987. Thereafter Ouedraogo had two consecutive successes at Cannes: In 1989 the FIPRESCI Prize was awarded for *Yaaba*, and in 1990 the second highest Cannes award, the Grand Prix du Jury, went to *Tilai*. In 1992 Sembene's *Guelwaar* and Djibril Diop Mambety's *Hyenas* were entered for the main competition at Cannes, which further underscores the prominence of countries such as Senegal and Burkina Faso at this film festival. Burkina Faso is a relatively poor African country but is one of the undisputed leaders in African film art (Botha 1994).

It is indeed difficult to do justice to the extent of African cinemas in this section. Since the Senegalese director Ousmane Sembene produced his first film, *Borom Sarret*, in 1964, a series of films followed (such as *Xala* and *Camp de Thiaroye*) which were very well received across the world. Since 1960 countries such as Tunisia, Egypt, Ghana, Burkina Faso, Zaire,

Zimbabwe, Senegal, Ivory Coast, Nigeria, Ethiopia and Mali produced films that caught attention worldwide. Apart from awards at Cannes, film auteurs such as Cisse, Hondo and Sembene won awards for their work at film festivals in Paris, Rome and Moscow. Nigeria is currently one of the largest video industries in the world with an annual video production of more than 800 titles.

As a result of apartheid and the international cultural boycott during the 1980s, South African academics and film-makers were excluded from the major African film festivals and congresses, such as the Pan African Film and Television Festival (Festival Panafricain du Cinema et de la Television de Ouagadougou, i.e. FESPACO) and the Carthage Film Festival (Journees Cinematographes de Carthage) (Botha 1994). The Pan African Film and Television Festival is held in Ouagadougou in Burkina Faso, and in 1993 nearly a million people participated in the programme which comprized 120 films shown at 13 venues. The Carthage Film Festival is held in Tunisia and is regarded as the display window of African cinemas. As a result of international isolation, South Africans during the 1980s were seldom exposed to these films as well as the debates on film aesthetics, distribution and other important issues on the African continent.

Academics such as Botha (1986) and Van Zyl (1985) argued during the mid-1980s for a closer link between the South African film industry and film industries elsewhere on the continent. In 1988 a watershed was experienced in South Africa when FAWO was founded. It was initiated by the Culture in Another South Africa (CASA) congress and festival, which were held in Amsterdam the year before. At the congress, the role of film-makers in the cultural struggle in South Africa was debated. Definite similarities were pointed out between South African initiatives and initiatives in other Third World countries, particularly in Africa, with regard to the establishment of an 'indigenous' film culture.

A further development led to contact between local and other African film-makers. In July 1990, the Zabalaza Film Workshop and Film Festival were held in London. Local directors, such as Elaine Proctor, and veteran African film-makers, such as Med Hondo and Gaston Kabore, were panel members during the panel discussion. For the first time, South African cinema was discussed and debated within the historical context of African films. A book on the link between South African and African cinema, titled *Images of South Africa: The Rise of the Alternative Film* by Botha and Van Aswegen was completed and published in 1992.

FAWO also started important initiatives: the training of potential young black film-makers in a so-called Community Video School (which evolved into the Newtown Film school); the distribution of films, including African films, in the townships by means of the Video Suitcase Project (which became the Film Resource Unit); and research on new structures for the local film industry which lacked a central statutory body responsible for securing continued government support for the industry. Voluntary researchers such as Danie Pieterse, Johan Blignaut, Martin Botha, Clive Metz and others studied the structure of various foreign film industries with a view of possible application of their findings in the South African context (Botha 1991; 1997b; Metz 1991; Moni 1991). Eventually the French structures, amongst others the Centre National de la Cinematographie (CNC), which was also successfully implemented in Burkina Faso, emerged as a viable model for South Africa (Pieterse 1991). At the congress of the ANC's Department for Arts and Culture in April 1993, the French structures and their success in establishing a true national film industry in France and Burkina Faso were illustrated and discussed.

Since the unbanning of the African National Congress, Pan African Congress and South African Communist Party and the concomitant political changes in South Africa, individuals in the local film and television industries worked closer together with their colleagues in Africa. At the 1993 Pan African Film and Television Festival in Burkina Faso three South African films, namely *Sarafina!* (1992), Jean Delbeke's *The Schoolmaster* (about racism in a small South African town) and Jürgen Schadeberg's *Have You Seen Drum Recently?*, a documentary on Sophiatown culture that was wiped out by apartheid in the 1950s, were included in the festival programme for the first time. In the sphere of television, Africa's United Radio and Television Network Association (Urtna), in collaboration with the pay-channel M-Net, broadcast the award ceremony, which was held in Nairobi, Kenya, as a television programme live across Africa. In order to stimulate the production of local films, M-Net also invited other southern African countries, such as Botswana, Lesotho, Zimbabwe and Namibia, to enter their work for M-Net's annual film competition. The competition was open to the whole African continent. In 1992 Gaston Kabore of Burkina Faso visited South Africa as guest of the *Weekly Mail*, and three of his films were screened at the newspaper's annual film festival, the Weekly Mail Film Festival (Botha 1994).

Since 1994 there has been progressively closer contact and co-operation between the film and television industries of South Africa and other African countries. Martin Botha incorporated African cinemas as part of the film studies modules at the University of South Africa in 1996 and between 2000 and 2005 at the CityVarsity School of Media and Creative Arts. During 2007 Botha started a third-year course in African Cinemas in the Centre for Film and Media Studies at the University of Cape Town that introduces students to the work of directors such as Djibril Diop Mambety, Youssef Chahine, Gaston Kabore, Ousmane Sembene and Gillo Pontecorvo. The course also examines contemporary issues in African cinemas, including cinema in South Africa during and after apartheid. During 2008 an African Cinema Unit was established by Botha at the same university.

The Department of Arts and Culture (DAC) and the NFVF of South Africa, in association with the Pan African Federation of Film-Makers (FEPACI), hosted the first African Film Summit as well as the General Congress of the Pan Federation of African Film-Makers in Johannesburg from 3 to 6 April 2006.[5] Over 150 delegates, including some of the most prolific film practitioners from the continent and the Diaspora, representatives of national and regional film associations, guilds and unions, continental and national government institutions and other key stakeholders, converged in Johannesburg to engage with each other and continued dialogue towards the streamlining of policies, strategies and activities aimed at developing the African audio-visual industry. Discussions towards the hosting of the summit initiated at the 2003 edition of FESPACO between the DAC, NFVF and FEPACI were on the basis of the recommendations of the African Union Commission's appeal for the participation of the African Union, the RECs (Regional Economic Communities), African governments, the private sector and the civil society to take appropriate steps, in conjunction with FEPACI, Urtna, FESPACO and all stakeholders, to hold consultations and conduct preliminary studies with a view to establish an African Commission on the Audiovisual and Cinema Industries as well as a fund to promote the cinema industry and television programmes in Africa (Decisions of the Assembly of the AU, Second Ordinary Session, 10–12 July 2003, Maputo, Mozambique). South Africa was requested by FEPACI to host the first African Film Summit.[6]

Through the various initiatives of FEPACI, which include the film festivals in Ouagadougou and Tunisia as well as inter-African co-operation in respect of co-production and interdependent distribution networks, South Africans have been progressively exposed to film debates and films that are released elsewhere in Africa and to which we have been denied access for many years. This contact was an enriching influence on South African film culture, especially with regard to the use of oral storytelling by a new generation of post-apartheid film-makers (see Chapter 12).[7]

Screen Africa, which has covered the South African film industry since the 1980s in its print and electronic publications, also attempts to expose local industry professionals to other African film-producing countries by means of news stories, articles and coverage of African film festivals.

Notes

1. Another notable production was *Shaka Zulu* (1986), the epic mini-series by William C. Faure.
2. See Botha and Van Aswegen (1992) for a list of Kevin Harris's awards.
3. See Gabriel (1989) for a comprehensive discussion on popular memory and cinema.
4. Information based on press releases about the death of Pretorius in 2007.
5. Information based on press releases by the NFVF.
6. FEPACI moved its offices to South Africa during the past decade. Sepati Bulane Hopa became the secretary-general of FEPACI.
7. See Diawara (1996) for a discussion on oral storytelling in African cinemas.

Chapter 10

Attempts to create a national film commission

The year 1994 could be regarded as a landmark for the South African film industry due to the historic democratic elections and the birth of a post-apartheid society (Botha 2003a; 2004). A comprehensive study by the HSRC into the restructuring of the entire South African film industry was completed and forwarded to the DACST (Botha et al. 1994). The report of 400 pages received widespread praise throughout the local film and television industry, especially by members of the FTF (Botha 1997b; 2003a; 2004).

The report acknowledged 15 years of efforts by individuals such as professors Pieter Fourie and Keyan Tomaselli and volunteers within FAWO to transform the structures of the film industry, especially the previous subsidy system. Ironically, in 1994 the industry was more unified than now with regard to a type of film federation speaking on behalf of various interests.[1] The FTF included bodies such as the FAWO, the NTVA, South African Scriptwriters Association (SASWA), Performing Arts Workers Equity (PAWE), African Film and Television Collective, Association of Community Arts Centres, Black Film and Television Foundation as well as the South African Film and Television Institute (SAFTI).

The HSRC research team recommended that state aid to the local film industry should be administered by a statutory body referred to as the South African Film and Video Foundation (SAFVF). Commercial viability should not be the sole criterion for government support of locally made films. All types of films, including short films, should benefit, and a developmental fund should be used to support first-time film-makers from previously marginalized communities (Botha 1997b; 2003a; 2004).

The underlying assumption should be that a diversity of film types would make the film industry as a whole more healthy, with France as an excellent example. A film industry that is focused exclusively on maximizing profit would inevitably become shallow and artless. In general the dilemma of the local film industry could be attributed to the fact that film was seldom regarded in South Africa as a cultural industry. Although film can be regarded as a commercial product, it should also be seen as a product of culture, such as indigenous literature, theatre, the plastic arts and music (Botha 1997b; 2003a; 2004; Pieterse 1991).

A sustained level of government/private sector aid to the post-apartheid film industry would be necessary to ensure the continued existence of South African cinema. Even the highly developed 'First World' film industries outside the United States, such as Canada, Australia, New Zealand, France and the Scandinavian countries, cannot survive without ongoing support from the state. This does not mean that financial support to the local film industry is sunk into a 'bottomless hole'. As in the case of Burkina Faso, one of the poorest countries in the world, but boasting a vibrant film culture, the South African public would reap the benefits of a healthy film industry on the levels of development, cultural reconstruction, progress and eventually prosperity for the country as a whole (Botha 1997b; 2003a; 2004; Pieterse 1991).

It was thus recommended in the HSRC study (Botha et al. 1994) that the proposed Film and Video Foundation should support all aspects of the film industry. The audio-visual industry forms an organic whole where each of the parts contributes equally to the overall success of this industry. Production, distribution, exhibition, training, archives management, research and information, visual literacy programmes and the promotion and marketing of locally produced films and videos are essential elements of the relationship between film practitioners and the public.

Following the democratic elections of 1994 in South Africa, DACST was established. This was the first time in South African history that a distinct and *separate* portfolio was established for arts and culture. Included in this portfolio is the film and video sector.

The South African minister of the DACST, Dr. Ben Ngubane, formalized an Arts and Culture Task Group (ACTAG), in August/September 1994, to counsel him on the formulation of policy for the newly established government. In November of 1995, four months after the final ACTAG document was published, Dr. Ngubane appointed a Reference Group to write up the Film Development Strategy document. This Reference Group comprised 14 disparate members: individuals from the film industry; academics such as Keyan Tomaselli; the head of the HSRC research study on the film industry, Martin Botha, as well as Beschara Karam. The Reference Group met over a period of 4 weeks to discuss the drafting of the document, using the ACTAG document as the foundation for this book. The first draft of the Film Development Strategy document appeared at the beginning of 1996, and a revised version was published later in the year. The writers proposed that the South African film and video industry be administered by a statutory body, known as the South African Film and Video Foundation (SAFVF).[2]

The Reference Group also acknowledged that film is a high-risk industry and that in many countries it is supported by the state for cultural and investment reasons. The Film Development Strategy committed DACST to the establishment of the NFVF, which was formed with the promulgation of the National Film and Video Foundation Act 73 of 1997. The rest is history. Thanks to the efforts of ACTAG and the writers of the White Paper the NFVF was finally established in 1999. One of the long-term aims of the foundation is to facilitate the placement of the South African film industry on a sound commercial footing and enable it to become internationally competitive (Botha 1997b; 2003a; 2004). Despite the fact that the White Paper was an uneasy blend of progressive and neoliberal thinking it remains a valuable document, which gave birth to a national film commission (see Saks, 2010, and Treffry-Goatley, 2010, for an invaluable critique of the White Paper and policy formulation process). The NFVF of South Africa is a statutory body mandated by parliament to spearhead the development of the South African film and video industry in a post-apartheid society. The NFVF was officially launched at Sithengi '99, the 4th Southern African International Film and Television Market.

The vision of the NFVF is to strive for a quality South African film and video industry that is representative of the nation, commercially viable and encourages development. The NFVF aims to support this by creating an environment that develops and promotes the South African film and video industry, domestically and internationally. As the primary mechanism for state assistance in the development of the South African film and television industry, the NFVF is the key institution for coordinating and promoting this industry.

The NFVF is guided by a council of 14 members, consisting of film professionals with diverse expertise in the film and television industry. The inaugural council, which was appointed on 8 April 1999, consisted of the following members: Shan Moodley (chair), Letebele Masemola Jones (deputy chair), Glynn O'Leary (executive councillor), Gal Batsri, Martin Botha, Carolyn Carew Maseko, Georgina Bonmariage, Mike Dearham, Eddie Khalipha Mbalo,[3] Pinkie Mseleku, Moosa Moosa, Lionel Ngakane, Talib Sadik and Sanjeev Singh.

Faced with a highly fragmented film and video industry the council had to translate the objectives of the Act into specific strategies which are sensitive to the needs of the industry. These strategies were as follows:

- Establish effective relationships with the Minister of Arts, Culture, Science and Technology and other government departments and regulatory bodies to influence policy and access funds
- Establish effective relationships with the National Lottery, private investors and international donors in order to access funds for the industry
- Build effective relationships with the film and video industry
- Initiate and support the development of diverse and effective education and training for the film and video industry – the foundation is mandated to conduct a feasibility study for the establishment of the South African National Film School
- To initiate, conduct and consolidate relevant research and communicate the findings to the industry
- To ensure domestic production and content growth
- To ensure the growth and sustainability of existing and new audience development initiatives
- To develop and implement effective domestic and international marketing and distribution strategies
- To create awareness of existing incentives in the film industry and actively promote additional incentives for the industry and to develop a mutually beneficial environment to attract international film productions
- To research, design and implement innovative fund disbursement approaches
- To promote a climate within which sustainable small, medium and micro-enterprise (SMME) development can take place
- To redress past imbalances in the industry by actively identifying and addressing these problems through all NFVF activities

- To establish conditions for the efficient and effective running of the council of the NFVF
- To establish an efficient and effective NFVF office that is capable of achieving the council's objectives.

In many ways the impact of the NFVF on the post-apartheid cinema was significant. The developments in post-apartheid cinema are discussed and analyzed in Chapter 11.

Notes

1. The current body is called SASFED or the South African Screen Federation. It is a federation of independent film, television and audio-visual content industry organizations and was constituted in March 2006.
2. The establishment of the NFVF and its role in the development of a post-apartheid film industry are documented by Botha (2003a).
3. Mbalo was the first chief executive officer (CEO) of the NFVF.

Chapter 11

Post-apartheid cinema

A positive development during the early 1990s was the perception from all sectors of the South African film industry that cinema has a vital role to play in the forging of social cohesion and the process of democratization and development that so urgently needs to take place (Botha 1995). In 1991 the FBF was established to address the problems of the industry. It was widely considered to be an important step in the consultation process that resulted in the creation of a single body in 1993, motivated by mutual interests.

In composition, the FBF represented the widest possible cross-section of industry interests, from producers and directors to writers, actors, musicians, technicians, agents, managements and studios (Botha 2003b). It also included both progressive and more establishment-oriented groupings, some of which have hitherto not been overly co-operative. The FBF described its prime objective as the creation of an environment in which its members could address strategic issues of common interest and to discuss such strategies with the state, political parties, cultural groups, broadcasters, distributors, exhibitors and others. The main aim was the establishment and development of a representative and indigenous South African film culture which would redress the political imbalance of the past to ensure all South Africans have equal access to film structures. From this consultative process, an interim consensus document emerged which tried to address the restructuring of the local film industry.

This resulted in the creation of the Film and Broadcasting Steering Committee in 1993, representing the eight major film organizations in local cinema. The Film and Broadcasting Steering Committee worked painstakingly for more than a year on proposals for a South African Film Foundation. The proposed structures were modelled on the French film structures in France and Burkina Faso. By mid-1994 the FTF emerged from the Broadcasting and Film Steering Committee (see Chapter 10).

Film production from 1990 to 1994 started to sharply decline after the termination of the B Subsidy Scheme as well as the tax-benefit system of the 1980s (see Chapter 8). The number of features dropped from 81 in 1990 to 9 in 1994 (Armes 2008). In March 1995 the A Subsidy system, which was based on box-office returns, also finally ceased to exist. As a result only seven features were made in 1995.

An interim film fund was announced by the newly formed DACST in May 1996 until a film statutory body was established (Botha 2004). Annually R10 million were distributed among various projects, which included funding for short-film-making. In 1998, for example, R110,000 was allocated to the development of short films and R1,010,000 for the actual production of short films. These grants had an important impact on the short film industry but did not really stimulate feature film-making. As a result only 45 features were made from 1995 to 1999 (Armes 2008). In 1999 the NFVF was finally established to support the local film industry. During 2000 the NFVF started to allocate funding to the local film industry, including the making of short films.[1] It was noted that the short film provided a training ground for aspirant film-makers and would make it financially viable to tell a diverse range of South African stories on film (Maingard 2007).

A short-film-making revival[2]

More than 500 short fiction and short non-fiction films have been made in South Africa since 1980. The themes of most of these films were initially limited to anti-apartheid texts. Since the late 1980s and early 1990s the makers of short films have also explored themes other than apartheid (Botha 1996; 2009). The short films of the 1980s consisted mainly of images against apartheid, but later efforts were lyrical and sensitive portrayals of the destruction of indigenous cultures and forced removals of people due to apartheid laws. Some films also attempted to explore those aspects ignored in official history books. In the late 1980s, particularly because of the Weekly Mail Film Festival, new themes were explored in short films, such as gay and lesbian issues and attempts by people to adapt to changes in South Africa. Animation films, including those by artist William Kentridge, were also made. These short films form part of the new, critical South African film art which emerged in the second half of the 1980s (see Chapter 8).

Various short films portrayed events which were conveniently left out of official South African history books and of a contemporary context in actuality programmes on national television under control of the Nationalist regime (Botha 1996; 2009). Therefore, they became guardians of popular memory in the socio-political process in South Africa. Some of these films portrayed the forced removals of communities from their places of birth under the laws of apartheid. Others confronted the viewer with the destruction of indigenous cultures due to apartheid. In *Dear Grandfather Your Right Foot Is Missing* (1984) director Yunus Ahmed created an imaginative and lyrical short documentary about the destruction of Cape Town's District Six.

Ahmed returned to the bulldozed landscape of his place of birth, and through innovative film techniques, he evocatively recalled the spirit of the formerly thriving 'coloured' community. Set to the haunting sounds of Jean Michel Jarre, the endless tracking shots mercilessly explored the desolate plains, as if filmic interrogation would restore this place to its former life. The film became a lyrical lament for a lost area lying on the right foot of Table Mountain (the grey old Grandfather of Cape Town).

Ross Devenish also made a short film about the movement of a family under apartheid's racial laws. In *A Chip of Glass Ruby* (1982) the Banjee family lived in a small house in an area of Johannesburg which was reclassified as a white residential area. Although the family had lived there all their lives, they were forced to relocate to a new Indian development. In *Cato*

Manor: People Were Living There (1989) director Charlotte Owen created a revealing and visually stunning history of Cato Manor, which was changed from a thriving and bustling active township of mixed African and Indian people to become its present unhappy ruin. *Last Supper at Horstley Street* (1983) is a moving short documentary and true drama of one family's poignant experiences when they were removed from their traditional home in District Six and their attempts to adapt to their new environment, which was without amenities or traditions.

One of the most moving explorations of popular memory is Lance Gewer's *Come See the Bioscope* (1994), a film about Sol Plaatje and his attempts at the beginning of this century to educate rural blacks about the Land Act of 1913. The film resembled the oral narrative structures of west African cinema (for example *Wend Kuuni* from Burkina Faso[3]) and led to several later attempts by young film-makers to explore oral storytelling in short films (e.g. Harold Hölscher's *iBali*, Garth Meyer's *Killer October* and *Bitter Water* as well as Teboho Mahlatsi's *Meokgo and the Stickfighter*). Aryan Kaganof's short *Western 4:33* (2002) is another compelling study of popular memory. It focuses on genocide of Herero people in Namibia during German colonial rule. Kaganof brilliantly uses images and sounds in his observation of a painful history.

In 1989 Melanie Chait's *Out in Africa* became the first South African film to deal with the gay liberation struggle in South Africa (Botha 2009). This short film is a moving tribute to two gay South African men, Simon Nkoli and Ivan Toms, who were respected internationally for their stand against apartheid. Dr. Toms was the first white South African to refuse to serve in the South African Defence Force; Simon Nkoli was one of the Delmas trialists. The film portrayed what it meant to be gay under apartheid and claimed that the South African liberation struggle is a movement for political as well as gay equality (see Chapter 12 for a discussion on the emerging queer cinema in South Africa).

Since the late 1980s the annual Weekly Mail Film Festival became an important forum for the screening of short films (Botha 1996). A short film competition also encouraged new and young film-makers to present their work at this festival. In the early 1990s short films about socio-political changes in South Africa and how people relate to them have become thematically dominant at this festival. In the 1980s the contours of South Africa's political landscape were transformed by massive black popular protest and government promises of a 'new' South Africa. Between black political mobilization and a state attempting to manage a disintegrating economy existed another reality – an embattled white working class struggling to defend a way of life in the face of loss of privilege based on race. Against this background, Guy Spiller's short film *The Boxer* (1990) explored the effect which wider socio-political changes in South African society had wrought in the intimate space of a white working-class family in Johannesburg. In particular, the film documented the hopes and fears of a young champion boxer in a society where the passage from youth to manhood involves entry into a world moulded by a violently defensive culture which is bound by a narrow-minded patriotism and captured by the rhetoric of right-wing politicians.

One of the most remarkable films about adapting to the changes in South Africa has been Catherine Meyburgh's *The Clay Ox* (1993). This visually stunning film portrayed the brief meeting of two young Afrikaners at the foot of the Drakensberg. He is a pacifist who is fleeing from military conscription. She is an activist who is preparing a suicidal bomb attack on a military target in Pretoria. In a highly symbolic landscape Meyburgh addresses the patriarchal, repressive society under apartheid. Afrikaner mythology is examined by using numerous symbols and references to Afrikaner history.

Throughout the 1990s further developments within the South film industry stimulated the production especially of short films, a significant development in the growth of the local film industry (Botha 2009). The pay-television station M-Net initiated a project titled New Directions to give talented first-time South African and other African film-makers and scriptwriters a break into the film industry. By 1999 M-Net's MagicWorks completed 20 short films and two features. This project has been a showcase for new talent in this country and has led to some outstanding short films, such as *Come See the Bioscope* (1994), *Angel* (1996) and *Salvation* (1998). First-time directors and screenwriters, some of them female, black or 'coloured', explored a diversity of themes. Director Khalo Matabane and scriptwriter Mtutuzeli Matshoba, for example, created an award-winning comedy *Chikin Biz'nis* (1995) about the vibrant South African informal economic sector, which provides millions of unemployed urban South Africans with alternative livelihood. Russell Thompson and Patrick Shai explored South Africa's culture of violence in *The Pink Leather Chair* (1996) and *Stray Bullet* (1996), while directors Dumisani Phakathi and Tamsin McCarthy highlighted intimate relationships against the background of the new South African democracy in *An Old Wife's Tale* (1998) and *Cry Me a Baby* (1998), respectively. Relevant social problems such as drug abuse (*Stimulation*, 1996) were also explored in these M-Net short films.

Angel. M-Net

Regional initiatives further encouraged short film production. The former Cape Film and Video Foundation[4] and SASWA in collaboration with DACST funded short films such as *Kap an Driver* (1998), a beautiful exploration of racial relations in the 'new' South Africa, and *Stompie and the Red Tide* (1998), about Cape Town's homeless. The Southern African International Film and Television Market (Sithengi), held every November in Cape Town till 2006, became an important forum for locally made features and short films. The first market took place in Longkloof Studios, and over 1000 delegates from 40 countries attended.[5]

The year 1998 highlighted an important pan-African short film initiative, called *African Dreaming* (Botha 2009). The array of six short films was a major co-production, the first of its kind on the continent, which drew on talent from Mozambique, Namibia, Senegal, Tunisia, Zimbabwe and South Africa. International funding came from the SABC, the Hubert Bals Fund in the Netherlands, cable channel La Sept/Arte in France, YLE TV2 in Finland, HIVOS and NCDO in the Netherlands, the CNC in France, the French ministry of co-operation and Video Lab in South Africa. Deals and contracts were co-ordinated by one of South Africa's leading producers, Jeremy Nathan, through his company Catalyst Films. The South African film *Mamlambo* (1997), a love story between a black boy and a Chinese girl, gave first-time female and black director Palesa ka Letlaka-Nkosi chance to direct a fiction film.

Since the past 12 years short-film-making in South Africa has received international acclaim. Among the short films, Gavin Hood's *The Storekeeper* (1998) stood out. It is a devastating portrait of the culture of violence in this country. Without relying on dialogue Hood tells the story of an elderly man who owns a small, isolated shop in rural South Africa. After several burglaries he takes the law in his own hands – with shocking consequences. Hood's film won as overall best short film at the Nashville Independent Film Festival. It also won the bronze for best dramatic short at the Houston International Film Festival.[6]

Another internationally acclaimed short is Teboho Mahlatsi's *Portrait of a Young Man Drowning* (1998), a short film about redemption. Mahlatsi commented about his film as follows:

> I'm interested in pushing the limits of reality and fusing it with the elements of magic, which have existed since the beginning of time and have been used in African communities in order to deal with the complexities of their existence. One of my dominant images, which I love using, is that of water: how water has been used to cleanse and baptise; and I used it a lot as metaphor for redemption in *Portrait of a Young Man Drowning*.

Mahlatsi completed his internship with Free Film Makers, a film collective in 1993, and has since worked on many projects, including the award-winning *Ghetto Diaries* (1996). Together with Angus Gibson, Mahlatsi wrote and directed the provocative 13-part television series *Yizo Yizo* (1999). *Portrait of a Young Man Drowning* won Mahlatsi the coveted Silver Lion at the Venice Film Festival in 1999.

Developments in South African film production since 2000

Since the collapse of apartheid it became important for South Africa to establish partnerships with other film industries (Botha 2003a; 2004). One such partnership has been with the European Union (EU) and its member states. Set within the context of the signed trade co-operation and development agreement between South Africa and the EU, the South African DACST together with the NFVF and the delegation of the EU in South Africa hosted a film symposium in November 2000 in Johannesburg. The participants of the symposium were drawn from the ranks of chief executive officers of the EU member states' film commissions as well as significant players in the South African film and television industry.

The objectives of the symposium were to develop and sustain robust co-productions between the EU member states and the South African film industry, to create varied products for the film and television markets of the territories concerned as well as to develop a framework that will ensure the strengthening of small and medium-size enterprise initiatives in the film sector. The aim was also finally to work towards the establishment of a financial framework for financing of co-productions between the EU and South Africa (Botha 2003a; 2004).

DACST also commissioned a study, which provided an overview of the current status quo of the South African film industry. The PricewaterhouseCoopers report (Nel 2000) concentrated on the core activities of film and television production across the film industry value chain. The study highlighted the areas of opportunity and growth in the South African film industry.

The results and recommendations were presented at the symposium. It was estimated that less than 15 productions companies produce more than 90% of all feature film and television productions in South Africa, although there are currently more than 150 registered producers in the country. The industry was also traditionally highly dependent on the commissioning activities of the SABC as the National Broadcaster for the majority of production work. According to the research, the revenue generated from television production currently constituted approximately 36% of the total annual film/television revenues.

The South African film industry generated close to R1.4 billion worth of production per annum at the beginning of 2000, but the funding provided by government was a mere R10 million per annum, implying a funding ratio of 0.7%. It was clear from this finding in the report that much can be done to increase the government-funding ratio (the ratio between the size of the industry and the amount of funding made available to the industry) if the South African film industry funding is to be comparable with international benchmarks.

The most significant trends shaping the South African film industry during the early part of the past decade were as follows:

- The emergence of black film-makers: Directors such as Zola Maseko (*The Life and Times of Sara Baartman*), Ntshavheni Wa Luruli (*Chikin Biz'nis – The Whole Story*), Akin Omotoso

170

(*God Is African*), Teboho Mahlatsi (*Portrait of a Young Man Drowning*), Dumisani Phakati (*Christmas with Granny*) and Norman Maake (*Home Sweet Home*) impressed local and international audiences with a number of documentaries, shorts and features

- The alignment and consolidation of the independent film production sector
- Past and recent surges of media donor funding for the development of documentaries
- International demand for South African conservation and wildlife productions
- Strong South African participation in international markets
- The signing of a co-production treaty between the NFVF and Canada and memoranda of understanding with countries such as India and Sweden as well as South African industry players such as M-Net and the Media, Advertising, Publishing, Printing and Packaging Sector Education and Training Authority (MAPPP-SETA)
- The realization and, in some cases, active steps towards the use of digital production formats and its applications thereof in an African setting
- The decrease in video hire activity
- The increase in video sell-through
- A newly re-regulated broadcasting industry that still needs well-defined monitoring mechanisms to drive measurements regarding local content quotas from a production point of view.

Feature film production exists on two levels: co-productions and locally made films. The most lucrative is the facilitation of international and foreign films that find South Africa to be a useful location in terms of flexible and original sites, and favourable exchange rate (Botha 2003a; 2004). Since 1995, at least five features are produced on average every year, for example, the British company Peakviewing's US$12 million production *Glory Glory* (2000), which was shot near Johannesburg. An epic western, it follows a renegade gang of women led by Hannah (Chantelle Stander) who embarks on a campaign of terror in Texas as a way of wreaking a kind of vengeance on a society they feel has failed to protect them from the ravages and degradation of the Civil War. Peakviewing has had a consistent production output since 1993. It includes family films such as *The Last Leprechaun* (1998) and *The Little Unicorn* (1998). Since 1999 it made another three films in South Africa: *Africa!* (1999) with Elizabeth Berkley and Patrick Bergin, about a model who is forced to survive in Africa, *Pets* (1999) starring Christopher Atkins as well as *Dazzle* (1999).

Another example of a foreign-financed film shot in South Africa was *Dr. Lucille* (2000), one of the first films to be made under the South African/Canadian co-production treaty. Budgeted at R20 million it depicts the true story of Canadian Dr. Lucille Teasdale, who with her husband, paediatrician Piero Corti, started a dispensary in Uganda and for more than two decades dedicated their lives to caring for the sick and wounded in the civil war.

Another significant co-production with Canada is *Proteus* (2003), with financing from the NFVF, Telefilm Canada and several Canadian broadcasters. Directed by John Greyson and Jack Lewis, it was produced by Steven Markovitz and Platon Trakoshis of Big World Cinema. Based on a true story, it is a period film that raises issues still of enormous relevance today.

Historian and film-maker Jack Lewis was fascinated by a court record in the Cape Archives, dated 18 August 1735, giving judgement in the case of two Robben Island prisoners. Dutch sailor Rijkhaart Jacobsz and Khoe tribesman Claas Blank received extreme sentences for what the court called 'the abominable and unnatural crime of Sodomy'. *Proteus* was one of 10 features which were shot in and around Cape Town in 2002. The film features five languages – English, Afrikaans, Dutch, Nama and Latin. (The film is discussed in the Queer Voices section of Chapter 12.)

According to the report by Nel (2000) the only South African company to make a significant number of films in South Africa during the 1990s and early 2000 was the Durban-based Videovision, which was responsible for landmarks such as *Cry the Beloved Country* (1994) and *Sarafina!* (1991). Most locally produced films were less successful than co-productions. While revenue generated from co-productions had increased at a rate of 63% per annum from 1997 to 1999, revenue generated from 100% local production had shown little growth in the same period. In fact, the number of local films released annually in South African cinemas declined from 1991 to 1999. South Africa had about 801 screens at the beginning of the past decade, dominated by Nu Metro and Ster-Kinekor (612 combined) as the two biggest players and including a couple of independents (189). Indications were that this number should stabilize and that any significant increase up to 2004 was improbable. In real terms, only 16 locally produced films have generated more than R6 million at the South African box office between 1980 and 2001. Most of these were slapstick comedies, such as *Mr. Bones, The Gods Must Be Crazy* and *Funny People*.

During 1997–99, when the DACST Interim Film Fund was in place, 1203 applications for grants were received, of which 414 projects received allocations worth over R30 million (Nel 2000: 21). The annual budget was R10,685 million; however, there was recognition of the need for a more coherent and strict monitoring system. Such a system was put in place by the NFVF Council in 2000.

The annual interim film fund project expenditure was as follows:

- 1997 – R9835 million
- 1998 – R10,225 million
- 1999 – R10,563 million

During these first 3 years the majority of the funding allocated by the DACST Interim Film Fund went towards production (41%), content creation (22%) and training (21%). With regard to the value chain activities, the following is evident of the projects initiated via the fund (1997–99):

- Content creation (R6928 million) – most of the funds (48%) were allocated to features, whilst the balance was mostly divided between television (23%) and documentaries (21%).

- Production and post-production (R13,507 million) – the major benefiting sub-sectors were documentaries (49%) and features (29%), with television a distant third.
- Training (R5946 million) – a good balance was created between institutional training (54%) and on-the-job or project-based training (46%).
- Promotion (R3312 million) – all the funds were utilized through promotion at international film markets and festivals.

When the NFVF took over the allocated funding by DACST a funding criteria document was drafted and made available to the film and video industry in 2000 for their input. Based on an extensive consultative process the funding criteria document was adopted by council as policy and implemented. Funding is provided in four broad categories:

- Education and training
- Development
- Production
- Marketing and distribution

Individuals, companies and organizations may submit funding applications to the NFVF for grants or grant loans, but specific conditions are applicable in each funding category. For each of the categories an advisory panel with relevant expertise in that area has been constituted.

On Saturday 11 August 2001 the NFVF hosted an industry meeting (Indaba) to present to the film and video industry research findings on matters such as film production, co-production and local content; finance, funding and taxation; marketing and distribution; as well as training and development. The way forward was also discussed with industry players and stakeholders.

The following findings from research input by the panels were an indication of the status of the South African film and video industry in 2001 and thus the challenges faced by the NFVF. The findings and recommendations are summarized for each field of research.

Production

- Theatrical film-making was at the time of the meeting not an industry.
- Television productions were inadequately funded and generally not of international standard.
- The commercials production industry was highly successful.
- The long format servicing industry had slowed down.
- The commercials servicing industry was lucrative but driving prices through the roof.

It was recommended by the researchers that once the new local content regulations of the Independent Communications Authority of South Africa (ICASA) were announced, the NFVF had to host a separate conference to address matters concerning South African content. The NFVF should drive a short film initiative and more investment should flow into audience development. Broadcaster partnerships for feature and short films had become crucial. A climate needed to be created for the growth of small independent production companies by increasing the number of productions commissioned from small production companies. The establishment of a regular cycle of commissioning of works by all the broadcasters, perhaps twice a year, could contribute to this climate. The NFVF must actively pursue co-production treaties with African and other international film industries. It was noted that no reference has been made by the researchers to the important potential of new media (Botha 2003a; 2004).

Finance, funding and taxation

- There has been an emerging domestic and international interest in the South African film and television industry.
- There was a visible growth in local and international co-productions.
- The historical experience of film investment in South Africa still carried a negative impression due to the A and B Subsidy schemes and tax-benefit system of the 1980s.
- Film financing facilities were still emerging.
- The financial services industry, however, remained cautious about the film industry as a viable investment.
- Broadcasters had not yet developed sophisticated finance and funding models.
- Local content regulations and audience demand had given rise to increased demand for South African product.

It was recommended that the NFVF should establish an advisory panel in terms of the NFVF Act with the participation of the Departments of Trade and Industry and Finance to investigate and make recommendations on funding and finance policy with respect to the following:

- Fair and generally accepted criteria for the allocation of NFVF funds.
- The improvement of accountability mechanisms for usage of government funding.
- The creation of distinct commercial and development funds.
- The establishment of a full-time finance and funding office within the NFVF.
- A substantive audit of all income tax allowances and trade and industry incentives as well as the National Lottery Fund.
- Investigating additional revenue sources such as withholding tax on royalties paid to foreign film distributors, box-office levies and incentives for private contributions to a National Film Fund.
- The liaison between the NFVF and SARS regarding the consistent application of Section 24F of the Income Tax Act,[7] including clarifying status and opportunities of Section

24F, and proposing amendments where necessary, and the role of the NFVF in assisting revenue practice through South African film certification.

- The consolidation of general Department of Trade and Industry subsidies and incentives through one NFVF office.
- The liaison with the Reserve Bank regarding criteria for forex approval in respect of export investment structures.
- Consistency and co-ordination with best international practice regarding co-production treaties, memos of understanding between the NFVF and foreign film commissions/ institutes as well as an analysis of international models capable of local application.
- Advise on strategy for marketing the film and video industry as a viable investment nationally and internationally.
- Investigate alternative sources of government funding.
- Liaison between the NFVF and ICASA on application of local content regulation.
- The development of a national strategy for public funding and private finance models for the film and video industry.

Significantly, questions were raised at the meeting about the possibility of the government creating additional tax incentives to boost the film industry (Botha 2003a; 2004). Examples cited of additional incentives included a payroll tax credit, which is used widely in other countries. Value added tax (VAT) is collected on cinema tickets, and it was suggested that this revenue be reallocated to the film industry. It was also suggested, as years ago in the HSRC report by Botha et al. (1994), that South Africa considers implementing a withhold tax on foreign films screened here. Concern was raised among conference delegates about the practices of certain investment companies that were exploiting South African incentives to finance foreign films without any benefit to the local industry. The South African government, together with the NFVF, needed to move towards the development of consistent national policies in support of finance and funding of the film industry. An integral part of this was mobilizing additional resources to increase the size of the NFVF Film Fund so that it is able to meet the needs of the film and video industry.

Marketing and distribution

- South African product distributors were insignificant in the global arena.
- Many South African films experienced no box-office success.
- International marketing strategies by South Africans were insufficient.
- Local producers focused on making and not selling films.
- Local films had difficult access to large markets.

It was recommended that the NFVF provide an infrastructure for global marketing strategies, that incentives are created for local broadcasters to promote South African films, that new media is involved in marketing and distribution strategies and that training providers add new media to film training courses.

Training and development

Many training institutions in South Africa had done little to address past imbalances in the film industry.

The NFVF had a clear mandate contained within the NFVF Act to explore the feasibility of establishing a National Film School.

From the industry input during and after the Indaba a NFVF Strategy for the South African Film Sector was drafted in 2002 and adopted by council.

The challenges faced by the NFVF at the beginning of the past decade were, however, enormous (Botha 2003a). The estimated size of the worldwide convergence market of entertainment and information and communications technologies was US$386 billion, which translates roughly into R3.8 trillion. South Africa's entertainment industry accounts an insignificant share of 0.3% to 0.5% of this wealth. Vigorous competition with the rest of the players to increase their share of this lucrative market is but one challenge faced by the post-apartheid film industry and a statutory body such as the NFVF. Fortunately, the film sector has been redefined as part of a cultural, knowledge and information industry. The cultural industries in South Africa have been singled out as one of the sectors with the potential to contribute to higher growth rate and job creation. The NFVF will have to play its part to ensure this success.

After the *Indaba* it received a 50% increase in its allocation in the 2001/02 financial year, enabling it to start the year with R18 million in its coffers. In addition, the Ministry of Arts, Culture, Science and Technology announced a further allocation of R35 million for the production of short and feature-length films over the next 3 years, which will also be managed by the NFVF. In 2004, R27 million was available for the funding of projects in the film and television sector. It remained far removed from the budgets of international commissions such as the CNC in France.

During 2002, for example, R8,916,145 was invested in the production of 15 documentaries, one feature, five short films, one television series, one animation production and the post-production of one project. Fifteen training institutions and 12 student applicants for bursaries were supported. Distribution and marketing grants were provided to six institutions/organizations and a further 39 grants for development of documentaries, features and television series were made available. In total 96 projects were supported and the first signs of success were visible: International acclaimed films such as *Promised Land* (2002) and Zola Maseko's *A Drink in the Passage* (2003) were co-funded by the NFVF.

At the 2002 Sithengi there were indications that South Africa and the NFVF will play an important role in contributing to film policy for parts of the African continent. From

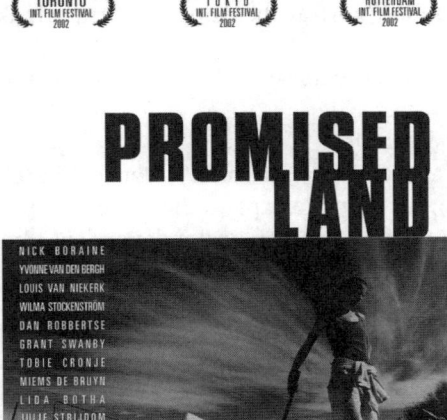

Promised Land. Moonnyeen Lee, David Wicht

11 to 13 November 2002 at the Sithengi Market and Festival the African Script Development Fund (ASDF) hosted a seminar on African cinema and television. This was attended by film-makers, academics, policy specialists, marketers, researchers, broadcasters, journalists and producers, both new and established, who discussed African cinema and television in the context of new departures in African co-operation and development.

Participants included representation from the South African film industry as well as producers from as far as the United States, Nigeria and Senegal. The representatives were from diverse backgrounds, including the public and private film sectors, academics and commentators from Southern Africa and elsewhere (Botha 2003a). At the end of the discussion, the participants made the following declaration (Botha 2003a):

We, the participants of the African Cinema Seminar;

GUIDED by the policies, priorities and strategies of the Sector for Culture, Information and Sport of SADC (the Southern African Development Community);

FURTHER GUIDED by the Organisation of African Unity (OAU) Cultural Charter for Africa; the Cultural Manifesto of Algiers (1969); the OAU Lagos Plan of Action for the Economic Development of Africa and the Final Act of Lagos (1980); Our Creative Diversity (1997); the UNESCO Stockholm Action Plan on Cultural Policies for Development and the OAU Dakar Plan of Action on Cultural Industries;

MINDFUL OF the crucial role of the Southern Africa Film and Television Workshops in Victoria Falls – Zimbabwe (1994 & 1995) and Harare, Zimbabwe (2001), in identifying that African film and television face major challenges such as:

- Lack of national policies, programmes and funding critical for encouraging and supporting the growth and development of film and television industries grounded in African social and cultural contexts;

177

- Serious limitation of production finance to enable local film and television producers to ensure that productions made in Africa accurately portray the culture and traditions of its people;
- Fragmented audio-visual industries that lack formal organization both at national and regional levels;
- Serious limitation of professional training opportunities;
- Broadcasters pay very low licensing fees for local productions to make it worthwhile for distributors of African films and television programming to expand their operations;
- Broadcasters are not willing to play the lead in the financing of local independent film and television projects;
- Lack of professional expertise in the management of markets and festival organizations;
- Limited availability of films and television productions dealing with children and youth audiences; and
- Limited availability of relevant industry information.

Agreed that:

1. The New Partnership for Africa's Development (NEPAD) is a pledge by African leaders, based on a common vision and a firm and shared conviction, that they have a pressing duty to eradicate poverty and to place countries, both individually and collectively, on a path of sustainable growth and development, and at the same time, to participate actively in the world economy and body politic.
2. NEPAD is a political tool and the Film Industry plays the part of being the critic, spiritual channel, inspiration, dream maker and conscience of NEPAD. As such it can convey messages to various audiences in a manner that they understand. African economic and political revival is one of the greatest challenges confronting Africa and the film and television industries in Africa have a fundamental role to play in overcoming these challenges.
3. Since NEPAD and African Union (AU) initiatives are new departures for African co-operation and development, they require new images for the vision. *We cannot create the future if we cannot visualize it.* The place of visual media is to create images that inspire and lead but also which analyse and reflect on processes and their success. Film and television are instruments for a new visual folklore. Filmmaking in Africa portrays images of Africa to the rest of the world but also conveys images of Africa to Africans themselves. For this reason, the film industry is finally attracting increasing levels of investment in Africa but needs support from African Governments with both policy formulation and financing.
4. Film and television writers should be telling stories based on the will and the resilience of our people and the present and the future we want to create. We need to tell the reality of Africa, its contradictions, its power, its poverty, its struggles, its successes and its failures. In summary the industry needs to provide an honest view and evaluation of ourselves.

Call upon:

a. NEPAD Secretariat to include the African audio-visual industry as a strategic component among its policies and programmes.
b. Pan African Federation of Filmmakers (FEPACI) and relevant organizations such as the South African National Film and Video Foundation (NFVF), Southern African Communication for Development (SACOD), Southern African Development Community (SADC), Southern African International Film and Television Market (Sithengi) and African Script Development Fund (ASDF) to organize a summit meeting to develop an African film and television strategic plan and appoint an African Film and Television Technical Task Force to present the strategic plan to the NEPAD Secretariat.
c. African Film and Television Task Force to organize a side event at the 2003 African Union Meeting of Ministers of Culture, Information and Broadcasting to advocate policy issues dealing with film, video, broadcasting, markets, festivals, training and institutional frameworks.
d. African governments to establish local content quotas for both cinema and television in their countries.
e. African governments to sign co-production treaties designed to promote film and television productions that foster better understanding and cooperation among the diverse cultures and people of Africa.
f. African broadcasters pool buying power and pay licensing fees that make it worthwhile for distributors of African films and television productions to expand their operations.
g. African broadcasters to develop infrastructure and support for production and broadcast of appropriate film and television programmes for children and youth in Africa.
h. African film and television producers to enter into dialogue with their national governments about the issues of growth and development of the local and regional audiovisual industries.

First signs of a revival

Ten years after South Africa had become a democracy the local film industry has started to blossom (Botha 2006b). At various international film festivals during 2003 and 2004, including FESPACO, Rotterdam, Berlin, Cannes, Genova, Zanzibar and the Commonwealth Film Festival, retrospectives of South African cinema, including features, shorts and documentaries, were held. Martin Botha, for example, assisted the 14th African, Asian and Latin American festival in Milan with a 40-year retrospective, which included 24 features, documentaries and shorts. The bold, socio-critical work of veterans such as Jans Rautenbach, Manie van Rensburg and Ross Devenish, landmark documentaries such as

Last Grave at Dimbaza, the seminal anti-apartheid cinema of the 1980s, Katinka Heyns's sensitive portraits of women in *Paljas* and recent work by a new generation such as Zola Maseko, Ramadan Suleman, Ntshaveni Wa Luruli and Teboho Mahlatsi were all on display. Those film-makers who made films against all odds in the apartheid years were combined with recent post-apartheid cinema, and in a way, the best of the past was juxtaposed with the present.

The South African government and local government in regions such as Gauteng, KwaZulu-Natal and the western Cape were quick to realize that the film industry offers the country huge earning potential and the creation of jobs. The government's national funding institution, the Industrial Development Corporation (IDC), had initially a fund of R250 million per annum earmarked for the film industry within South Africa. The IDC provides financial assistance by means of loans. Parallel with this, the South African Department of Arts and Culture and the NFVF have made grants of R60 million available to film-makers during the first 5 years of the past decade, including documentaries. The IDC, for example, contributed to the budget of Craig and Damon Foster's documentary feature *Cosmic Africa* (2003). Shot on High Definition this visual masterpiece explores and sheds light on traditional African astronomy. Using oral storytelling aesthetics the film vividly captures the remarkable personal journey of African astronomer Thebe Medupe through the ancestral land of Namibia's hunter-gatherers, the Dogon country of Mali and the landscapes of the Egyptian Sahara Desert (Botha 2006b). This seminal work swept eight awards at the 2003 NTVA's Stone Awards ceremony and received ecstatic acclaim at the Ten Years of Freedom Festival in New York in 2004.

Cosmic Africa. Damon and Craig Foster

Apart from *Cosmic Africa* several outstanding documentaries were made and screened in 2003/04. One was impressed by the poetic beauty of *A Fisherman's Tale* (2003), a 26-minute personal narrative documentary film set in Kalkbay, Cape Town. Initially it starts as the story of a young man who takes his father's fishing lines and goes out to sea in the hope of finding what the ocean means to the fishermen. The young man's story is addressed to his mother. But then the film takes another direction and becomes a moving reflection on the despair and hopelessness of these people's lives as globalization takes its effect, leaving entire South African subsistence-fishing communities on dry land. Structurally it is amazing to note how the personal narrative about the author's inability to communicate with his father, and the emotions that he could never articulate to his mother, is seamlessly integrated with the harsh conditions of the fishing community. With funding from the NFVF director Riaan Hendricks has realized this project after 3 hard years (Botha 2006b). Like in the case of the Foster Brothers (*Cosmic Africa* and *The Great Dance*) Hendricks's documentary is enough proof that documentary work could be personal and poetic, and still succeed as non-fiction.

Documentaries in the post-apartheid South Africa have indeed moved away from the stark political texts of the 1980s to become more personal (Botha 2006b). Screened all over the world *Project 10*, a series of documentaries which examine the personal experiences of 10 years of democracy in South Africa, became a landmark in local documentary film-making. *Project 10* was developed and commissioned by the public broadcaster SABC1 and supported by the NFVF, the Maurits Binger Institute and the Sundance Institute (Pichaske 2007). *Project 10* consisted of 13 narrative documentary films exploring intimate and personal experiences of the film-makers and their characters, such as Minky Schlesinger's *Belonging* (2004), a personal essay of Kethiwe Ngcobo about her struggle to find a place for herself in the New South Africa after growing up in Britain as the daughter of political *émigrés*, as well as Gillian Schutte and Sipho Singiswa's *Umgidi* (2004). In *Umgidi*, film-maker Singiswa prepares to undergo a delayed rite of passage ceremony while his younger brother refuses to participate, arguing that the tradition has no relevance to him as a modern, gay man. More than a collection of films, the project was meant to help nurture a new and more diverse generation of film-makers and encourage a shift from history and politics towards more in-depth personal narratives about the South African nation's transformation (Pichaske 2009).

A major contributor to the stimulation of documentary film-making in South Africa has been Encounters, the annual international documentary film festival, which includes workshops on documentary production (Botha 2006b). Several tertiary institutions such as the Centre for Film and Media Studies at the University of Cape Town also offer comprehensive courses on documentary film-making. In addition to the higher profile festivals and markets, the South African documentary industry now finds support and training opportunities through a variety of professional networks and workshop events. One of the most long standing of these is South African Communications for Development (SACOD), which was created in 1987 and includes members from 12 southern African countries. The SACOD Forum provides a rare opportunity for professionals to engage in critical study and debate – from viewing groundbreaking new films from the region to discussing latest developments regarding ethics, aesthetics and distribution, and getting critical feedback on their own work (Pichaske 2009). Important developments include the establishment of the South African Documentary Film-Makers Association (DFA), which was launched at the 2007 Encounters Film Festival with the goal of creating a body to nurture and represent the interests of the industry. Already the DFA has attracted a wide membership, established important links to industry partners including Encounters and lobbied on behalf of its members on important industry issues such as government funding and SABC policies.

In 2004 and 2005 the feature film industry seemed to experience a revival. The NFVF was able to co-fund the production of more than 10 feature films, most of which were submitted to the Cannes Film Festival in 2004. Investor confidence in South African features with local themes had been demonstrated by the US$15 million budget of the crime drama *Stander* (2003), the story of a disillusioned policeman in the apartheid years who became a bank robber. Another case was the lyrical period drama *The Story of an African Farm* (2004), which received funding by multiple investors, including the Rand Merchant Bank, IDC, Sasani Group, the NFVF, executive producer Izidor Codron and producer Bonny Rodini. Made for R20 million *The Story of an African Farm* is based on the classic novel by Olive Schreiner. Visually beautiful it tells the story of the dramatic impact of a stranger on the

Forgiveness. Jeremy Nathan, DV8

lives of three children on a remote farm. Richard E. Grant is splendid as the opportunistic stranger, who plays the members of the farm community off against each other. Veteran director David Lister expertly combines serious drama with comedy.

The IDC provided 35% of the budget for John Boorman's *In My Country* (2004), a 15 million euro adaptation of Antjie Krog's account of hearings at South Africa's TRC. The script, by South African-born Ann Peacock is told through the eyes of a *Washington Post* journalist (Samuel L. Jackson) sent to South Africa to cover the hearings. Juliette Binoche plays Anna Malan, an Afrikaner poet covering the hearings for radio.[8]

The DV8 project, initiated by Ballistic Pictures' Kobus Botha, Joel Phiri of ICE Media and Avatar Digital's Jeremy Nathan, made its first impact with Ian Gabriel's *Forgiveness* (2004).[9] DV8 had more than 300 submissions in response for script proposals. Eight scripts were selected to be shot in South Africa in the DV format. DV8 was working on an average of US$250,000 in production costs, excluding blowing up and development. Initial funding for the project was provided by the Hubert Bals Fund, but then the NFVF also came on board. Brilliantly shot by Guilio Biccari *Forgiveness* tells the story of an apartheid-era policeman (played by Arnold Vosloo) seeking redemption for crimes he committed against a coloured family in the windswept landscape of the Atlantic West Coast. Biccari won the Best Cinematography Award at the 25th DIFF, and the film also picked up the Audience Choice Best Film Award and shared the Best South African Feature Film Award with Ntshaveni Wa Luruli's multi-award winning *The Wooden Camera* (2003). Also co-funded by the NFVF Wa Luruli's poetic film is very much a rites-of-passage story. The plot deals with a young black boy, Sipho, who finds a video camera and then disguises it as a homemade wooden camera so that he can film life in the Khayelitsha Township. It is one of the first films from South Africa to build a navigable road between the youth of the townships and of upper class South Africa. It also vividly deals with marginalized communities in post-apartheid South Africa (see Chapter 12).

The Wooden Camera. Richard Green

By dealing with marginalized voices *Yesterday* (2004) is a milestone in post-apartheid cinema (Treffry-Goatley 2010). Directed by Darrell Roodt and arguably his best film since *Jobman*, *Yesterday* is the simple story of a young mother who lives in rural KwaZulu-Natal with her pre-school child. Her migrant labourer husband works on the mines in Johannesburg. The woman takes ill and after many attempts to visit a local clinic learns that she is HIV positive. As a masterpiece of understatement Roodt and producer Anant Singh movingly highlights the difficulties that impoverished rural people who have AIDS encounter and the devastating effects of social stigma. The film was screened to high acclaim at the 2004 Durban International Film Festival (DIFF).

Yesterday forms part of an injection in feature film-making coming from the pay channel M-Net's initiative titled *Movie of the Month*. The broadcaster was putting up R1.35 million per feature and hoped that local producers would bring other financing to the table. In the case of *Yesterday* producer Anant Singh co-produced the film, and it was shot for R10 million in KwaZulu-Natal on Super 35mm. Another striking film from this initiative is *Skilpoppe* (2004), a moving drama about a family reeling from a devastating personal tragedy, as seen through the eyes of the teenage daughter. The film powerfully taps into the being of contemporary South African youth – where tragedy is a part of life and growing up can be a brutal but beautiful experience.

The success of numerous South African features at international film festivals finally became a reality from 2004 onwards. At the 55th Berlinale Mark Dornford-May's *U-Carmen eKhayelitsha/Carmen in Khayelitsha* (2005), an adaptation of Georges Bizet's opera set in the Cape Town Township of Khayelitsha and sung in Xhosa, was a surprise winner of the Golden Bear. The production was originally intended for the stage by the talented company *Dimpho Di Kopane*. By transferring the larger-than-life characters and their torments to a township milieu and a set of shacks at the Spier Estate near Cape Town, director Dornford-May tries to integrate the documentary style of shooting with the stylized nature of opera. Unfortunately the characterization is not always convincing. The best quality of the production lies with Giullio Biccari's mobile and inquisitive camera work.

A few weeks after the triumph at the Berlinale South African cinema struck further gold at FESPACO. Zola Maseko's *Drum* (2004), a visually stunning chronicle of South Africa in the 1950s, won the Golden Stallion. *Drum* depicts life in Sophiatown before the apartheid government bulldozed the beacon of non-racialism by the end of the fifties. It tells the story of Henry Nxumalo, a reporter of *Drum* magazine, and his reportage on the slave camps at Bethal Farm. American Taye Diggs gives a fine central performance

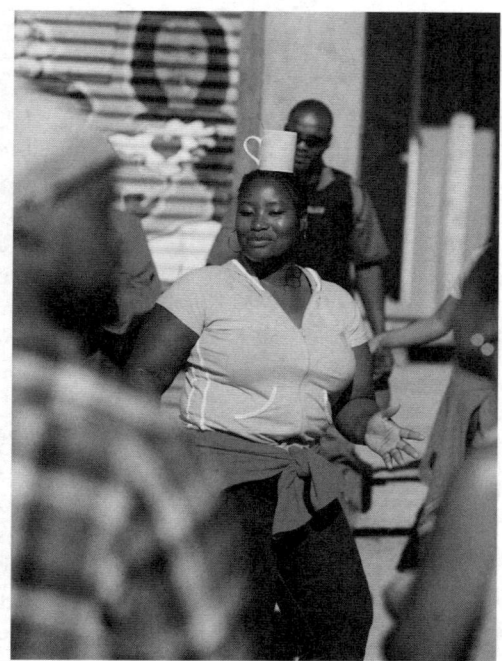

U-Carmen eKhayelitsha. Michael Auret, Spier Films, Ross Garland

as the investigative reporter, but the script lets the film down with clichés and anachronisms (see Treffry-Goatley, 2010, for an analysis of the film). Local critics questioned the film's claims to historical authenticity and ultimately the best thing about *Drum* is its wonderful art direction and period reconstruction by Eddy Ketilsson, Lisa Perry and Susan Vermaak, who deservedly won the Prix du Meilleur Décor at FESPACO as well. Despite the mixed critical response to Maseko's first feature film, it won several more awards – a Silver Dhow, as well as the FIPRESCI Prize at Zanzibar 2005, and the Best South African Feature Award at the 26th DIFF.

Maseko was born in exile in 1967 and educated in Swaziland and Tanzania. He studied at the National Film School at Beaconsfield in England. Apart from his numerous award-winning documentaries and shorts Maseko also directed an 11-part series for the SABC titled *In Search of Our History*. The capturing of popular memory lies at the heart of his work, which is demonstrated by his moving documentary *The Life and Times of Sara Baartman* (1998). In the 19th century Sara Baartman, a young Khoi-san girl, was taken abroad to Europe, where she served as both a servant and a curiosity to satisfy the European obsession with Khoi genitalia. After 5 years of sordid exhibition in the capitals of Europe, she died in Paris and her body was donated to scientific research. She was only 25. After her death she was dissected and her brain and genitals where preserved in formalin in a back room of the Musee de L'Homme in Paris. Recently her remains were returned to South Africa to be buried. Maseko made a follow-up titled *The Return of Sara Baartman* (2003).

Two other South African features also triumphed at FESPACO. Ramadan Suleman's multi-award winning drama *Zulu Love Letter* (2005) won several awards, including the Best Actress Award for Pamela Nomvete. The film is set in a democratic South Africa where some wounds are left unhealed. Tormented by the haunting images and grief of her country's apartheid past, single mother and journalist Thandi (played by Nomvete) has difficulty communicating with her estranged daughter, Mangi. The 13-year-old child is deaf and dumb due to the beating that the pregnant Thandi received at the same time her friends were murdered by an apartheid hit squad. Like in many features and documentaries South Africa's painful pasts are revisited.[10]

Suleman was born in Durban in 1955 and has been living in France since the 1980s. He is a graduate of the Centre for Research and Training in African Theatre in Newtown. In the early 1980s he was intensively involved in alternative theatre, becoming a founder member of the Dhlomo Theatre, the first black theatre in South Africa. Towards the mid-eighties he studied film in South Africa and France after the theatre's closure by the apartheid authorities. During this period he experimented with a Super-8 camera and made two short documentaries. From 1987 to 1990 Suleman studied at the London International Film School, majoring in directing and scriptwriting. His short film *The Devil's Children* won various international awards. *Fools* (1996), his first feature, was the winner of a Silver Leopard at the Locarno International Film Festival. *Fools* examines some of the critical issues in contemporary South Africa before the healing process could begin. Patrick Shai

Max and Mona. Jeremy Nathan, DV8

plays a middle-aged teacher, who has slipped into a life of alcoholism and is forced by a young student activist to re-examine his life.

Quite satisfying on narrative and aesthetical level is first-time director Teddy Mattera's *Max and Mona* (2004), which won the Prix Oumarou Ganda at FESPACO. It is one of the few black comedies to emerge out of South African cinema and is a wonderful treat, a perfectly balanced combination of grief, love and death. The principal character, Max, is treasured by his village, since he has inherited an extraordinary gift as a professional mourner. Inciting the ancestors, Max can reduce the stoniest heart to a flood of tears. He must, however, follow his calling to study medicine in the big city of Johannesburg. When in the city, Max realizes that he cannot pay his study fees in time, and on top of this, he is saddled with a complaining sacred goat, called Mona. Max tries to get money from his Uncle Norman. Norman agrees only if Max is using his God-given talents for his financial redemption at various city funerals. Mattera and his co-writer Greg Latter deservedly won the Best Screenplay Award at the 2004 Cape Town World Cinema Festival. The film also won Best South African feature at the 2005 Apollo Film Festival in Victoria West.

The most prominent feature of 2005 was Gavin Hood's *Tsotsi*, a South African/Great Britain co-production. *Tsotsi* made history at the 2005 Edinburgh Film Festival by becoming the first film in more than 7 years to win both the Standard Life Audience Award for most

Tsotsi. Paul Raleigh, Gavin Hood

popular film and the Michael Powell Award for Best Film. Based on the only novel written by Athol Fugard, the film depicts the story of a young boy orphaned at the age of 9 and forced to claw his way to adulthood alone in the sprawling townships of Johannesburg. In the violent world he inhabits, Tsotsi lives forever in the moment. An impromptu car jacking resulting in the accidental kidnapping of an infant forces him to confront his own humanity. The film is an emotive and very powerful journey in which the central character learns to confront the demons of his past while also coming to terms with the reality of his own destiny. *Tsotsi* was submitted as South Africa's official entry in the foreign film category for the 2006 Academy Awards. *Tsotsi* won Best Film at Edinburgh and Audience Choice Awards at Edinburgh, Toronto, Los Angeles, Denver and Washington. It also won the Critics Jury Award for Best SA Film at the Cape Town World Cinema Festival, with lead actor Presley Cheweneyagae winning Best Actor, and it took the Oscar for Best Foreign Language Film. In retrospective Hood's multi-award winning drama has been the climax of the South African New Wave that started in 2004 and till 2006 resulted in several international awards for local features, documentaries and shorts.[11]

Back to reality after the revival

Sadly the non-renewal of the special feature film fund by the DAC stifled the South African New Wave and as a result feature film production declined remarkably. From 2000 to 2006 only 80 South African features were made – in stark contrast to the 186 of the 1990s, 735 of the 1980s and 236 of the 1970s (Armes 2008). As the most important national institution for the development and promotion of the South African film and video industry, the NFVF currently needs about R325 million per year to do a proper job. Unfortunately its annual allocation in 2009 was a mere 39 million with which it has to cover its administrative expenditure as well as funding obligations.[12]

As a result of limited government funding many exciting new and veteran film-makers were unable to rely on the NFVF to fund their projects. Darrell Roodt's *Faith's Corner* (2005), winner of Best South African Feature at the 2006 Apollo Film Festival, is one of several examples. The film follows the life of Faith, a homeless beggar and a single mother of two young sons. They live in an abandoned car in an alleyway in central Johannesburg. Faith spends her days begging for money from disinterested commuters on the streets. Darrell Roodt's experimentation with film form is remarkable: Shot in the style of the silent cinema, complete with intertitles to capture the dialogue, the film sensitively confronts social issues of poverty and joblessness in South Africa. It is a vivid combination of social concern and formal experimentation. By using the silent format it almost makes a statement that social conditions for the poor have not changed over the decades (Botha 2011). Roodt's *Meisie/ Girl* (2007) is a slice of life about a girl in a rural community who is prevented from going to school by her father, who believes that she should spend her days tending goats instead. Shot in the style of neorealism the film features wonderfully natural performances by non-professional actors from the remote community of Riemvasmaak, on the edge of the Kalahari (Botha 2011).

Several other award-winning features also received no NFVF funding: Khalo Matabane's innovative blending of documentary and fiction in *Conversations on a Sunday Afternoon* (2006) deals with refugees and xenophobia. Gustav Kuhn's *Ouma se Slim Kind/Granny's Clever Child* (2006) examines relationships in the 1940s and how the dominant Afrikaner culture at the time destroyed any hope of non-racialism. Winner of Best Feature at the 2007 Apollo Film Festival, *Son of Man* (2005) is a refreshing retelling of the Gospels within the setting of a South African township.

Ouma se Slim Kind. Gustav Kuhn

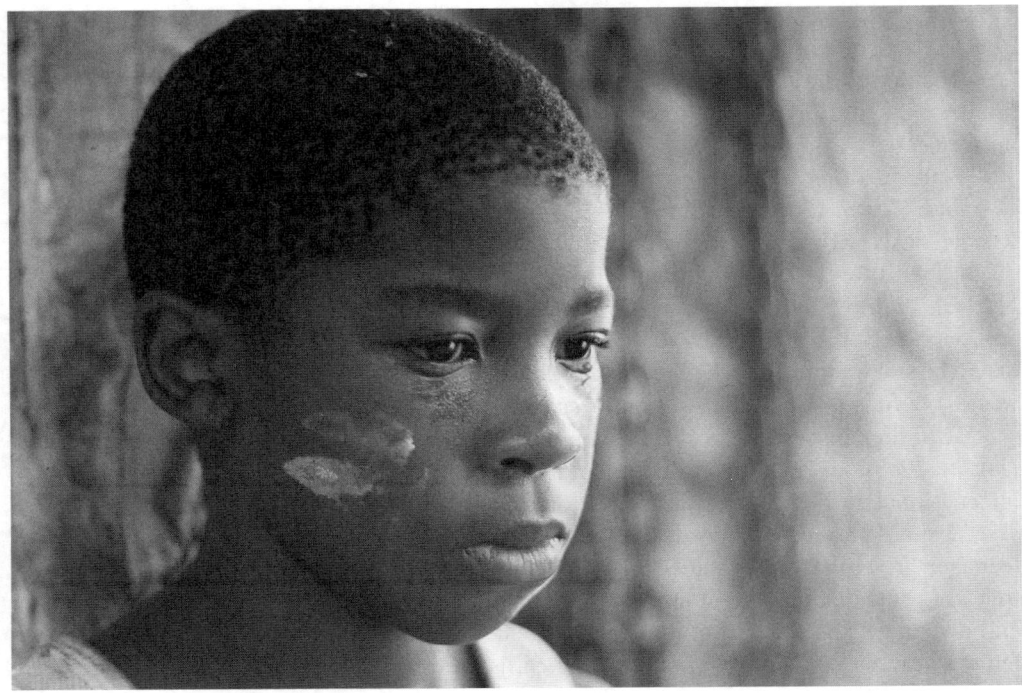

Son of Man. Spier Films, Michael Auret

189

Zulfah Otto-Sallies explores conflict in a Muslim family in the neorealist *Don't Touch* (2006). Otto-Sallies is an important new female voice in South African cinema. Although her film career started only recently, her involvement in the other arts dates back to the 1980s – as writer, playwright and composer of musicals. Her musical *Diekie vannie Bo-Kaap* was presented at the Baxter Theatre in Cape Town and the Grahamstown National Arts Festival. It was followed by even greater success: Productions such as *Rosa, Koesiester Mentality, Echoes from the Ghettos* and *Rainbow and the Moon Princess* played to full houses.

Her direct involvement in the film industry started at the CVET, of which she was the director in the mid-1990s. Her short *Raya* impressed with its delicate portrait of three generations of women from the Bo-Kaap community, a world that has been almost invisible in the past in South African cinema. The criminal past and leaving it behind is the theme of *Raya* (2001), a story of these women, their struggles and reconciliation. In the 2003 edition of *Variety's International Film Guide* Martin Botha called *Raya* 'a visually beautiful insight into a closed, conservative community not often represented on our screens'. *Raya* won an award at the Apollo Film Festival in 2000. *Don't Touch* explored that community further. Some of the themes of *Raya* are also further explored in her documentary for *Project 10*, namely *Through the Eyes of My Daughter* (2004). Otto-Sallies is fascinated by her 15-year-old daughter who, although she was born in the same neighbourhood as her mother, has developed an original view of the world. Mother and daughter get to know another in the documentary through the intermediary of video.

Sadly, the funding limitations of the NFVF impacts on the most acclaimed directors. Ross Devenish, who received international awards for *The Guest* and *Marigolds in August* (see Chapter 6), has been constantly struggling since his return to South Africa in 2002 to finalize new film projects. His script based on a novel by Zakes Mda, *Ways of Dying*, has been rejected by the NFVF.

Co-productions, always a strong component of the film industry, however, continued. *Goodbye Bafana* (2007) by director Bille August and starring Joseph Fiennes and Diane Kruger deals with the relationship between Nelson Mandela and his white prison guard on Robben Island. It received a lukewarm reception at the 2007 Berlin International Film Festival. Phillip Noyce's *Catch a Fire* (2007) managed to avoid a didactic and issue-driven approach to South African history and instead concentrated on the human elements that drive the story about Patrick Chamusso (played by Derek Luke), who was apolitical until he was wrongfully jailed in the apartheid years.

One of the outstanding post-apartheid productions of this decade has been *The Mothers' House* (2005), a 76-minute documentary by Francois Verster, which won numerous international and national awards.[13] Astonishingly intimate, overwhelming and shocking, *The Mothers' House* is a record of 4 years in the life of Miché, a charming and precocious teenager growing into womanhood in post-apartheid South Africa. Living in a 'coloured' township outside Cape Town, she has to face not only life in a community beset by gangsterism and drug abuse but also what it means to break the cycle of violence imprisoning her own female-only family. Miché's mother Valencia is an ex-Struggle activist, now unemployed,

HIV positive and about to give birth to a third child. Dominated by unresolved conflict with her own mother Amy, she increasingly directs her own problems onto her daughter. The film gives the viewer a powerful insight into three generations of women striving to untie the knots that bind and to find peace and love amongst all the hurt and anger within their community.

From 2008 onwards two contrasting developments in South African film-making became evident: On the one hand government funding in the form of grants by the South African NFVF remains hopelessly inadequate. In stark contrast to the limited financial role of the NFVF were the remarkable individual achievements by a new generation of South African film-makers, who have managed to secure alternative funding for their projects. In several cases these young film-makers also succeeded in reaching significant South African audiences on the mainstream circuit.

An example is Ralph Ziman's *Jerusalema* (2008), a realistic and unwavering look into the gritty underbelly of crime, corruption and transgression in the new South Africa.[14] The film chronicles the rise and fall of Lucky Kunene (Rapulana Seiphemo), who from a young age always wanted a BMW and a sea view, but coming from a poor family in Soweto the odds were stacked against him. Lucky moves to Hillbrow, where he becomes a real-estate crime boss. By 11 September 2008 *Jerusalema* has made R1.2 million at the South African box office. It is one of the few South African films, apart from the Leon Schuster comedies, to reach the R1 million mark.

Acclaimed Zimbabwean director, Michael Raeburn, also could not rely on the NFVF to finance *Triomf* (2008), the story of a dysfunctional family living in the poor white suburb of Triomf, built on the ruins of the black community of Sophiatown, just before South Africa's first democratic elections in 1994. The film received acclaim at the Cannes Film Festival as well as the DIFF, where it received the Best South African Feature Award. After being rejected (like many other local films) by Ster-Kinekor, one of South African film distributors, *Triomf* secured a local theatrical release in February 2009.

During the past few years Ster-Kinekor has rejected most local films about South Africa's apartheid past and instead focused on contemporary comedies. Some performed very poorly at the box office: *Running Riot* (2006), a comedy by Koos Roets about the antics of two men in the Comrades Marathon, opened with 83 prints and attracted a mere 91,974 attendances. *Bunny Chow Know Thyself* (2006), about a trio of stand-up comics spending a weekend at a rock festival and messing up their sex lives in various ways, had 20,197 attendances by August 2008 despite opening with 16 prints.

Box-office successes occurred within the established Afrikaans-language market and continued the escapism of the 1970s: *Poena Is Koning* (2007), a very crude farce about secondary school pupils and their obsession with sex, grossed R2,447,025 by August 2008. *Bakgat!* (2007), an Afrikaans-language version of the average US school comedy, grossed R2,864,820.[15] Apart from *Jerusalema* and these Afrikaans-language comedies only *Faith Like Potatoes* (see Chapter 8) grossed more than R1 million at the local box office. *Faith Like Potatoes* targets the religious market and earned R3,580,335 at the box office.

Despite Ster-Kinekor's reluctance to distribute historical dramas, feature film-makers continued to explore South Africa's painful past in notable productions. Shamim Sharif's *The World Unseen* (2008) is a sensitive story of two Indian–South African women who fall in love in the racist, sexist society of apartheid South Africa in 1952. Junaid Ahmed's *More Than Just a Game* (2007) is a touching drama that tells of how political activists who were unjustly imprisoned on Robben Island in the 1960s rose above their incarceration through the creation of a football league. For years, political prisoners had to fight for the right to play football on the island, with men secretly playing the game in their cells with balls made of pieces of paper, cardboard and rags held together with string. The island's authorities finally gave in, granting inmates the right to play football in 1965. The prisoners then built their own goals and would swap their drab prison garb to play on Saturdays in the colours of their teams. The Makana Football Association was formed in 1966.

Anthony Fabrian's *Skin* (2008) is based on the true story of Sandra Laing, a black girl born of two white Afrikaner parents, Abraham and Sannie (Sam Neill and Alice Krige), and traces her life from her childhood up to her adult life. As a child, her parents try to integrate Sandra into a South African educational system that does not allow the inclusion of black children. Given that her birth certificate indicated a 'white' status, she was able to attend school initially but was later classified as 'coloured' and rejected.

Confessions of a Gambler. Ross Garland

Fortunately Nu Metro, another important film distributor, seems less reluctant to screen South African films, for example, the award-winning *Confessions of a Gambler* (2007), a fascinating portrait of a Muslim woman who struggles with her gambling addiction, enjoyed a successful theatrical release. Nu Metro is also now the venue of choice for the organizers of the annual Encounters International Documentary Film Festival as well as the Out in Africa Gay and Lesbian Film Festival, events which were hosted on the Ster-Kinekor theatrical circuit.

In the past few years Ster-Kinekor received harsh criticism for a lack of films from a diversity of film cultures on the so-called Cinema Nouveau circuit. As a result specialized DVD rental venues and film festivals have become important platforms for world cinema. In this regard the first edition of the Cape Winelands Film Festival in Cape Town in 2008 was an important development in ensuring that South Africans are exposed to quality films from around the globe. The festival successfully included retrospectives of the work of Ingmar Bergman, Ousmane Sembene, Francois Ozon and Youssef Chahine, and was the first film festival in South Africa to award an M-Net Lifetime Achievement Award to the late master Ousmane Sembene.

Since its inception in 2005 the Department of Trade and Industry's Film and Television Production and Co-production scheme has been instrumental in growing the film industry.

M-Net Lifetime Award (posthumous) for Ousmane Sembene (Sembene was already dead and a delegate from Senegal received the award on behalf of Sembene's family). Cape Winelands Film festival

More than 37 features, including South African-born Neill Blomkamp's international hit *District 9* (2009), benefited by this rebate incentive scheme. Blomkamp's sci-fi spectacle about aliens – who, with their spaceship stranded above Johannesburg, have to endure a daily routine of unemployment, gangsterism and xenophobia in a squalid Johannesburg shantytown, shot straight to the number one spot in the United States and made US$37 million in the opening weekend.

In 2009 this allegorical film about recent xenophobia in post-apartheid South Africa had raked in US$109,444,336 at the US box office, US$14,336,708 in foreign box office, and US$123,781,044 worldwide. The film undoubtedly drew international attention to the talent and skills to be found in the South African film industry.

To date Department of Trade and Industry's film and television production incentive programme had approved 81 productions for a total rebate of R387.5 million, including the local box-office hit *White Wedding* (2009). Director Jann Turner's romantic comedy about a groom and his best man, who race against time for the wedding ceremony in Cape Town, opened the 2nd Cape Winelands Film Festival and received a standing ovation. During its first week of release on the circuit the film grossed over R1.1 million at the box office. It had since run for 11 consecutive weeks in a total of 43 cinemas in South Africa. *White Wedding* is South Africa's official selection for entry into the Foreign Language Category of the 82nd Academy Awards (Oscars) in 2010.

Shot in Durban and Inanda, director Madoda Ncayiyana's *My Secret Sky/Izulu Lami* (2009) tells the story of two orphaned children, Thembi and Khwezi, who travel to Durban to find a priest who admired their mother's hand-woven mats and encouraged her to enter them in a craft competition. When they arrive in the city, however, they encounter a group of tough street children led by Chilli-Boy (Tshepang Mohlomi) and learn the hard way that the city is a dangerous place. The film won several international prizes, including the Dikalo Award for Best Feature Film at the Pan African International Film Festival in Cannes, the Audience Award for Best Feature Film at Spain's Cinema Africano de Tarifa Film Festival and the Best Actress Award for Sobahle Mkhabase, who was 10 years old when the film was shot as well as the SIGNIS Award for Best Film at the Zanzibar International Film Festival

My Secret Sky/Izulu Lami. Julie Frederikse, Vuleka Productions

One of the outstanding films of 2009 is *Shirley Adams*, a feature-length project co-produced by the London Film School (LFS) with Centropolis Entertainment and South African production house DV8. It is the final LFS project of Oliver Hermanus, who graduated in 2009 with the film. Set in Mitchell's Plain in Cape Town, it is the sensitive story of a mother who struggles to rehabilitate her son after he is paralyzed by a gunshot wound. Denise Newman's portrayal of the mother is one of the highlights in South African cinema. Hermanus scooped Best South African Feature Film and Best First Feature Film at the DIFF for his film, and Newman picked up the Best Actress Award.

Other recent cinematic jewels are Claire Angelique's *My Black Little Heart* (2008), a beautifully shot tale of a heroin user stuck in a Durban seaside vortex of decrepit flats and abandoned office blocks littered with self-mutilators, ex-cons, gangsters, street delinquents, hustlers and addicts; and the South African–Australian co-production *Disgrace* (2009), starring John Malkovich. Steve Jacobs' award-winning adaptation of J.M. Coetzee's novel about a Cape Town professor, who settles with his daughter in the Eastern Cape and gets caught up in the complexities of post-apartheid racial relationships, divided local film critics because of its representation of race.

In 2009 South African cinema was highlighted at the 7th Ischia Global Film and Music Fest in the form of an exhibition on the 113-year history of South African cinema. This unique collection of film stills, posters and DVD clips had been the result of collaboration between the director of the Cape Winelands Film Festival, Leon Van der Merwe, and the South African National Film Archives. The exhibition on South Africa's film heritage demonstrated to an international film audience that among the decades of film escapism, racist films and government propaganda, South African cinema produced cinematic jewels.

Nevertheless, despite recent successes such as *District 9, Jerusalema* and *White Wedding*, the economic viability, cultural diversity as well as gender and racial inequality of the film industry remains a site of public concern (Treffry-Goatley 2010). At the 2009 NFVF Indaba Clarence Hamilton, Head of Production and Development at the NFVF, presented statistics on South African film production since 1994. A total of 615 documentaries were made from 1994 to 2008, with 2003 and 2004 as the most prolific years (154 productions). White directors still dominate production at 68% compared to black directors at 32%. Male directors constituted the highest percentage at 61% compared to females at 39%.

In addition to the NFVF's research results Kristin Pichaske's doctorate study on the process of racial transformation within South Africa's documentary film industry drew multiple conclusions. Thanks largely to the legacies of apartheid, the already high barriers to entry into the documentary field are considerably higher for people of colour in South Africa. For this and other reasons, black South Africans remain more often the subjects of documentaries than their makers. Overcoming this barrier must be a long-term priority, as it is the only means by which an equitable plurality of voices may reach South African audiences (Pichaske 2009). This persistence of racial inequity has fuelled tensions throughout the film industry. In particular, white film-makers who seek to document black subjects face mounting criticism, regardless of the purity of their intentions or methods. These tensions

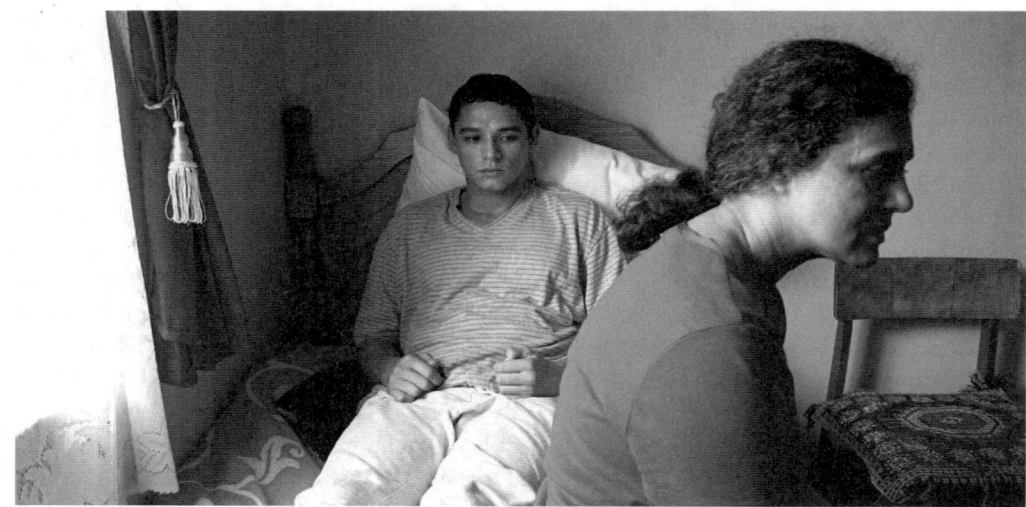

Shirley Adams. DV8

are ultimately a burden on the industry as a whole, and the inability to look past race has inhibited progress. Pichaske (2009), however, argued that while racial parity must remain the film industry's ultimate goal, the intent, integrity and approach of the film-maker is ultimately a more significant determinant of representational accuracy than the colour of his or her skin. In particular, the following three factors are critical to accurate and ethical representation, regardless of the socio-economic status of the film-maker's vis-à-vis subject:

1. First-person and/or reflexive approaches to documentary storytelling which help frame documentary narratives as subjective – that is representations of one film-maker's viewpoint as opposed to objective representations of pure, unadulterated fact.
2. The cultivation of meaningful relationships between film-maker and subjects that endure beyond the scope of the project – the presence of which elevates the film-maker's level of understanding and empathy towards his or her subjects and also helps ensure a sense of responsibility for their long-term well-being.
3. Collaboration between film-makers and subjects in a manner that subjects have greater agency in determining the construction of their images. This strategy helps to mitigate both concerns regarding power imbalance and inaccuracies that may arise through the practice of outsider storytelling.

With regard to feature film production the NFVF research department estimated that from 1994 to 2008 132 films were made. Representation of black directors is quite low at only 15%, compared to white directors at 85%. Representation of female directors is also quite low at only 18%, compared to male directors at 82%. An average budget for documentaries

Exhibition of South African Cinema at Ischia Global Film and Music Festival. Cape Winelands Film Festival

is about R900,000, with budgets ranging from R52,000 to R2.8 million for the largest budget. The average budget for feature films is R24.3 million, with budgets ranging from R60,000 (e.g. Akin Omotoso's *God Is African*) to R171.3 million (e.g. *Hotel Rwanda*). The average budget of feature films excluding official and unofficial co-productions is slightly lower at R9.1 million, with budgets ranging from R60,000 to about R40 million. The average box office for South African feature films in the specified period is R2.5 million. This is very low compared to the average budget of R24.3 million. Box-office figures ranged from R8000 (e.g. *Boesman and Lena*, 1999) to highest grossing figure of R34 million for *Mr. Bones 2: Back from the Past*, released in 2008. The sad reality is that 22% of local feature films grossed less than R100,000 at the South African box office and the highest percentage of films (40%) grossed between R100,000 and R500,000.

Thanks to digital technology[16] the post-apartheid cinema is currently enjoying a revival. But the industry also faces major challenges as mentioned in the introduction of the book. Despite the establishment of the NFVF and significant positive initiatives such as the Film Resource Unit[17] during the 1990s to develop audiences for South African films, local film-makers in general are still struggling to find an audience for their work. The poor local performance of internationally acclaimed films such as *A Reasonable Man* (1999), *Chikin Biz'nis – The Whole Story* (1998) and *Hijack Stories* (2001) leaves one with a feeling of déjà vu.

[A film industry or, in more ambitious terms, 'a national cinema'[18] is ultimately dependent on the number of people who are willing to pay for it. Without a paying audience, whether it is cinema, television, video or new media exhibition, there can be no industry to speak of. With a total population of approximately 49 million people South Africa has a tiny cinema-going audience, measured at approximately 5 million people with a rapidly growing television-consuming public penetrating approximately 49% of the total number of South African households (Botha 2004).

In the future audience development will become more and more crucial to build audiences for the post-apartheid cinema. South Africa's film industry has been held to ransom for decades by the developed markets' funding and exhibition models, content and distribution strengths and worldwide dominance of the Hollywood studios (Botha 2004). It has been estimated that Hollywood product dominates 99% of screen time in South African cinemas. South African film-makers have to compete with films by independent American, British and Australian film-makers as well as the Middle East, Latin America and Asia for the remaining 1%.

Other challenges facing the post-apartheid industry are the inaccessible film exhibition sites that are outside the reach of the majority of South Africans, the limited concentration of theatres in metropolitan areas and the general lack of culturally specific, community-based film exhibition points and product. According to research by the NFVF, audience attendance at South African cinemas is decreasing at an alarming rate to the extent that exhibitors have had to close down cinemas, especially in townships. Some independent cinemas in townships have been converted to churches. Various factors contribute to this decline, including the increase in the range of entertainment media, especially a wider range of television content, door price increases, unemployment, crime and a lack of effective marketing strategies (Botha 2004).

Some theatrical distributors such as UIP owned by international studios merely serve as a 'courier service' between international studios and local exhibitors. They do not have a quota system for local content distribution and exhibition. The rationale that informs their decision on whether to acquire and exhibit a product is based on the commercial viability of the product. Criteria used to determine viability is sometimes out of touch with South African and African realities, especially if one studies the cultural role of cinema within African communities. In this regard one could also look at the South Korean cinema regarding its struggle to fight American dominance. The unfair competition and massive marketing budgets of Hollywood studio backed film releases reduce the chances of South African box-office success at the cinema level. The introduction of incentivized screen quotas for domestic and African film theatrical releases thus becomes a necessary intervention. France and South Korea are important case studies in this regard.

Through audience development programmes South African distributors and exhibitors can ultimately create a demand for local content on the screen, video hire, video sell thru, pay TV, free TV and public broadcasters, both locally and internationally. There is a definite need for aggressive marketing of South African films in people's home communities and the generation of local media enthusiasm around promotion of local product. Local film journalists and critics are also to be encouraged to support local product. It is a fragile industry, especially in the face of globalization.

Within this context the demise of audience development initiatives, such as Film Resource Unit (FRU), during the past decade is a matter of concern. Other important platforms for South African as well as African films also ceased to function such as Sithengi and the African Screen at the Labia independent cinema in Cape Town. Film organizations, which formed part of the FTF initiatives of the early 1990s (see Chapter 10), such as SASWA and NTVA, also closed their doors.

Notes

1. See Botha (2003a).
2. For the purpose of this book short films are defined as audio-visual material on film, video or DVD which is shorter than 60 minutes in duration.
3. See Diawara (1996) for a discussion on oral storytelling in African cinema. Chirol (1999) provides an analysis of the narrative structure of *Wend Kuuni*.
4. A new structure, the Cape Film Commission (CFC) was established in 1999.
5. Sithengi was later incorporated into the Cape Town World Cinema Film Festival.
6. Hood later won an Oscar for *Tsotsi* (2006).
7. Section 24F of the Income Tax Act provides taxpayers with a deduction on taxable income on any amount invested by the taxpayer in the production, post-production or international marketing of a South African film. However, if an investment is made on the basis of credit or loans, or is otherwise not paid for in the relevant tax year of assessment, the taxpayer will only be allowed to claim a deduction to the extent that he or she is at risk in respect of future income derived from the exploitation of the film.
8. See Evans (2007) and Treffry-Goatley (2010) for an analysis.
9. Marx (2007) provides an excellent discussion on *Forgiveness* by comparing the film with documentaries by Mark Kaplan on the TRC.
10. See Maingard (2007) for an analysis of *Zulu Love Letter*.
11. See Dovey (2007) for an excellent analysis of *Tsotsi*.
12. In February 2011 the NFVF announced that the South African government has heeded its call for an increase in its budget allocation. The additional budget allocation is R135,218,000 allocated for the period 2011–13. The additional annual allocation to the NFVF for the financial year 2011/12 is R33,538,000, taking the total amount allocated to R74,879,000. The additional amount for 2012/13 is R42,750,000 and the total allocation is R86,158,000. For 2013/14 the additional amount will be R58,930,000, taking the total allocation to R104,725,000. The allocation was made to the NFVF in alignment with the government's New Growth Path (NGP) in order to create jobs and address skills shortage in the industry. Needless to say the new annual amounts are still far removed from R325 million per year suggested in the NFVF's Value Charter.
13. Description is based on production notes by director Francois Verster.
14. See Marx (2010) for an excellent analysis of *Jerusalema*.
15. The recent Afrikaans film revival includes more than 20 features since 2008.

16. See Treffry-Goatley (2010) for a discussion on digital developments in South African film-making.

17. When still operating the Film Resource Unit (FRU) reached audiences of at least 300,000 to 500,000 per annum, free of charge. FRU played a significant role in local film audience development but ceased to exist in 2007 due to financial problems.

18. Like the term 'nation', 'national cinema' is a complex and somewhat problematic term. This is mostly due to the fact that the concept of nationality varies according to different geographies, histories and cultures. The concept of a 'national cinema' is further compounded in the South African context where film industry fragmentation, a small production output and European and American monopolization have resulted in claims that there 'is no national cinema' to speak of (Botha 2004).

Chapter 12

Themes and aesthetics of post-apartheid cinema

P ost-apartheid cinema is characterized by the emergence of new voices and a diversification of themes (Botha 2007; 2009). An exciting generation of male or female, gay or heterosexual directors has emerged. Many films explore the realities of South Africa from various ethnic perspectives, and soundtracks include several of South Africa's eleven official languages. One thinks of a new generation of film-makers[1] such as Zola Maseko (*The Life and Times of Sara Baartman, Drum*), Ntshavheni Wa Luruli (*Chikin Biznis – The Whole Story, The Wooden Camera*), Oliver Hermanus (*Shirley Adams, Skoonheid*), Mark Dornford-May (*U-Carmen eKhayelitsha, Son of Man*), Gustav Kuhn (*Ouma se Slim Kind*), Rehad Desai (*Born into Struggle, Bushman's Secret, The Battle for Johannesburg*), Donovan Marsh (*Dollars and White Pipes, Spud*), Stefanie Sycholt (*Malunde, Themba – A Boy Called Hope*), Akin Omotoso (*God Is African, Rifle Road*), David Hickson (*Beat the Drum*), Teboho Mahlatsi (*Portrait of a Young Man Drowning, Yizo Yizo, Sekalli sa Meokgo*), Dumisani Phakhati (*Christmas with Granny, Waiting for Valdez*), Ramadan Suleman (*Fools, Zulu Love Letter*), Meganthrie Pillay (*34 South*), Sechaba Morojele (*Ubuntu's Wounds*), Gavin Hood (*A Reasonable Man, Tsotsi*), Zulfah Otto-Sallies (*Raya, Don't Touch*), Teddy Mattera (*Max and Mona, Stay with Me*), André Odendaal (*Skilpoppe*), Tim Greene (*Boy Called Twist*), Riaan Hendricks (*A Fisherman's Tale, The Last Voyage*), Khalo Matabane (*Chikin Biz'nis, Conversations on a Sunday Afternoon, State of Violence*), Jason Xenopoulos (*Promised Land*), Madoda Ncayiyana (*The Sky in Her Eyes, A Child Is a Child, My Secret Sky*), Portia Rankoane (*Tsietsi, My Hero*), Thabang Moleya (*Portrait of a Dark Soul, Case 474*), Willem Grobler (*Considerately Killing Me*), Louis du Toit (*When Tomorrow Calls, 'n Roos vir Mari*), Tristan Holmes (*Elalini*), Garth Meyer (*Killer October, Bitter Water*), Inger Smith (*The One That Fits Inside the Bathtub, Love Poem, Road to Pride*), Harold Holscher (*iBali, 'n Sprokie, The First Time*), Neill Blomkamp (*Alive in JHB, District 9*), Dean Blumberg (*Under the Rainbow, Black Sushi*), John Warner (*Note to Self*), Brett Melvill-Smith (*Tracks*), Bryan Little (*Tagged Toilets, Fokofpolisiekar*), Nina Mnaya (*Life Is Hard*), Matthew Cowles (*The Tooth Fairy*), Claire Angelique (*My Black Little Heart*), Joshua Rous (*Discreet*) and Norman Maake (*Soldiers of the Rock, Homecoming*).

The cinema of marginality

For the first time South African audiences are exposed to certain marginalized communities, such as the homeless in Francois Verster's remarkable documentary *Pavement Aristocrats:*

Boy Called Twist. Tim Greene, Oscar Phasha

The Bergies of Cape Town (1998), the Himbas of Kaokoland in Craig Matthew's *Ochre and Water: Himba Chronicles from the Land of Kaoko* (2001),[2] AIDS victims in *Shouting Silent* (2001), the gay subcultures of the fifties and sixties in *The Man Who Drove with Mandela* (1998), street children in *Hillbrow Kids* (1999), prison inmates in Cliff Bestall's *Cage of Dreams* (2001) and the San in the Foster Brothers' visual poem *The Great Dance* (2000). The latter has already won more than 35 international and national awards, the most for a single film in the history of South African cinema.[3] Wynand Dreyer's trilogy of TV documentaries about ordinary lives on the Cape Flats, *Ravensmead, A Piece of Life, A Piece of Death* and *Steel upon Steel*, is a lyrical and moving document.

The term 'marginality' will be used in this section to describe the poor, economic and social conditions of individuals within a society, social classes within a nation, or nations within the larger world community. Here it also refers to poverty-stricken groups left behind in the modernization process. They are not integrated into the socio-economic system and their relative poverty increases.

A gallery of marginal lives is seen in a variety of features, documentaries and shorts[4]:

1. Homelessness and poverty[5]: *Angel, The Wooden Camera, The Flyer, Under the Rainbow, Boy Called Twist, Stompie and the Red Tide, Pavement Aristocrats: The Bergies of Cape*

Town, Malunde, Hillbrow Kids, Faith's Corner, Tsotsi, Boesman and Lena, Tracks, Azure, Life Is Hard, Zimbabwe, Meisie, My Secret Sky.

2. AIDS orphans: *Shouting Silent, The Sky in Her Eyes, A Child Is a Child, Lucky, Zimbabwe, Life, Above All, Nikiwe.*
3. AIDS victims: *Yesterday, It's My Life, Beat the Drum, Considerately Killing Me, Themba.*
4. Gays and lesbians: *Proteus, Property of the State: Gay Men in the Apartheid Military, The Man Who Drove with Mandela, Skilpoppe, Apostles of Civilised Vice, The World Unseen.*
5. Cultures under threat: *Ochre and Water, The Great Dance.*
6. Foreigners in South Africa and xenophobia: *The Foreigner, Conversations on a Sunday Afternoon, A Shadow of Hope, The Burning Man, District 9.*
7. Victims of institutionalized violence during apartheid: *Zulu Love Letter, Ubuntu's Wounds, Forgiveness, Red Dust, The Gugulethu Seven, What Happened to Mbuyisa?, Between Joyce and Remembrance, Betrayal, Drum, Skin, The Cradock Four.*
8. Victims of colonial racism: *The Life and Times of Sara Baartman.*
9. Victims of child rape: *And There in the Dust.*
10. Intellectually challenged youths and the community's discrimination: *Ouma se Slim Kind.*
11. Victims of drug addiction: *Ongeriewe, My Black Little Heart.*

Marginalized communities finally have a voice in our post-apartheid cinema. Over the past 15 years one has observed the remarkable revival in short-film-making. Among the M-Net New Directions series Barry Berk's lovely film on the homeless, *Angel* (1996), and Dumisani Phakati's poetic coming-of-age tale *Christmas with Granny* (1999) and especially *Waiting for Valdez* (2002) tower above the other shorts. Berk's *Angel* focuses on a group of homeless people in Cape Town. By contrasting their desperate situation with the beauty of the city and its surroundings, Berk has created a very moving portrait of people living on the margin of South African society (Botha 2009). Phakati's *Waiting for Valdez* is a visually eloquent evocation of a twisted society seen through a child's eyes. Set against the backdrop of forced removals in the 1970s the film deals with the popular memory of many South Africans who lived in that dark period. The film deals consciously with themes about identity, especially racial identity and its complexities (Maingard 2007). But the film is also a lyrical, poignant tale of a young boy torn between his love for his dying grandmother and the desire to sneak out for nightly street recitals, around a drum fire, of movies his friends have seen at the local cinema.

One of the most impressive recent short films which examines the impact of AIDS on South African society is Willem Grobler's multi-award winning *Considerately Killing Me* (2005). Winner of Best South African Short (Newcomer) at the 2006 Apollo Film Festival the short is the tragic tale of love and loss. It takes an introspective look at the life of John, a young South African film-maker who has to deal with issues common among young adults today. John is confronted with the unstable political climate of southern Africa and the rest of the world on a daily basis. He struggles because the local film industry is difficult to break

Considerately Killing Me. CityVarsity, Evert Lombaert, Willem Grobler

into, and in trying to escape from the harsh realities of this world he submerges himself in a sea of hedonism, which results in his HIV/AIDS condition. The film's artistic quality is largely owing to Grobler's sensitive direction and Evert Lombaert's excellent cinematography.

On a very ambitious scale the southern African film initiative *Steps for the Future* included 36 documentaries and short films about how individuals are confronting their lives and how societies have to change under the impact of HIV/AIDS (Pichaske 2009; Saks 2010). These compelling stories reveal the effect of the HIV/AIDS pandemic on the lives of individuals, families, communities and nations. Diverse perspectives are presented through the eyes of a range of people and communities. Madoda Ncayiyana's short *The Sky in Her Eyes* (2002) is an example. It won the Djibril Diop Mambety Prize in 2003 at the Cannes Film Festival. The film, co-written and co-directed by Ouida Smit and Madoda and produced by Julie Frederikse, was also selected for screening at numerous international film festivals, including Sundance, Tampere, Siena and Banff as well as at the United Nations General Assembly Special Session on Children. The film was shot on Super-16mm and developed and produced as part of *Steps for the Future*. It is an immensely moving portrait of a young rural girl, left behind after her mother dies of AIDS. Madoda, however, uses a remarkable poetic approach to a harsh reality. Ncayiyana is actually a veteran of radio and television productions, as a director, producer and actor. He was the first black actor hired to work full-time in a South African performing arts council and the first black director of a Natal Performing Arts Council

Yesterday. Anant Singh, Videovision International

production. He has written and performed at theatre festivals throughout Europe and South Africa, including the Edinburgh Festival, where one of his plays won the prestigious Scotsman Award, and South Africa's Grahamstown Festival, where his acting and writing won awards. He was also the co-founder of Theatre for Africa in Johannesburg and the director of the Maningi Theatre Workshop in Durban.

Ncayiyana co-hosted a daily radio talk show with Julie Frederikse and co-wrote a book for young people titled *Careers in Media*. His creative partnership with Frederikse dates back to 1993 when they began writing for radio and in 1995 co-hosted the daily national talk show. Since 1996 they have been writing together for television and Vuleka Productions was born.

Marginalized communities thus finally feature in South African cinema after a silence of more than 90 years owing to colonialism and apartheid. Of major importance in this regard is the cinema of director Darrell James Roodt (*Sarafina!, Yesterday*). Roodt's recent films (*Yesterday, Faith's Corner, Meisie, Lullaby*) have all explored marginalized female characters (Botha 2011). His film *Zimbabwe* (2008) continues the director's studies about vulnerable women challenged by politics and social circumstances. Armed with only a Sony PD150 camera and no budget whatsoever Roodt successfully made a film about an 18-year-old AIDS orphan who travels to South Africa in an effort to support her and two siblings. Apart from the main character's traumatic story, the film vividly reflects the bleakness of a Zimbabwe in ruins.

Another significant film is *Faith's Corner* (2005). The film follows the life of Faith, a homeless beggar and a single mother of two young sons. They live in an abandoned car in an alleyway of central Johannesburg. Faith spends her days begging for money from disinterested commuters on the streets. Darrell Roodt's experimentation with film form is remarkable: Shot in the style of the silent cinema, complete with intertitles to capture the dialogue, the film sensitively confronts social issues of poverty and joblessness in South Africa. It is a remarkable combination of social concern and cinematic experimentation. By using the silent film format it almost makes a statement that social conditions for the poor in the world have not changed over the decades (Botha 2009; 2011).

Both the Oscar-nominated *Yesterday* (about AIDS) as well as *Meisie*, a multi-award-winning film, focus on poverty in rural South Africa. *Meisie* (Girl) is a slice of life about a girl in a rural community who is prevented from going to school by her dad who believes that she should spend her days tending goats instead. Shot in the style of neorealism the film features wonderful natural performances by non-professional actors from the rural community of Riemvasmaak, on the edge of the Kalahari (Botha 2011).

These films display Roodt's cinematic humanism in his representation of (black) women on the edge of post-apartheid society, which do get a voice in his work. At the same time his deviation from the Hollywood classical narrative structure has resulted in fascinating experimentation with form – neorealism and oral narrative structures in the case of *Meisie* and partly *Yesterday, cinema vérité* in *Zimbabwe* and the silent film with avant-garde elements in *Faith's Corner* (Botha 2011).

Yesterday is in particular a fine example. It tells the story of a young black mother with AIDS. Within the temporal frame of the story, which is barely a year, Yesterday's life undergoes radical change. Physically, socially and existentially, her fortunes are profoundly altered when she becomes ill (Horne 2005). The significance of time is also seen in the importance of history in Yesterday's experience. There is considerable irony in the belief of Yesterday's father that the world of yesterday was better than the world of the present, since the tragic turn his daughter's life takes is directly linked to events in the past. The importance of time also features in the chronological structure of the narrative which is explicitly marked by the naming of the seasons as they pass. This sequencing device creates a sense of the relentlessness of the passage of time and the inexorability of death. Roodt brilliantly depicts a socio-political milieu characterized by rural poverty, an inadequate primary health care system, a lack of a support base, community stigmatization, domestic violence, a lack of formal education as well as a lack of empowerment (Botha 2011; Horne 2005; Treffry-Goatley 2010).

Significantly, however, the film is about the main character's growing sense of empowerment, not her misery. Although she is representative of nameless millions with no status in the social hierarchy of South Africa, Roodt inverts the social order, adopting the discourse of transformation in the duration of the film (Horne 2005; Treffry-Goatley 2010). His achievement, as in the case of *Meisie*, is the representation of a character, who ultimately transcends her marginal status. *Yesterday* remains an important, progressive addition to the post-apartheid cinematic repertoire. Furthermore, Roodt's application of certain neorealist elements in the film might also be seen as a breakthrough in an industry where the pervasive influence of Hollywood is evident, not only in the distribution, exhibition and consumption practices of the country but also in the widespread application of the classical narrative conventions in cinematic production (Botha 2011; Treffry-Goatley 2010).

Another notable filmic representation of the AIDS pandemic in South Africa is Ingrid Gavshon's *Nikiwe* (2004). It is a poignant story of three orphans and their triumph of survival against all odds. Nikiwe, only 15 years old, looks after her brothers, Peter (12) and Mgungu (10). Their mother died of AIDS in 1997, and their father abandoned the children to live with another woman. They live in Acornhoek, a desolate, poverty-stricken, sprawling village surrounded by luxury game lodges bordering the Kruger National Park. Beautifully filmed over a year in *cinema vérité* style, the viewer gets an intimate glimpse of Nikiwe's life as she becomes a woman while she searches for her identity, struggles with the stigma of being an orphan and tries to keep the family together. Although life is hard and they have so little, their lives are filled with both joy and despair. The film explores their lives and the film-makers' dilemma as she struggles to document the children's lives without stepping in to rescue them.

One of South Africa's best-known documentary makers, Francois Verster has built a successful career on documenting the lives of marginalized South Africans. His first film, *Pavement Aristocrats: The Bergies of Cape Town* (1998), presented a graphic portrayal of homeless people living on the streets of Cape Town. *When the War Is Over* (2002) is an equally gritty portrait of two freedom fighters struggling to come to terms with life after the Struggle. In 2004, Verster made the Emmy Award-winning *A Lion's Trail* (2002), which tells the story of Solomon Linda, a Zulu musician who wrote the internationally famous song 'The Lion Sleeps Tonight' but was denied a share of the songs immense profits. Verster's greatest achievement to date is *The Mothers' House*, which was released in 2006. In the film, Verster and his long-time producer Neil Brandt again document life on the margins of South African society. This time the focus is on the troubled relationships between Amy, Valencia and Miche Moses – three generations of women living in the Bonteheuwel Township on the Cape Flats. The emphasis is on Miche, the youngest, and

The Mothers' House. Francois Verster

how her life is shaped by the violence that surrounds her, her mother's HIV status and other problematic aspects of her environment. Weaving together pivotal scenes from her formative years, Verster creates a coming-of-age story that centres on the question of whether Miche will break free from the negative cycles of behaviour in her family and community and take advantage of better opportunities (theoretically) afforded to her in a newly democratic South Africa (Pichaske 2009).

Made over a period of 6 years, *The Mothers' House* was an exhaustive project on many levels. Verster shot more than 110 hours of tape with the family, working almost entirely alone and recording both sound and images himself – a practice driven not only by budget constraints but also by a desire to maintain intimacy with the family. Pichaske (2009) describes *The Mothers' House* as a classic participatory/observational documentary. Most of the film's content consists of unscripted observational scenes, shot and edited with the aesthetic aims of realism in mind. As a result, the film has a way of pulling audiences into a state of suspension of belief and absorbing them in the narrative. It draws much of its power from its sense of intimacy with the characters. This stems largely from Verster's close relationship with his subjects and the therapeutic nature of their conversations. Their trust in him is apparent in the scenes they have allowed him to film and deeply personal thoughts they express to him on camera. This sense of emotional intimacy is also reflected in Verster's shooting style, which includes many extreme close-ups of his characters that highlight their facial expressions and other emotive details.

The most popular criticism of *The Mother's House* is that it perpetuates negative stereotypes, presenting a damaging picture of poor, black women and perpetuating stereotypical notions that South African townships are filled with violence, poverty, drug use and HIV (Pichaske 2009). Certainly these social problems are all a part of the film, just as they are all a part of Miche's reality. Yet the film's portrayals are sufficiently complex and mixed with positive imagery that it constitutes a false reduction to accuse it of stereotyping. *The Mother's House* not only gives voice to three generations of black women but also defies the tradition of representing African women as ignorant and victimized. The family is clearly strong and in control, despite their difficult circumstances. More importantly, *The Mother's House* takes pains to properly contextualize the Moses family's problems within the broader social context of post-apartheid South Africa. Audience reactions to the *The Mother's House* have, for the most part, been very positive. In South Africa, the film impressed audiences and won best documentary awards at the Sithengi, Durban International, and Apollo film festivals as well as at the SAFTA.

Confronting the past and the present

Another important theme in post-apartheid cinema is how South Africans are dealing with the traumatic past and how they are adjusting to the dramatic socio-political changes in contemporary South African society (Botha 2007; 2009).

Narratives about the apartheid past

The first decade after apartheid was an intense period of revelation and introspection for most South Africans. After the media censorship and political repression of the 1980s, the hard truths of apartheid were finally being aired, and South Africans had a lot of processing to do. The idea of reclaiming history and telling stories that could not be told previously became a significant part of the national ethos, which emphasized airing apartheid's dirty laundry (Pichaske 2009).

The practice of recovering popular memory rose to an intense level in 1996, when the TRC began hearing its first cases. The proceedings were broadcast regularly on the SABC and national radio – the first time an international truth commission would be broadcast to the public (Pichaske 2009). South African film-makers adopted the theme, using their newfound journalistic freedom to craft more detailed accounts of apartheid than could be made previously. Films like Lindy Wilson's *The Gugulethu Seven* (2000) and Mark Kaplan's *Between Joyce and Remembrance* (2003) elevated the complexity and production value of South African documentary film by combining some of the documentary traditions of the 1980s (didactic stance, 'expert' testimony, a single 'objective' argument) with more creative, narrative techniques (*The Gugulethu Seven* taking on the formal qualities of a detective mystery while *Between Joyce and Remembrance* introduces an element of personal essay).

Master Harold…and the Boys. Spier Films, Michael Auret

Ubuntu's Wounds (2003) is a landmark in our post-apartheid cinema. While several local documentaries have dealt with the TRC,[6] Sechaba Morojele's film was the first attempt outside documentary film-making to examine the effectiveness of the process, and it questions whether real forgiveness is possible in response to truly inhuman acts. And it is a considerable achievement to raise and examine these questions in less than 35 minutes. The film also shows off Morojele as an actor's director, eliciting strong performances from his ensemble cast (Botha 2009).

Zola Maseko's moving *A Drink in the Passage* (2003) is a powerful short film about a touching encounter between a white and black man in South Africa in the 1960s. A celebrated black sculptor recalls the curious events, which led him to share a drink of brandy with a white family during the height of apartheid. It is a complex contemplation on the personal dimensions of enforced segregation and the power of art to transcend the divide (Botha 2009).

Lonny Price's *Master Harold ... and the Boys* (2010), based on playwright Athol Fugard's early life in South Africa, is not a simple retelling of an incident from his past. Rather, Fugard has presented a personal experience that extends to universal humanity. If it were simply a polemic against the policy of apartheid, it would already be outdated now that significant change has transformed South Africa. Instead, Fugard wrote a play about human relationships that are put to the test by societal and personal forces. Set in the shadow of apartheid South Africa in the 1950s, *Master Harold ... and the Boys* focuses on the relationship between a young white boy, his alcoholic father who has one leg and the two black men who work in his parents' Tea Room in Port Elizabeth. Through his humiliation about his father and day-to-day life with Sam (Ving Rhames) the young boy Hally (Freddie Highmore) learns lessons in life, respect and tolerance. Some of Athol Fugard's most guarded and shameful memories of his life in Port Elizabeth make this film touching and a very memorable story.

The trauma of the British concentration camp strategy during the Anglo-Boer War

At the end of the 1990s South Africans participated in the centenary commemoration of the Anglo-Boer or South African War (1899–1902). The Anglo-Boer War broke out on 11 October 1899 between the two former republics (Free State and Transvaal) and Britain. As the war escalated Britain brought reinforcements from Australia, New Zealand and Canada as well as some volunteers from other British colonies. The war lasted 3 years with a very high casualty rate on both sides. Since the governments of the Free State and Transvaal were both elected by the white population, historians in the past generalized it by calling it a 'white man's war'. Apart from the fact that a war cannot be waged in a country without affecting all who live within its borders, recent archival research has proved that the black inhabitants of the two republics were affected more than was generally accepted (Le Roux 2009). Both sides used these people as scouts, labourers and even, at times, armed them, thus using them in a fighting capacity. The scope of the war was the biggest thus far on South African territory and one of the greatest thus far waged by Britain in southern Africa. The

Boer forces had a potential of 54,000 men but never more than 40,000 were employed at once, whilst the British forces grew to 450,000 at the height of hostilities.

According to historians 7792 British soldiers were killed on the battlefields and 13,250 died from disease. On the Boer side 6000 died in military action and 26,370 women and children perished in the British concentration camps. The number of deaths of blacks in concentration camps has been estimated at 20,000 or more. Of special importance is the final phase of the war, after the capitals Bloemfontein and Pretoria were captured and the Boer forces resorted to guerrilla warfare. In an effort to contain the guerrillas the British adopted a two pronged strategy: the so-called scorched-earth policy and the removal of the Boer women and children to concentration camps. It was during this phase of the war that the suffering of the black people intensified. Since about 30,000 farms were destroyed, livestock killed and crops burnt, the farm labourers and their families were taken to refugee camps. Because there was also fear amongst the British that those black farmers who farmed independently may supply the Boer commandos with victuals or that their livestock might be commandeered, these farmers were taken to concentration or labour camps. As the

Feast of the Uninvited. Garth Meyer, M-Net

Feast of the Uninvited. Garth Meyer, M-Net

main reason for the war was the British desire to gain control of the gold mines in the Witwatersrand, there was a need to build a labour force with which to reopen the mines as soon as the state of hostilities allowed it. Forced labour camps were introduced and black labourers were concentrated therein.

The conditions in these camps were appalling. Epidemic diseases, malnutrition, insufficient medical care and dreadful sanitary arrangements resulted in the high death rate. In the white camps the death toll rose to 26,370 of the approximately 100,000 inmates. In the black camps the official British figure was just over 14,000, but recent research proves that a figure in excess of 20,000 deaths among the 120,000 inmates of these camps is acceptable. The traumatic memory of this war became an important theme in several post-apartheid productions such as Herman Binge's documentary *Scorched Earth* (2001), which examines the British concentration camp strategy during the war period as well as director Katinka Heyns's *The Feast of the Uninvited* (2008).

In the first century of South African cinema few film-makers addressed the trauma of the concentration camps. The narrative of *Die Bou van 'n Nasie* (1938) includes a brief reference

Feast of the Uninvited. Garth Meyer, M-Net

to the Anglo-Boer War, but nothing is mentioned about the concentration camps and the death of more than 26,000 Afrikaner women and their children. Afrikaans-language films in the 1960s such as *Die Kavaliers* (1966) and *Krugermiljoene* (1967) about the Anglo-Boer War were nostalgic and romantic period dramas, and in the case of the latter even involved songs by Gé Korsten, Min Shaw and Brenda Bell. In Ross Devenish's masterful *The Guest* (1977) the traumatic memory of the war and the burnt farms is referred to in a conversation between Eugène Marais and Tant Corrie:

Marais: Veld is looking good, Tant Corrie.
Tant Corrie: Ja, but it needs rain. Just remembering what it looked like when we first came. Nineteen hundred and five: homestead burnt down, bare veld. We outspanned and put up our tents where the kraal is now. Bitter hearts. The two boys still small; myself out of the concentration camp; doors as long a prisoner of war. We had nothing when we stared … except that bitterness.
Marais: Which camp, Tant Corrie?

Tant Corrie: Turffontein. The race course. Ja. Two years. The longest two of my life. Not even the drought in nineteen ten and nineteen eleven seemed to last as long. It wasn't the Almighty's mercy we were waiting for, but an end to man's stupidity. (Fugard & Devenish 1992: 101–02)

During the 1980s Dirk de Villiers became the chronicler of the Anglo-Boer War as well as the concentration camps in *Arende* and *That Englishwoman* (see Chapter 8).

Herman Binge's *Scorched Earth* (2001) draws on over 80 interviews conducted in both Britain and South Africa to examine the scorched-earth policy which led to the destruction of more than 30,000 farms and the subsequent relocation of Boer women and children as well as blacks to British concentration camps (Bickford & Mendelsohn 2003). The documentary formed part of M-Net's television series on the devastation the war had on non-fighting civilians, especially women, children and the elderly (Le Roux 2009). Binge made extensive use of testimonies, photographs and conversations with several historians such as Fransjohan Pretorius and Albert Grundlingh to contextualize the historical events and narratives of trauma.

Director Katinka Heyns and writer P.G. du Plessis's *The Feast of the Uninvited* (2008) focuses on several families on both sides of the conflict, who were traumatized by the war and the concentration camps. Starring an impressive ensemble of fine actors such as Jana Cilliers, Marius Weyers, Anna-Mart Van der Merwe, Cobus Rossouw, Rika Sennett, Louis Van Niekerk, Albert Maritz, Neil Sandilands, Marcel Van Heerden, Paul Luckhof, Hykie Berg and Stian Bam the 350-minute production was commissioned by M-Net's Marida Swanepoel and produced by André Scholtz.

Cobus Rossouw serves as a narrator, who fulfils various functions for the duration of the narrative. He reflects on to what extent the stories in the mini-series are able to capture collective memory. He provides an important contextualization of the historical events which frame the narrative. The narrator even engages the characters about their motives of joining the war as well as their post-war memories. It is a non-linear narrative structure, which attempts to understand the sweeps of history by focusing on the stories of ordinary people. At the beginning of the almost 7-hour epic the narrator invites the audience to a game of history. The approach is imagining ordinary people and their stories during and after the war experience. The characters are thus based on the imagined lives of various families, and the narrator admits that they could not be representative of the wider spectre of real-life participants in the war. The post-modern approach of screenwriter P.G. Du Plessis is ultimately highly successful and contributes to a very rich experience. The film examines in a very nuanced way a range of themes: the bitterness among Afrikaners after the war, ideological and class differences among Afrikaners as well as traumatic memories of war, especially by various female characters. Ultimately the narrator argues that how do we really tell the story of collective pain when it is on this scale. For example, 22,000 children died in the concentration camps in less than three years. In the end we cannot really recall the pain of history. We can only put cold numbers to it, but statistics cannot move us. Numbers only astonish the brain, but the soul is left untouched.

Challenging stereotypes of Afrikaners

During the past decade attempts were made by young Afrikaner film-makers to separate themselves from the so-called traditional Afrikaner culture (especially of apartheid) and to re-employ signifiers of that culture as a way to rebel against it (Nel 2007; 2010). These tendencies in a new generation of film directors are to re-employ cultural signifiers, discredit the parental figure (which is associated with the apartheid past) and, in some cases, to present the black 'other' as a key to salvation. It is primarily the result of the loss of narratives of certainty, which collapsed with the transition to democracy in South Africa (Nel 2007: 1).

When Tomorrow Calls (2002) is an important short film by a young graduate, Louis du Toit. He graduated at one of South Africa's film schools, the CityVarsity School of Media and Creative Arts. In only 11 minutes the poetic and highly symbolic narrative depicts an old order of the apartheid years making way for a new dispensation of hope and reconciliation in the story of an Afrikaans boy and a Xhosa boy facing each other as human beings (Botha 2005; 2009). Shot in Afrikaans and Xhosa the film also depicts an Afrikaner nuclear family clearly characterized by the absence of the mother and a father belonging to the past and unable to assist his son to adjust to the changing socio-political landscape of a post-apartheid South Africa. These cultural indicators are surprisingly also present in the Afrikaans short

When Tomorrow Calls. CityVarsity, Louis du Toit

Swing Left Frank. CityVarsity, Grant Appleton, Johan Nel

films of a new generation of directors: Rudi Steyn's *Senter* (2003), J.-H. Beetge's *Triomfeer* (2001), Danie Bester's *Skitterwit* (2003) and Johan Nel's *Swing Left Frank* (2002). Despite working independently from each other, the same images of the Afrikaner nuclear family in a post-apartheid society appear in these exciting shorts, especially with regard to the absence of the Afrikaner mother (Botha 2006c; 2009). Nel (2007) argues that the prevailing doctrine currently appears that Afrikaner fathers are portrayed as patriarchal, aggressive and archaic, while mothers are marginal or absent and that black characters offer liberation. In *When Tomorrow Calls* and *Senter* the implied message is that a new generation of Afrikaners must learn to cooperate with their black counterparts in order to fit in with the new South Africa.

Especially Johan Nel's work is important as deliberate deconstructions of the soothing images of white Afrikaners in South African cinema of the 1970s. As mentioned before, with a few exceptions Afrikaans-language films ignored the socio-political turmoil of the period as well as the realities experienced by black South Africans (Botha 2009). Most Afrikaans-language films communicated by means of obsolete symbols that had little multicultural communication value. They painted a one-sided and stereotypical portrait of the Afrikaner, leading to a misconception about whom and what the Afrikaner was (Botha 1996; 2007; Botha & Van Aswegen 1992). Furthermore, the negative portrayal of blacks as a servant class in these films is a visual symbol of the deep-seated apartheid ideology. Nel has attempted to look at Afrikaners in all their ugliness and multi-facets: In a series of short films, ranging from *Malpit* (2001) to his best *Swing Left Frank*, the idealized image of the white Afrikaner is challenged and analyzed in a critical manner.[7]

In *Swing Left Frank* (2002) Frank Nel is an ex-soldier, who is caught having sex with a black woman by his wife. She kicks him out of the house, and he leaves with a caravan to visit his ex-army friend, who owns a caravan park at the coast. His friend suffers from post-traumatic stress and delusionally relives combat (Nel 2007). While staying at the resort Frank encounters Nomvula, the water spirit, who ultimately liberates him from earthly possessions and offers him transcendence. At the end of the film he enters the ocean where Nomvula takes his hand. They disappear into the deep.

Nel (2007) argues that it seems as if material possessions are representative of Afrikaner privilege, which burden men in the post-apartheid milieu. Nomvula operates as a potential signifier of an exotic black culture, which is foreign but alluring to Frank. The manner in which Frank experience transcendence through her echoes a similar motif of the troubled Afrikaner finding emancipation by bonding with a black character as seen in *When Tomorrow Calls*.

Some of the most interesting features indeed deal with the response of the Afrikaner community to the new democratic South Africa. One of the most powerful features since 1994 deals with an estranged Afrikaner community of white supremacists. In stark (almost black and white images) *Promised Land* (2002) depicts desperate minorities who, trying to retain their apartheid ideologies in the face of a new, democratic South Africa, have retreated into self-inflicted isolation and marginalization. On seeing *Promised Land* for the first time, one realizes again that there has been a bifurcation within Afrikaner culture (Botha 2006a). There is a clear split between the 'old' and the 'new'. Contemporary Afrikaners have been forced to make a choice after 1994 – to choose between racial separation and assimilation and to acknowledge all the ideological ramifications that come with that decision. *Promised Land* depicts both sides of this equation. It portrays the death of one era and the birth of another. In doing so *Promised Land* depicts the advocates of separatist ideology quite cruelly (Botha 2006a; Botha & Lelievre 2004).

With the same expressionist brilliance Ken Kaplan uses black comedy and the horror genre in *Pure Blood* (1999) to look at a group of white supremacists who are trying to revive the old order of the apartheid years. The images of Afrikaners in *Pure Blood* and *Promised Land* are an important alternative to the idealized portrait of Afrikaners in the Afrikaans escapist cinema of the 1970s (see Chapter 3).

Rina Jooste's documentary *Afrikaner, Afrikaan* (2009) is an interesting exploration of a multicultural South African society today. Afrikaans music is used as the vehicle to portray Afrikaner identity and culture, focusing on the minority group of Afrikaners, once the elite ruling class, and the shifts they have had to undergo from an apartheid to post-apartheid period. The preoccupation with Afrikaner identity has been taken up by the youth but is also present in older generations and is evident in the booming record sales in the Afrikaans music industry. Inextricably bound to Afrikaner identity is the Afrikaans language, which many feel is under threat. A form of protest which began in Afrikaans music manifested in the 'Voëlvry' movement of the late 1980s, protesting against the apartheid government. Today, Afrikaans protest music involves the struggle of the so-called marginalized Afrikaner

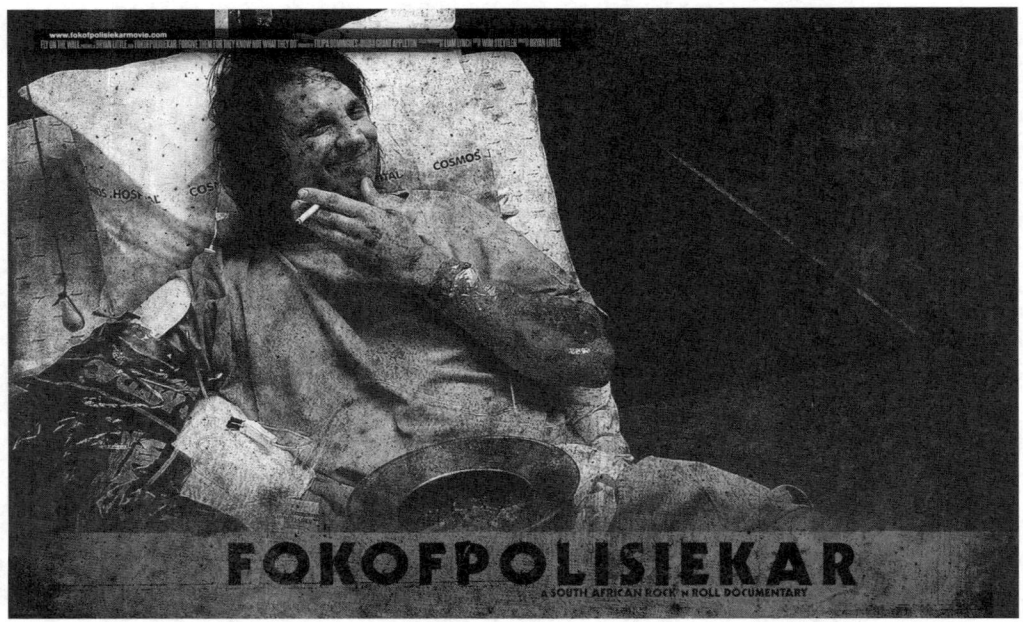

Fokofpolisiekar. Bryan Little

to hold on to their identity and culture. A fine line is drawn between racial identity and racial supremacy. The documentary features three well-known Afrikaans musicians and media personalities from opposing viewpoints: Sean Else, known for his popular song *De la Rey*; Johrné Van Huyssteen, from the band disselblom, and the controversial media personality Deon Maas.

Bryan Little's documentary *Fokofpolisiekar: Forgive Them for They Know Not What They Do* (2009) presents the strongest attempt yet by young Afrikaners to separate themselves from traditional Afrikanerdom (especially of apartheid), to rebel against it and to discredit the parental figure (which is associated with the apartheid past). Between 2003 and 2007 the band Fokofpolisiekar (translated as 'fuck off police car') was at the forefront of not only renewal in Afrikaans youth culture but also the growth of South African rock music (Nel 2010: 127). Little's film is an excellent documentation of their career and presents an interpretation of Afrikanerdom as an illusionary identity, which was maintained through brainwashing by the church, schools and the apartheid government. By viewing traditional Afrikaner culture as something founded on deception Little's film draws significantly on counter-cultural attitudes towards the perceived falsity of society (Nel 2010). At the same time the film expresses an admiration for a community of young Afrikaners who perform rebellion.

Contemporary stories of black lives

Post-apartheid features are also dealing overwhelmingly and by necessity with the lives of black South Africans (Botha 2006a). Two examples are Ntshaveni wa Luruli's *Chikin Biznis – The Whole Story* (1998) and *Hijack Stories* (2000). *Chikin Biznis*, an internationally acclaimed film (Best Film at the Montreal Film Festival and Best Screenplay at FESPACO 1999), follows the fortunes and blunders of middle-aged Sipho, who gives up his menial work at a Stock Exchange-listed company to embark on a new venture: the lucrative trade of chicken business. Sipho not only faces stiff competition from others in this informal sector, but he also has to deal with his family as well. Fats Bookholane deservedly won Best Actor at FESPACO 1999. Surviving in the 'informal sector', but in this case, in a milieu of crime, is also one of the themes of Oliver Schmitz's *Hijack Stories*. Completed in 2000 it took 3 years to get a theatrical release in South Africa, a fate faced by several of the post-apartheid features (Botha 2004).

Several post-apartheid features such as *Tsotsi, Jerusalema, Dollars and White Pipes* (2005), *Dangerous Ground* (1996) and *Crime – It's a Way of Life* (2009) construct black masculinities within a context of crime, gangsters and poverty.[8]

A welcome alternative to these representations of South African black males is on display in the recent documentary work by Liz Fish. In *Urban Cowboy* (2008), for example, the main character, Kendre Allies, come from what he calls a very 'tough time'. He is the product of a broken home, was a member of the notorious Cape Flats Young Americans gang and was the school bully. He left school in Grade 10 and started as a stable hand at the Oude Molen riding school. Today he owns the school with 38 horses and is a beacon of hope in a harsh urban environment for both children and horses alike.

Lastly, another representation of black lives in a South African context drew its inspiration from a Shakespeare text. Minky Schlesinger's 2008 project *Gugu and Andile*, a mini-series and feature, which she co-wrote and directed, won three prizes at the African Movie Academy Awards in Nigeria, including Best Picture in an African language. The film was selected for competition at FESPACO in Burkina Faso and won first prize for Best Youth Film at the Lola Kenya Screen and Best South African Feature at the 3rd Cape Winelands Film festival. The year is 1993. Democracy is at hand and South Africa's townships are burning. Gugu, a 16 year old from a Zulu family, falls in love with Andile, an 18-year-old Xhosa youth. Their love is frowned upon by both communities. Based on Shakespeare's *Romeo and Juliet*, *Gugu and Andile* is a film about love, death and reconciliation.

Director Minky Schlesinger started out as a researcher/writer/director of documentaries in the early 1990s, winning music documentary of the year at Cannes Midem for *We've Got the Power!* and a Star Tonight Award for the TV series *Our Kind of Jazz*. Selected for M-Net's New Directions initiative in 1998, Schlesinger wrote and directed her first short drama *Salvation*, screened widely locally and abroad. Through the 2000s Schlesinger directed both TV documentary (*Women and War*, filmed in Uganda, Bosnia and Israel/Palestine) as well as drama (*To the Bitter End*, part of the *Saints, Sinners and Settlers* series). Her 2004

Gugu & Andile. Neil Brandt, Minky Schlesinger

documentary *Belonging*, on which Schlesinger served as co-director, cinematographer and sound-recordist, premiered at the Berlinale and screened at festivals in Rio, Milan, New York, Amsterdam, London, Flanders, Durban and numerous others. Schlesinger went on to write and direct on the TV drama series *Home Affairs*, working on all five, 13-part seasons. *Home Affairs* has garnered three International Emmy nominations, was selected in competition at BANFF, the Rose d'Or, Roma Fiction Fest and is still broadcasting on South African television.

Rehad Desai's perspective on past and present

Director Rehad Desai's documentaries serve as important examples of how South Africans are dealing with the traumatic past and how they are adjusting to the dramatic socio-political changes in contemporary South African society. His *Born into Struggle* (2004) is a personal documentary about the film-maker's relationship with his well-known father, a leader in the South African liberation movement, set against the backdrop of the struggle for a democratic South Africa and the transition from apartheid to freedom. The story is in essence a father/son story covering three generations, Desai's own 17-year-old son included. The film shows the love, opposition, aggression and conflict involved in a father/son relationship. The setting combines to create a political and at times highly emotional world.

In 1963, the director's father, Barney Desai, a political opponent of the apartheid regime, fled into exile. Rehad Desai's mother, pregnant with him, began her labour under harsh questioning by the security police. At 9 months the director was exiled to England. Later, his father would remind him that he was born into struggle, that a life of politics was his destiny.

By 1966 Barney Desai had joined the PAC of Azania, an avowedly militant organization. In exile, Desai's parents began to slide into alcohol dependency. Family dysfunction largely contributed to a pattern of drug dependency amongst his siblings. His parents, Barney in particular, instilled in the children a sense of duty and belonging to South Africa. High levels of racism in Britain led them to believe they were South African, drummed home by their parents, whilst in reality they had become Black Britons.

Desai's father and he had a special relationship, both devoting their lives to the struggle against apartheid. Yet their differences began to emerge as his political identity formed. As an adolescent Rehad Desai threw himself into the fight against racism and capitalism. His father had come to believe that apartheid could be successfully usurped by a caring capitalism. In contrast he held that apartheid could and should be replaced by a socialist society. Father and son returned together to South Africa in 1990 at different points of their respective political journeys. In Desai's mind his father became the pragmatist and he the idealist.

More comfortable culturally with progressive whites but politically more akin to black Africans, Desai became aware of how British he was. His father's political stature constantly reminded him of the responsibility that went with the name. He launched himself into far left politics and mass struggle, while Barney found himself leading a militant liberation movement.

Back in England, Rehad Desai's son suffered a similar experience of racism and lack of paternal attention. His need to belong led him at 16 to leave his mother and join his dad in South Africa in 2001, closely followed by Rehad's British-born younger brother who 'came home' to develop his identity and heal his drug addiction.

Rehad Desai's father killed himself through drinking in 1997. His death sent the director into clinical depression. Desai recovered and left organized political activity and entered television as a current affairs journalist. It led to a meaningful self-appraisal and significant life changes. As a film-maker, Desai remained rooted in oppositional politics. Several of his documentaries are examining questions about life and identity in post-apartheid South Africa, for example, *The Heart of Whiteness* (2005). Determined to find out what white identity means to South African whites – and why social segregation remains important – the director embarks on a road trip across South Africa with a light spirit and an enquiring mind. His aim is to find and talk to those white South Africans who are so terrified of being swamped by Africa that they purposely isolate themselves from all races in a town called Orania. From the very onset, until he is standing next to the sculpture of Hendrik Verwoerd in the heart of Orania, Desai gently challenges the ordinary whites he meets, be they teachers or janitors, English middle class or Afrikaans farmers. They are friendly and personable, yet invariably each clings fearfully to the trappings of their identity and their entrenched views with resigned bitterness.

A portrait of contemporary South Africa – Sea Point Days

One of the most fascinating portraits of contemporary life in South Africa has been producer Neil Brandt and director Francois Verster's impressionistic documentary *Sea Point Days* (2009). Alongside the southernmost urban centre in Africa, which separates the city from the Atlantic ocean, exists an unusual strip of land.[9] The Sea Point Promenade – and the public swimming pools at its centre – forms a space unlike any other in Cape Town. Right here, slightly away from the hustle and bustle of the city centre, life is paraded in all its forms: over-made-up power-walkers, homeless persons, rent boys waiting for the next pick-up, trendy teenagers as well as elderly ladies. Black, brown, white, young, old, locals, tourists, rich, poor, Jews, Muslims, Christians, stylish, tasteless – they are all here, arriving from apparently nowhere to join the ritual of walking a man-made path along the sea.

At the core of the promenade lies the Sea Point Pavilion, a complex of municipal pools built over a large landscaped lawn during the 1920s. If the promenade is the place where people from all walks of life parade their identities, the pool is where these are, in a sense,

Sea Point Days. Neil Brandt, Francois Verster, Pierre Crocquet

levelled. As clothes are removed, bodies of all shapes and hues are openly on display, and different races come into close bodily contact. Bloated pink bodies splash close to small brown ones; visiting European models lie topless on towels close to carefully clad Muslim women overseeing family picnics underneath the stinkwood trees.[10]

Even in post-apartheid South Africa, the type of proximity and interchange amongst very different people found on the promenade and at the pool is unique. Personal and interpersonal identities are still far from clear in this country – and here they seem to be negotiated in unusual ways on a daily basis. In this everyman's land between ocean and city, the most bizarre and unexpected things happen everyday.

Using innovative film language, quirky charm and a combination of film formats, director Verster's essayistic and often visionary film captures not only the societal blend particular to this part of Cape Town but also the conflicts and difficulties underlying it. Intimate and original vignettes alternate with powerful scenic shots, archive footage and observations of life, all leading towards a comprehensive and surprising view on what it means to be South African right now. *Sea Point Days* presents a fresh and compelling vision of South Africa through an extraordinary public space in a time of transition. It is a film that explores memory, nostalgia, identity and the right not only to space but also to belonging and happiness.

An experimentation with form

With South African formal film training providers mushrooming since the 1990s some very interesting work has been produced from the directing graduates (Botha 2005). In many ways there is more originality and an ability to explore the potential of the medium on display in the short films of these upcoming directors than in an entire decade of local film-making in the 1970s!

Film schools have become vital in a post-apartheid South African cinema to expose students to international cinema as well as to focus on the technological, social, aesthetical and political highlights in the development of cinema in all its facets (Botha 2005). Apart from skills training South African film schools have the responsibility to nurture new voices in an industry that has a long history in which many voices were silenced – those from the black majority, women, gays and lesbians.[11] Film is not only for getting bums on seats but also a means of self-expression by voices, which were silent during the apartheid years.

Some award-winning short films from graduates should be mentioned here:

Dean Blumberg

When one first saw *Black Sushi* (2003) as part of the adjudicating panel of the 2003 Apollo Film Festival,[12] I was immensely impressed by the sensitivity and delicate handling of the subject matter. Here is the story of a black male, Zama, whose old comrades immediately try to draw him back into the criminal world after he is released from prison. Caught up in the cyclic nature of crime and punishment Zama's life seems headed for the same unfortunate conclusion until he becomes attracted by the mysterious art of sushi making. It is a stroke of genius that Blumberg pulls off this narrative device, and in the end the short film becomes a beautiful meditation on cultural identity and multicultural communication, for which it deservedly won a special award at the 14th African, Asian and Latin American Film Festival in Milan (Botha 2005).

After several years as a production assistant, while successfully finishing a Bachelors Degree in Commerce at the University of the Witwatersrand, Blumberg enroled at AFDA (South African School of Motion Picture Medium and Live Performance), where he completed both a Bachelors and Honours Degree in Motion Picture Medium. More important, his talent is on display in a few short films, which have won numerous international and national awards. *Black Sushi* was chosen as the Best Student Film at the 2003 Apollo Film Festival. It was also screened as part of the 10 Years of Freedom Festival in New York in May 2004. It toured several festivals around the world, from Manchester to Mexico City.

Even more impressive, if judged by international critical acknowledgement, is *Under the Rainbow* (2002), a poetic recreation of actual events which took place in the inner city of Johannesburg. It is a story of two young men on their nightly prowl, which inevitably turns tragic. In Blumberg's own words the film is about 'people under the rainbow. There were a lot of people that got left behind' in the new South Africa. 'They didn't go over the rainbow – they got left underneath it.'[13] In a blending of *cinema verité* and poetic realism the film is a gritty portrayal of contemporary urban South Africa, a meditation on the dreams of a dismembered sector of our population and their inevitable search for a better life. The film won numerous awards, including the Fiction Award at the Short Ends World Film Schools Festival in London and a Certificate of Mention at the 7th International Festival of Film Schools in Mexico City (Botha 2005).

Unlike France and Poland where graduates from film schools have a better chance to move into the film industry as young directors (Kieslowski is a very good example) South African directing graduates are very much out in the cold after they leave the safe environment. In a way they are marginalized and the opportunities to obtain hands-on experience on longer formats such as features are limited. Blumberg at present is working for a production company, Freshwater Films, and will be working on commercials. Over the past year he worked on three feature film scripts, one being a full-length version of *Black Sushi*. He is also working on a documentary rooted in the subcultures of Johannesburg. So far his film images consisted of looking at the urban landscape of that city with all its angst but with hope and even optimism.

Harold Holscher

At the 25th Stone Awards Evening in 2003 of the NTVA Harold Holscher's short *iBali* not only picked up a Stone Award for overall excellence but also garnered craft awards for directing, acting, cinematography and animation. The film is a magnificent blending of magic realism and African mythology, with touches of the urban alienation of Michelangelo Antonioni (Holscher is an admirer of *Zabriskie Point*), the surrealism of Djibril Diop Mambety and the beautiful compositions of Stanley Kubrick. Holscher states that *iBali* 'came from an idea of living one's heritage, one's culture' (Botha 2005). He is fascinated by myths and fables, especially in the cinema of Mambety and Kusturica. The plot of *iBali* conveys how African heritage is passed from generation to generation through the art of storytelling. It is a mythical tale about a boy discovering the essence of water.

The film is one of the first from a local film school which actually explores the possibilities of orality in South African film narrative. It aims at an indigenous mode of aesthetics, and judged by the national and international recognition, seems to succeed. *Ibali* was selected for the 14th African Film Festival in Milan and formed part of the best of the shorts compilation. It was also selected for the Commonwealth Film Festival in Manchester and also toured the United Kingdom as part of the best of the festival. It was invited to the 7th Genoa Film Festival as well as the 2004 Cape Town World Cinema Festival (Botha 2005).

Holscher graduated from the CityVarsity School of Media and Creative Arts with a list of awards that testify to his talent. In 2002 his experimental musical narrative *In Progress* won

iBali, Harold Holscher, CityVarsity

awards for directing and the overall production. In the same year he received awards for *'n Sprokie*, another 'fairytale like *iBali*', characterized by exquisite visuals (another craft award), shot on 16mm. Adapted from an Afrikaans story it tells the sad tale of a woman waiting for her son to return from the war in Angola, but he will never return and the war has been lost (Botha 2005).

In December 2003 Holscher had the opportunity to do the storyboards for *U-Carmen eKhayelitsha* in Cape Town. As in the case of Blumberg he is working on feature-length scripts and has finished a short film about compassion, titled *The First Time* (2010). He does not consider himself to be a very good writer: 'The ideas are in my head. I just can't put it down on paper. I have to paint them, visually.'[14] It is the visual quality which makes his shorts so special.

After graduating from film school Holscher still found a very fond interest in the myths and mysticism of Africa. He started reading the works of Credo Mutwa, the last African sanusi (sangoma) and keeper of the Zulu secrets. In his readings Holscher found this ancient dark mysterious world so many people do not know of and got more and more fascinated with Africa.

He met a producer named Renier Ridgeway who also shared this common interest. They started talking about making a film and pretty soon started exploring the stories and heritage of one of the most ancient cultures on earth, the Khoi-san.

It became apparent after meeting with all the parties involved that this was not going to be an easy task since there are many schools of thought surrounding this fascinating tribe, their culture and their history. They met with the local community in Upington and told them their story. Approval was given and the script was written. The film *The First Time* explores the ancient art of compassion and the beauty and complexities of first-time experiences. It is a tale told around the campfire trying to capture the essence of a small family living on the southern tip of this continent.

It was going to be a difficult task getting hold of authentic members of the community, seeing that so few are left in Africa. Then one day Holscher's brother phoned and said he found the bushman. His name is !Gubi and he is 98 years old. A scientist did a study on his blood and came to the conclusion that his bloodline stems from one of the oldest families of the San people. He and his son Johannes came along for the journey.

The location of Elands Bay holds significant value and was picked not only for its sheer beauty but also for its rich cultural history. It was a holy place where the mountain meets the sea (Baboon Point) and where there was abundant fresh water for families to live in complete commune with each other. The ancient rock paintings in the caves tell of a land rich with food and game (like the eland) where many families lived, a very appropriate location.

Cinematically it was important to let the Bushmen and the location guide the film to keep it as authentic as possible. Shot on 4:2:1 ratio with old Cook lenses it gives that epic feel of an old American western but with an African twist.

John Warner

Another graduate of CityVarsity School of Media and Creative Arts John Warner has so far won no less than eleven local awards for his short films, music videos and advertisements. His greatest achievement to date is a short titled *Note to Self* (2001), which won Gold and a craft award for directing at the 2001 NTVA Stone Awards ceremony. The film was screened in the official Ten Years of Democracy in South Africa retrospective at the 7th Genoa Film Festival, and Warner was an invited guest (Botha 2005).

Highly ambitious for a final-year 35mm student production *Note to Self* is a surreal, almost Lynchian, glimpse of the traumatic past still haunting our present. Two stories, one about a young man who kidnapped a girl the other about two lovers who intend to meet for a Valentine's dinner, are seamlessly integrated into a dreamlike narrative. It is also a textbook of inter-textuality: In only twelve minutes references are made to *Blue Velvet, The Cell, Wild at Heart* and *Natural Born Killers* (Botha 2005; 2007; 2009). But this post-modern piece remains Warner's own original vision and has been acknowledged as such by the juries, who gave him an award for his direction. Technically it surpasses the majority of final-year student productions by local film schools. It was selected in 2003 as one of the Best of RESFEST Africa and was screened in Durban, Cape Town and Johannesburg to a very warm reception, especially from young audiences. Wherever it was screened in Cape Town audiences were stunned by the technical quality and beauty of the surreal images. *Note to Self* displays another characteristic in Warner's body of work, namely the deliberate subversion of movie genres. Throughout his shorts Warner played around with genre conventions and making references to various film examples.

Garth Meyer

Garth Meyer is a world-renowned photographer specialising in large format photography. His work over the past 20 years has been predominantly dedicated to exposing the majestic

Killer October. Garth Meyer, CityVarsity

Bitter Water. Garth Meyer, CityVarsity

essence of the African continent and in so doing ensuring a legacy for himself in the visual halls of history. By means of stunning visuals and an evocative sound design Meyer tells the story of a young boy, who loses a loved one to an unknown disease in *Killer October* (2004). The film hints at AIDS, which currently ravages Zimbabwe and could be the 'killer' of the title. The boy embarks on a mythical journey to find a resting place for the ashes of his parent. Documentary and African myth are impressively integrated in this short, which had its South African premiere at the Apollo Film Festival in Victoria West, where it won Best South African Short Film, and its African première at Zanzibar in 2005.

Meyer's *Bitter Water/Marah* (2006) is even more impressive than *Killer October*. The 37-minutes short explores the link between old beliefs in supernatural forces and modern social deterioration as a result of failing morals in a rural community. The approach is magical realism. Two parallel plots involve a boy's story of revenging his sister's death and the more subliminal story of the *inyanga*'s[15] power to 'make' a child for himself by using his powers. Oral storytelling is vividly explored and a documentary and dramatic approach to the subject matter is seamlessly integrated. The editor and sound designer Douw Jordaan's contribution to the film is impressive. The film won two awards at the 2007 KKNK Film Festival, one for Best South African Short and a second for Meyer as Best Young Artist.

Meyer was the stills photographer on the set of Katinka Heyns's *The Feast of the Uninvited* (2008). His images, which vividly capture the spirit and visual sensibility of the production, have been reproduced in this book.

Oral storytelling

Oral storytelling in recent short-film-making has reached an aesthetic peak in Teboho Mahlatsi's *Sekalli Le Meokgo/Meokgo and the Stickfighter* (2007). Visually ravishing this innovate short tells the story of Kgotso, a reclusive, concertina-playing stickfighter, who encounters the spirit of a beguiling woman, Meokgo, and rescues her from an evil horseman. Kgotso lives a solitary life high up in the Maluti Mountains of Lesotho. Whilst tending sheep and playing his concertina, he sees a beautiful and mysterious woman staring at him dreamily from the water. This story of unrequited love and sacrifice captures both the cruelty and the beauty of African magical beliefs. The film is in fact a fable that draws equally on Mozart's opera 'The Magic Flute' and the living power of magic in traditional African cultures. Mahlatsi brilliantly uses bold, iconic images to build an elemental conflict worthy of a Sergio Leone western.[16]

The work of Craig and Damon Foster

One needs to mention the work of the Foster Brothers for their bold experimentation with form. Brothers Craig and Damon Foster grew up in a wooden bungalow on the Atlantic Ocean, near the tip of Africa. They have travelled extensively, living and working in remote villages and wilderness areas in 10 African countries. They have more than 16 years of filming experience in Africa. Their primary intent lies in telling stories with the voice of

The Great Dance. Damon and Craig Foster

Africa herself and in creating film experiences that enable the viewer to gain an intense and deep insight into the natural and cultural dynamics of this ancient continent (Foster et al. 2005). They explore the timeless and universal themes of the relationship between man and animal, and the relationship between them and the environments that they share. The result is a portrayal of a reality that is rarely represented. Together they have over 40 international awards for film-making in the areas of photography, editing, writing, directing and human/animal interaction.

The Great Dance: A Hunter's Story (2000) is characterized by stunning visuals. The film is the winner of more than 35 international awards. It is a visual poem on the San hunters, who sustain a small band of nomads in the Kalahari Desert. Strictly speaking not a conventional documentary the film-makers have intercut documentary footage with highly original and semi-abstract material so the hard core of fact is surrounded with lyrical evocations of San legends, creating an intriguing visual texture. Black and white footage has been combined with richly coloured images, giving the film a poetic dimension rarely seen in documentaries (Van Vuuren 2007).

As an example of oral storytelling the Foster Brothers constructed the narrative out of the words of one of the main characters in the film, !Nqate Xqamxebe. The story is about three hunters and their personalities, their love for and belief in their traditional hunting practises, their passion for the land they live on, their extraordinarily sophisticated knowledge of the environment and ecology of the Kalahari, their cultural mythologies and ritual practices, their trouble with government and the prohibitions on their hunting, their sadness at the disappearance of their cultural practises in the face of sweeping change brought on by modernity, and their religious beliefs. All of these elements of the three hunters' stories are related back to the central thread of narrative that brings the film together – that of the hunt, particularly the hunt-by-running (Van Vuuren 2007).

Closely shadowing each sequence of hunting and tracking in the film is the telling of stories by means of the oral tradition. The three hunters read the signs left around the carcass of a pregnant steenbok, which has been killed by a leopard. They retell the story for the camera, often acting out the actions of the animals. Their stories are illustrated by a variety of stylized sequences created by the film-makers, usually in black and white that identify the images as 'flashbacks'. Here the Foster brothers' technical innovations with digital cameras produce unique camera angles, shooting from the bodies of animals, so that the viewer has a strong idea of the movement of the animals. Dramatic sequences are created that reconstruct the movement of animals as they hunt, the eating of their prey or the fevered chaos of vultures gobbling the remains of a carcass (Van Vuuren 2007). The hunters also narrate to the camera, sitting around a fire. During these sequences they discuss their god, and their religious beliefs as well as their holistic, tradition-bound approach to hunting. Their words are not fed through the narration of !Nqate but are translated on screen in subtitles. These fireside oral narrations are important because they provide an opportunity

Cosmic Africa. Damon and Craig Foster

Iceman: The Lewis Gordon Pugh Story. Damon and Craig Foster

for the other two hunters, Karoha and Xlhoase, to speak. They also allow for an intimate, 'real-time' connectedness with the hunters (Van Vuuren 2007).

At the end of the film !Nqate asks what will become of their traditions, now that everything is changing. Close-ups of his children's faces illustrate the point. They are filmed ghost like in the flickering light of the fire. The film closes with a mosaic of stylized images: slow-motion dancing, lightening in the sky, a man framed against a vast horizon, clouds and fire, and finally a single ember from the fire that is picked up and flung out into the night. The glowing coal lands on the ground and is filmed in close-up as its heat slowly fades away (Van Vuuren 2007). *The Great Dance* seems to be an attempt to show value in a culture at a time when that value is being rapidly eroded by poverty and dispossession.

Oral aesthetics are also at the core of the narrative structure of *Cosmic Africa* (2003), based on the personal odyssey of African astronomer Thebe Medupe. Based on his words the film chronicles his journey into the African continent's astronomical past and in the process unveiling the deep connection Africans have with the cosmos. Thebe is an astrophysicist and during his journey he gathers the earlier cosmologies of our ancestors (Foster et al. 2005). Grant McLachlan's powerful musical score enhances the poetry of the film.

The Foster Brothers' recent explorations include *Iceman: The Lewis Gordon Pugh Story* (2008), which serves as a visual experience of Lewis Gordon Pugh's attempts to draw attention to the oceans and raise awareness about climate change.[17] The film documents the extraordinary physiological and psychological journey of Lewis's long-distance swims in the freezing waters of both the South and the North Pole. Lewis Pugh has 10 seconds before he plunges into the freezing Arctic Ocean, where he swims a kilometre across Antarctica, wearing nothing but a Speedo and a swim cap, a feat never thought possible. 'Ordinary' humans would probably die within minutes in this icy water. The film raises questions such as how can his naked body cope with these conditions for so long, and why on earth would anyone want to do such a thing. With the support of cutting-edge science and an incredible ability to believe in himself he hopes to unify the potential of mind and body. Pugh has gone where no one has gone before and achieved a new understanding of the human body.

The Nature of Life (2009) is an epic documentary feature film that tries to provide solutions to humanity's greatest challenge yet – Global Climate Change. So far all we have heard is that climate change is the biggest ever environmental crisis and that it has been caused by our unsustainable approach to living. *The Nature of Life*, however, sets out as a great inspired clarion call to humanity, telling us that there is hope and that there are ways to adapt to and overcome this crisis. The documentary encapsulates a vision of hope that stems from the heart of Africa and expands globally, highlighting groundbreaking examples of sustainable development all over the world, inspired by the examples of Africa and the natural world. The microcosm of the 'cradle of civilization', Africa, will spill into the entire world, introducing the audience to a group of extraordinary humans and companies who are challenging past models of sustainability and creating a new legacy of elegant design, technology and rediscovered indigenous wisdom.

In 2010 the Foster Brothers premièred their documentary *My Hunter's Heart*. The film, shot over three-and-a-half years, explores the world's most ancient shamanic culture and how it is now on the brink of extinction. It tracks the Khomani San of the Central Kalahari, the oldest living indigenous tribe in the world and who are genetically linked to every human being on planet earth. In modern times, their traditional nomadic way of life has changed, and westernization has severed their link to the land and the animals. The film follows younger members of the clan as they embark on an epic journey to try to recapture some of the knowledge and skills of their ancestors. The children feel there is no future and the elders are faced with haunting reminders of their past. The film was produced by the Foster Brothers as well as Anant Singh and Helena Spring. The music is composed by multi-award winner Trevor Jones.

Animation

Any overview of the revival in recent South African film-making is incomplete without a brief reference to an exciting animation cinema which has been emerging since the 1980s. The most important exponent is the artist William Kentridge (Botha 2009). At the Twelfth Durban International Film Festival four of his short animation films were presented under the title *Animations by William Kentridge 1978–1989*. Kentridge used various techniques in creating these animation shorts. His Soho Eckstein saga depicts the battle between Soho

Eckstein (property developer) and Felix Teitlebaum. One of the shorts in the saga, *Mine*, subtly but scathingly indicts the mining industry. *Monument*, animated by means of a charcoal technique, chronicled the life of Soho as a civic benefactor. The whole saga has been assembled into a full-length feature film *9 Drawings for Projection*, which was screened for the first time in South Africa in 2004.

In recent animation shorts such as *The Shadow Boy* (2007) and *The Mbulu's Bride* (2006) by Justine Puren oral storytelling, African mythology and animation are creatively integrated.

Queer voices

Under apartheid gay and lesbian voices in film and television were also silenced. In a seven-year study of the depiction of gays and lesbians in African, Asian and Latin American cinema Martin Botha (2003b; Botha & Swinnen 2010) has noted that homosexual experience is unique in South Africa, precisely because of South Africa's history of racial division and subsequent resistance. South African gay identities have been formed by a long history of racial struggle. These gay identities were also deformed by an oppressive system, which classified homosexuals into those with freedom and those without. Apartheid legislated who South Africans were, where they could live, with whom they could associate and even what kind of sex they could have. Asserting a lesbian and gay identity in South Africa became a defiance of the fixed identities – of race, ethnicity, class, gender and sexuality – that the apartheid system attempted to impose upon *all* of South African society (Gevisser & Cameron 1994; Peach 2005; 2007).

No other film in South African film history chronicled the lives of lesbian and gays in the way the full-length documentary *The Man Who Drove with Mandela* (1988) has done (Botha 2003b). Winner of an award at the Berlin International Film Festival it was directed by Greta Schiller and researched by Mark Gevisser, co-writer of the outstanding compilation on South African lesbian and gay lives, *Defiant Desire* (1994). It is a semi-biographical portrait of Cecil Williams, who was being 'chauffeured' by Nelson Mandela on the day the future president was arrested. Williams was a communist and ANC activist. He was a dedicated campaigner and recruiter of ANC members, and he was also flamboyantly gay. Williams was well known in the Johannesburg of the fifties, as a socialite and a successful director of plays that belonged to the great liberal tradition of the earlier part of the century. He directed some of the country's top actors in their youth, staging contemporary classics in the city's lost and forgotten Library Theatre. One indigenous work remains notable. Called *The Kimberly Train* – directed in 1959 – it was about a love affair across the apartheid divide. In those days, because theatres were segregated, the white actress playing a coloured woman darkened her make-up by a couple of shades (Botha 2003b).

The facts surrounding Williams's life during the apartheid era in the fifties and sixties are conveyed to the audience via excerpts from a biographical one-man play performed by Corin Redgrave. It is filmed on a set, with highly theatrical lighting, and Redgrave's sensitive performance as Cecil Williams gives one a keen sense of this openly gay man. These performed fragments are integrated within interviews with party activists, who worked closely with Williams, by his colleagues in the theatre, black and white, and by wonderful archive footage of South African history over the past 40 years, which contextualizes Williams's life vividly. But it is not just the life story of Cecil Williams. It is a fascinating, deeply moving chronicle of how political and intellectual dissenters of the 1950s and 1960s lived and operated in South Africa. The audience glimpses the way the shebeens in the townships and the nightclubs worked, and how theatre in its unique way became a voice for the marginalized (Botha 2003b).

The film becomes a wonderful kaleidoscope of stories fitted vividly together but hinged on the fact that on the day Mandela was captured the comrade in the car with him was a white gay man, whose lifestyle was known to prominent leaders like Walter Sisulu and Mandela in the ANC and the South African Communist Party. Albie Sachs, an ANC activist, told Gevisser during his research phase that if one wants to understand why the older generation of ANC comrades is so receptive to the notion of gay equality in the constitutional debate one needs to go back and look at the role that Williams, a gay man and a communist, played within the liberation movement (Botha 2003b).

Gevisser's groundbreaking research into South African gay and lesbian lives forms the foundation of *The Man Who Drove with Mandela* and his book *Defiant Desire* (Gevisser & Cameron 1994). One overwhelming conclusion in his research points to the fact that there is no single, essential 'gay identity' in South African society. It also destroyed the claim that homosexuality is a bourgeois western phenomenon which contaminates the purity of African civilization. Homosexuality exists and flourishes in so-called black communities and cultures of South Africa, despite oppression. By the mid-1950s, the times depicted by *The Man Who Drove with Mandela*, gay subcultures existed in major cities like Johannesburg, Cape Town and Durban. The rapid urbanization of especially whites offered urban gays and lesbians away from their families and predominantly conservative home communities, a way to 'come out' as part of a gay subculture. With the exception of Cape Town, where there had been a gay culture based in the Cape Malay communities, these subcultures were mostly white, male and middle class. In South Africa's apartheid history, however, the move of whites into cities was paralleled by a system of black migrant labour: single-sex compounds, where men were divorced from home communities, basically created opportunities for homosexual encounters.

The end of the Second World War saw a larger percentage of single people living away from their families. Hillbrow, in Johannesburg, with its high-density accommodation, became an obvious neighbourhood for single people, and many gays moved there. Lesbians, despite being ignored by anti-gay legislation in South Africa, experienced far greater pressure to remain closeted and had far fewer public meeting places than men. While women's organizations focused on workplace rights and anti-apartheid struggle during the fifties and sixties, it did not address issues of sexuality or situate itself within feminist ideology. Without a feminist movement and virtually no subculture to refer to lesbians found it more difficult than gay men to find a space. On the whole, lesbian social life at the time revolved around private parties in private homes, while white gay men had the opportunity to interact in pubs and public places, such as parks or at the beachfront in Durban or Cape Town. 'Coloured' gay men became very much the texture of District Six, a racially mixed neighbourhood in Cape Town, which was finally demolished by apartheid (Gevisser & Cameron 1994). A lot of activities were centred along Hanover Street, where many gay men rented rooms and socialized by going on 'salon crawls' – visiting the many gay hairdressing salons. Gay life thrived in District Six, Athlone, Woodstock and Salt River, and a drag culture evolved here. Within the 'coloured' communities of Cape Town there were all-gay drag sports clubs, such as the District Six Netball Team, which participated in the women's league. These netball teams, like the drag performers, have been a constant in the Western Cape 'coloured' culture and have their latest incarnation in the Lavender Hill Netball Team, which was competing on the Cape Flats during the 1990s!

The history of gay life in Western Cape 'coloured' communities is beautifully captured by two documentaries of Jack Lewis, namely *Sando to Samantha aka the art of dikvel* (1998) and especially *A Normal Daughter: The Life and Times of Kewpie of District Six* (1997). Gay life has flourished over the years in these communities, probably since sexual dissidence is more tolerated in a hybrid, Creole society like that of South African 'coloureds' than in supposedly coherent societies with strong patriarchal mythologies and traditions, like those constructed by the African and white Afrikaner nationalist movements in South Africa . However, there was very little interaction between the 'coloured' and white gay communities in Cape Town. And only in the 1980s did black men and women begin to play an active role in gay politics (Botha 2003b).

There is a long history that remains as yet unwritten of the repression and regulation of sexuality by the Apartheid State during its more than four-decade hold on power (Gevisser & Cameron 1994; Peach 2007). Out of fragments, sensational press reports and oral histories a historical researcher will probably one day reconstruct a narrative which will deal with gay and lesbian oppression in South Africa as well. Racist legislation and iron-fisted rule have, since the earliest days of Nationalist Party rule, gone hand in hand with an obsessive interest in sexual policing. This policing was based on the values of Christian Nationalist apartheid ideology: the need to keep the white nation sexually and morally pure so that it had the strength to resist black communist onslaught. Sex laws drafted during the heyday of apartheid in the fifties and sixties prescribed tough penalties for a range of sexual offences. Apart from notoriously criminalizing interracial sex, the Immorality Act of 1957 also made everything from prostitution, to soliciting for immoral purposes, to sex with mentally retarded persons illegal and punishable by prison sentences of up to 6 years. In 1985, the racial provisions of the act were altered, but its other provisions were kept intact.

Freedoms of sexual speech and association were virtually unheard of until the ANC-led government came into power in 1994. Before that historic event the South African Publications Board censored any representations of sex or any sexual views that stray too far from what is defined as moral within a narrow, conservative world view (see Chapter 4). In practice this means, among other things, that anything with the sole purpose of providing sexual stimulation – such as sexy pictures or writing – was undesirable and hence illegal. Even educational videos on safe-sex practices for gay men experienced censor problems as late as the beginning of the 1990s.

Concerted attacks on the gay community in South Africa from the mid-sixties consisted of occasional incidents of victimization and the launching of a vigorous legislative campaign against it (Gevisser & Cameron 1994). The trigger of the campaign was a police raid on a house in Forest Town in Johannesburg in January 1966, where 300 gay men were dancing and kissing. It was recommended to the Minister of Justice that laws should be tightened to combat homosexuality. The issue was taken to parliament. A select committee of parliamentarians was established, at the minister's request, to look into the matter more closely. The report of this investigation, the only serious policy-making initiative to ever come from the Nationalist Party government on the issue of homosexuality, was published in 1968. It stated that homosexuality was spreading because older men and women were seducing teenagers. A gay action group, formed in the aftermath of the party raid, paid legal and expert witnesses to make representations. The anti-criminalization lobbying was not wasted, since the committee was talked out of the idea of new laws aimed at gay sex in general. However, the committee did go ahead with reactionary recommendations regarding gay parties and sex with teenagers. Any sexual acts between men at a party were to be banned, including kissing; the age of consent for male homosexual acts was to be raised from 16 to 19 years, and the manufacture or distribution of any article intended to be used to perform an unnatural sexual act was to be prohibited. These recommended amendments to the Immorality Act were passed into law in 1969. Just after the legislation was passed a clampdown on outdoor meeting places for gay men as well as routine police surveillance of gay clubs, bars and parties occurred, deep into the seventies and eighties.

Despite initial hostility the authorities agreed in 1990 to allow a lesbian and gay pride march through the streets in the metropolitan centre of Johannesburg. Censorship, however, regulated writing and audio-visual expression regarding gay lives until the first democratic government came into power in 1994. Before 1994 the censorship of gay material was severe. Magazines, such as popular US gay journal *The Advocate*, and books widely available in other countries were regularly banned, simply because they assumed there is nothing wrong with being gay or lesbian. Lesbian and gay publishers and book importers faced an uphill battle for survival. Otherworld Books, an independent book company, based in Cape Town, was but one example. Since it catered predominantly for the lesbian and gay market, it imported books on sexual theory, history, politics and culture. As late as 1992 Customs House in Cape Town confiscated every shipment of books bound for Otherworld, claiming possible contraventions of South African censorship laws.

In November 1993, in the waning days of Nationalist Party rule, representatives of 20 South African political parties, including the ANC, approved a draft constitution for a post-apartheid South Africa. The new constitution featured a Bill of Rights outlawing discrimination on the basis of a number of personal characteristics, ranging from race and gender to age and physical disability. It also included sexual orientation: South African gays and lesbians were at last considered as a part of this country. With countries like the United States of America still far from enacting gay civil rights protection, in just a few short years South Africa is leading the world with the most progressive constitution regarding gay and lesbian equality. It is still a long way to create total equality, since homophobia is still rife in rural South Africa and townships, and the vast majority of the population still lives in dire poverty. The country will struggle for many years to come to address the imbalances left by apartheid, also within the film industry, which is still predominantly white (Botha 2003b).

Homosexuality is almost non-existent in South African cinema up till 1985. The Afrikaans-language cinema has few images of openly gay characters (see Chapter 3). One could attribute this to the conservative attitude of Afrikaners at that stage towards the films. Afrikaners wanted their ideals visualized in these films. This idealistic conservatism was characterized by an attachment to the past, to ideals of linguistic and racial purity and to religious and moral norms. Homosexuality had no place in this world view (Botha 2003b). The films had to subscribe to these conservative and homophobic norms in order to be successful at the box office. The films seldom attempted to explore a national cultural psyche. As such, they were a closed form, made by Afrikaners for Afrikaners, with little or no attention to their potential to say something important about their society to an international audience (Pretorius 1992). The type of realism that could have analyzed Afrikaner culture in a critical manner was avoided. Instead use was made of folk stereotypes that showed the Afrikaner as chatty, heart-warming and lovable in a comedy tradition or as beset by emotional problems that had little to do with society but much to do with the mainsprings of western melodrama about mismatched couples overcoming obstacles on the path to true love (see Chapter 3). Afrikaans characters were always heterosexual, and although a film like *Forty Days* (1979) hinted at the 'perverse' homosexual subculture of Hillbrow, this subculture is not really given any human face and remains something sinister. Another film, *Seuns van die Wolke* (1975), presented audiences with vague homoerotic images of half-naked men, but nothing daring was portrayed. The story is set against the Second World War and deals with two hostile pilots. When they are forced to rely on each other for survival a strong friendship develops between them. There is a hint of a possible homoerotic bond, but it is never really explored. Afrikaans-language films also ignored the socio-political turmoil as well as the realities experienced by black South Africans under apartheid (see Chapter 3).

Even in the 1990s Afrikaans-language cinema and television struggled to offer viewers any three-dimensional gay characters. In the comedy *Lipstiek Dipstiek* (1994) the two gay characters (in supporting roles) are a stereotyped, flamboyant sissy and a villainous yuppie, who end up with each other. In *Kaalgat tussen die Daisies* (1997) drag queens in an unrecognizable gay pub are appearing before old heterosexual men with no gay men in sight and the leading gay character turning out to be an undercover cop, who is playing gay as a drag queen to finalize a case! Leon Schuster's slapstick comedies (*There's a Zulu on My Stoep*, 1993; *Sweet 'n Short*, 1991; *Panic Mechanic*, 1996) are full of homophobic and derogatory fag jokes and references. Only recently gay characters were introduced in popular daytime television soap operas such as *Egoli*.

In many respects, the early 1980s signified an opening up for South Africa, socially as well as politically (Gevisser & Cameron 1994). At the beginning of the decade, President P.W. Botha began instituting a 'reform' programme (which was balanced with heightened repression) and, in the aftermath of the Soweto upheavals in 1976, a massive upsurge of black liberationist activity swept through the townships. For the very first time since the Nationalist Party came to power in 1948, there was a tangible sense that the decades of white Afrikaner Calvinist rule were coming to an end and that the strict apartheid packaging off of people would give way to a more liberated and integrated society. Those years, despite two state of emergencies, saw the beginnings of deracialization and the establishment of anti-apartheid counter-cultures, which vociferously questioned the religious and political restrictions of the previous 40 years. Within gay politics gay movements such as Lesbians and Gays Against Oppression (LAGO), which became the Organisation of Lesbian and Gay Activists (OLGA) as well as black gay activist Simon Nkoli's Gay and Lesbian Organisation of the Witwatersrand (GLOW) became part of the broad democratic movement.

In the 1980s two South African features were made with gay characters: Cedric Sundström's thriller *The Shadowed Mind* (1988) and Helena Nogueira's lesbian love story *Quest for Love* (1987), set against political turmoil in Southern Africa. The latter starred two popular Afrikaans actresses, Jana Cilliers and Sandra Prinsloo. Prinsloo played Dorothy, a marine biologist, and Cilliers the political journalist Alexandra. The film used flashbacks to create a rhythm between Alexandra's memory and her current self-discovery, climaxing in her reunion with Dorothy. Voice over and letters are also used to suggest Alexandra's verbal control over experience and her analysis of the political and sexual worlds in which she finds herself. It is a complex structure, but Nogueira manages to create a film of emotional power, which also presents us with three-dimensional lesbian characters (Botha 2003b).

The film starts with the arrest of Alexandra and her lover, Michael, for accusing South Africa of military intervention in Mozania/Mozambique. Alexandra emerges from prison a year later, goes to Mozambique to stay with Dorothy and finds she has to wait 2 weeks for her friend's return. This waiting period forces Alexandra to reflect on her relationships, her ideological position and her attempts to come to terms with Africa. Dorothy, however, has become an integral part of Africa through her deeds as biologist. While one woman is experiencing conflicts regarding her role, the other is at ease with herself and her sexual orientation (Botha 2003b).

The flashbacks mostly concern discussions and arguments between Alexandra and Dorothy regarding the values of political activism against those of political common sense and pragmatism. Alexandra favours intellectual engagement. Dorothy chooses community involvement. She returns to her home country to try and help the people with her scientific knowledge and ecological and humanitarian concerns. Nogueira's portrayal of a lesbian love affair against the background of South Africa's military destabilization campaigns in neighbouring countries is one of the highlights of new South African gay cinema. More than

10 years after its first release in 1988 the film still comes across as a powerful and complex portrait of political and sexual themes within a contemporary South African setting.

Set in an extremely unlikely therapy centre for weird sexual malfunctions, *The Shadowed Mind* (1988) offers images of full-frontal male nudity and homosexual behaviour among inmates (Botha 2003b). Shot in disused railway warehouses in Pretoria, director Cedric Sundström created a stylized horror movie. The script, however, was written in a space of one week, which unfortunately led to weak characters and a very loose narrative structure. Dialogue was improvized but is never really convincing. The film tries to delineate the blurred lines between sanity and madness. Homosexuality, thus, is placed within that context. The asylum becomes a microcosmic battlefield in which a war of emotions is waged between the inmates. In that respect Sundström is successful: An atmosphere of menace is maintained throughout the film, and the style and photography is sometimes breathtaking. But the film cannot escape the old psychoanalytical notion that homosexuality is an illness, and finally, the bisexual male character, who engages in sex with another male, is brutally murdered. Not surprisingly *The Shadowed Mind* was banned for general release or festival screenings in the 1980s in South Africa. It was never released commercially in South Africa, and one only saw it on video during the end of the apartheid years (see Chapter 8).

Under apartheid many voices were thus silenced and marginalized in the film and television industries: blacks, women, gays and lesbians (Botha 2003b). In 1989 Melanie Chait's *Out in Africa* became the first South African film to deal with gay and lesbian liberation struggle in South Africa. This short film is a moving tribute to two gay South African men, Simon Nkoli and Dr. Ivan Toms, who were respected internationally for their stand against apartheid. Dr. Toms was the first white South African to refuse to serve in the South African defence force. Simon Nkoli was one of the Delmas trialists. The film portrayed what it meant to be gay under apartheid and claimed that the South African liberation struggle is a movement for political as well as gay equality. Nkoli was arrested after a rent boycott demonstration in his home township of Sebokeng and was held in custody for 2 years before being charged, with 21 other prominent United Democratic Front activists, with treason. He became a *cause célèbre* after his arrest: The confluence of his open homosexuality and his imprisonment as a soldier against apartheid made him immensely appealing to liberation-oriented gay organizations around the world (Botha 2003b; Peach 2007). In Canada the Simon Nkoli Anti-Apartment Committee became a critical player in both the gay and anti-apartheid movements. Gay film-maker John Greyson directed a short Canadian film, *A Moffie Called Simon* (1986), which became a confirmation of solidarity with the jailed activist.

Through Nkoli's imprisonment progressive members of the international anti-apartheid movement were able to begin introducing the issue of gay rights to the ANC. The highly respectable Anti-Apartheid Movements of both Britain and the Netherlands took up Nkoli's cause, and this was to exert a major impact on the ANC's later decision to include gay rights on its agenda for a democratic South Africa. By 1986 Nkoli was formally charged with murder but acquitted during the ensuing trail. In Beverley Ditsie and Nicky Newman's *Simon & I* (2001) Nkoli's relationship with fellow activist Beverley Ditsie is portrayed. It is a moving story of their battle against prejudice in any form, an effort which played an important role in ensuring constitutional protection of gay rights (Botha 2003b).

Even more remarkable is Brian Tilley's *It's My life* (2003). Shot over 5 months, this co-production with France chronicles the activist activities of Zackie Achmat. Achmat took on the world's largest pharmaceutical companies and the South African government, fighting to ensure affordable treatment for people living with HIV. Initially his organization, the Treatment Action Campaign (TAC), joined the South African government in a court case against pharmaceutical companies hoping to facilitate a legal framework allowing for affordable anti-AIDS medication, but victory in court resulted in disappointment as the government refused to act on the advantages offered by the victory. Achmat, himself HIV positive, stunned the world by refusing to take medication as leader of the TAC because of his moral convictions: He took a controversial stance that he would not take anti-retroviral drugs until the government set up pilot anti-retroviral programmes at community clinics in all of South Africa's nine provinces (Botha 2003b).

An important new voice in the creation of a South African gay and lesbian cinema is Luis DeBarros. DeBarros was a third-year BA student at the University of the Witwatersrand when he made *Pretty Boys* (1992), a film about two male prostitutes. The film explores the possibility of prostitution as a positive experience. His next film, *Clubbing* (1993), revolves around six, 20-something-year-old friends who meet one evening before they go out clubbing. DeBarros captures the decline of a white ruling class in a society in which the rules are changing. They must come to terms with a future of uncertainty, a future no longer assured of privilege. Among the characters is an attractive gay male couple, who comes across as three-dimensional. They are probably the first non-stereotypical male gays on South African screens (Botha 2003b).

DeBarros's *Hot Legs* (1996) is a revenge fantasy, which revolves around Tim, a young gay doctor who wants to take revenge on Dave, a man he once loved, by holding him captive in a motel room for 6 days. Together the two characters relive their past and look at how they became the people they are. Although psychologically troubled, both characters are attractive, non-stereotypical gays. They do not fall in the traps of either being sissies or villains, just two human beings trying to sort out their conflicts within a homophobic society. DeBarro's voice is loud and caustic; the audacity with which he tackles taboo subjects in a homophobic society can be seen as inspirational for other film-makers and for the fearless use of the medium to disseminate information about life in multiracial/multi-ethnic South Africa. Since the late 1990s DeBarros has been working on a feature on male homosexuality in South Africa, *Pressure*, but due to funding problems the end result has yet to be seen (Botha 2003b).

One of the most important local gay film-makers is Jack Lewis, who won acclaim for his two oral histories of gay subcultures in Cape Town. *A Normal Daughter: The Life and Times of Kewpie of District Six* (1997) depicts gay life in the former District Six through the memories and snapshots of the main character, a drag queen. In District Six, gays were an accepted part of a racially and religiously diverse community. Long before the emergence of the post-Stonewall gay scene in Cape Town, life in District Six was open and out. From the main protagonist's hairdressing salon the gays organized elaborate drag balls, cabaret performances and concerts. They colonized clubs, prepared food for weddings and funerals, styled everyone's hair and looked after the neighbours' children. Lewis captures this vibrancy lovingly by means of a collection of snapshots and interviews (Botha 2003b). But sadly, Cape Town's District Six was physically destroyed by the apartheid government in the 1970s.

The sense of loss is also sensitively depicted in another oral history by Lewis, titled *Sando to Samantha: Aka the Art of Dikvel* (1998). The video combines interview material with dramatized footage to reconstruct the life of Sando Willemse, a drag queen who served in the South African Defence Force until he was dismissed because of his HIV status. He turned to prostitution to survive and found friendship and support in a community of drag queens working in Cape Town streets. He died of HIV-related causes in 1996 aged 22. In this film, Lewis allowed Sando to narrate his own story in a beautiful blend of moving personal testimony and subversive commentary on South African politics (Botha 2003b).

Lewis is also the co-founder of the South African Gay and Lesbian Film Festival (with Nodi Murphy). It started because he was active with the founding of ABIGAIL (Association for Bisexuals, Gays and Lesbians), the first black-led gay organization in Cape Town. It was always a majority black-run organization. It did not attract many whites. To raise money for the organization he started taking some of the videos that he had acquired to places like Jazz Art and Don Pedro's to be screened. According to his summation, this venture made him to discover that the white gays from affluent 'Camps Bay, Bantry Bay and Clifton were prepared to roll up to Jazz Art and sit on the bloody floor on crates to watch gay movies/Queer movies, on video projector and stay around for a drink and so-on'. In the most profound proclamation yet, Lewis's frankness is hereby affirmed:

I must say that in that period there was a special atmosphere broadly round in South Africa at that time and it got even to this type of a gay set. Today I think that they are more than ever-sunk back into their self-satisfied, self-congratulatory complacency where they bitch and moan about South Africa at every level and do fuck-all and are generally a pain in the *gat* for everybody. But at that time the whole anti-apartheid movement, the internal pressure of the ANC, the movement in the country, what was happening in negotiations, even they, and I think they must be one of the most inert layers of society imaginable, despite their Queerness, were kind of moved. Everything was kind of special at that time and bathed in a special rainbow aura and nothing was quite real.

It was a revolutionary moment in its own way, although the revolution was a very muted one, in terms of what had originally been envisaged for South Africa, but none the less, the enormity of what was happening, the former government voluntarily surrendering power, got to people, and at the Queer level people felt that something was happening. They came out to these festivals and mini-programs and stayed all afternoon ... and sat down and talked ... It was those screenings, of which there might have been half a dozen or more ... that gave the impetus to form the formation of the festival.[18]

The first Out in Africa Gay and Lesbian Film Festival took place in South Africa in 1994, just after the new government came into power. The event was captured vividly by American lesbian director Barbara Hammer in her documentary *Out in South Africa*, (1994) which became one of the first local media portrayals of black gay and lesbian activities. The media silence regarding township gays were finally shattered. Lewis's intention was to create a black audience for the festival by promoting gay films to township gays and lesbians. According to him,

> It will be a small audience to begin with but it will be an audience of their friends, family, organisational contacts, to come along and see what [someone's] done. Because they know the director and they like him or her, and he or she's a cultural figure for them. And the word will get out and next time he/she does a film the audience will be bigger and in that way we will build a black audience for our festival.[19]

Lewis's other contribution to South African cinema includes facilitating postgraduate courses offered at tertiary institutions, which combine practical and theoretical aspects of gay film-making.

An important milestone in post-apartheid cinema is Lewis's *Proteus*, the beginning of a visible gay/lesbian cinema in South Africa. The film is a collaborative effort between Lewis and John Greyson, building on the oral histories background of Lewis and the subversion of

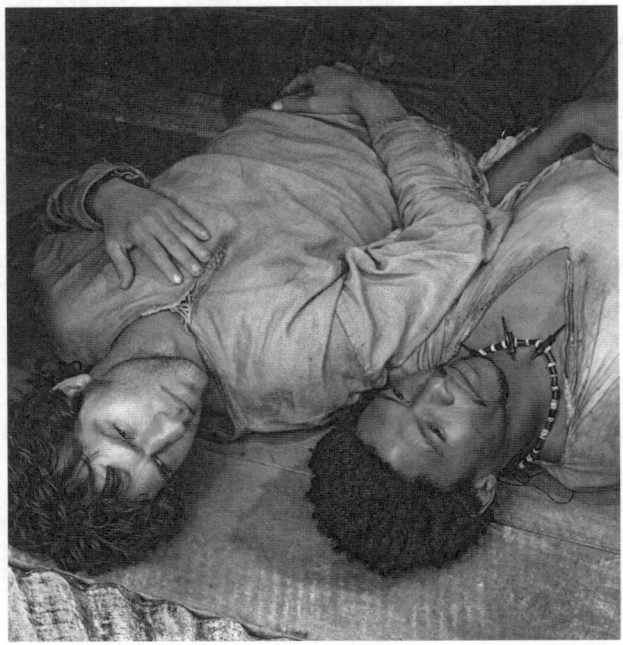

Proteus. Steven Markovitz

Proteus. Steven Markovitz

the period drama in previous Greyson films such as *Lilies* (1996), which is an adaptation by Michel Marc Bouchard and Linda Gaboriau of Bouchard's own play *Les feluettes*. It depicts a play being performed in a prison by the inmates. It covers a wide historical span (1912 to 1952) as the group of men in prison confront a bishop with his brutal response to their awakening homosexuality many years before.

Notions that homosexuality is un-African, an import of the western society, are brilliantly challenged in *Proteus*. Based on a true story, it is a period film that raises issues still of enormous relevance today. Historian and film-maker Jack Lewis was fascinated by a court record in the Cape Archives, dated 18 August 1735, giving judgement in the case of two

Robben Island prisoners. Dutch sailor Rijkhaart Jacobsz and Claas Blank, a Khoe tribesman convict, received extreme sentences for what the court called 'the abominable and unnatural crime of Sodomy'. Hees (2007) points out that, while based on extant court records, *Proteus* can hardly be read as a realistic account of the social construction of gender in the eighteenth century. The tension in the film between the attempt to *depict* the (historical) narrative of the prisoners as reflected in the court records of the time and the desire to *explain* their story with reference to a now suspect taxonomy is what generates and sustains its particular version of 'realism'. *Proteus* intends to generate a discourse on history, sexuality and identity construction. The way *Proteus* uses anachronism, for example, insistently draws attention to the film as a constructed historical discourse.

According to Hees (2007) the film departs radically from the norms governing the use of filmic space and time, and it does so precisely as a way of interrogating 'the relationship of past to present'. The film is based on court records of the time. The opening credits state it is 'based on a true story', but it quickly becomes evident that historical authenticity is not what the film is striving for. *Proteus* opens by first signalling that past very clearly, then it almost immediately disrupts our sense of the historical period very deliberately – the key juxtaposition that we have to make sense of at the beginning of the film is South Africa in 1735 and court stenographers in 1964. Greyson and Lewis indicated that they specifically referenced 1964 because that was the year that Mandela was incarcerated, but indicators such as the sixties court stenographers complete with cat-eye glasses and beehives also evoke this period when South Africa was drifting towards becoming a police state. In fact, Sergeant Willer's khaki uniform is that of the early apartheid period (as opposed to the later blue uniform). He is a key figure in the torture and incarceration of Claas Blank and Rijkhaart Jacobsz; at the start of the film we see him looming over Claas in the water-cell – the image is a chilling fusion of real and imaginary fear and anxiety, as will become clear – but for a South African viewer, at any rate, the khaki uniform is a powerful signifier of the growing state oppression (Hees 2007). The figure standing with Sergeant Willer, however, is dressed in an eighteenth-century military uniform.

The opening sequence indicates that the narrative is located in the decade between 1725 and 1735. The opening images on screen are of protea flowers intercut with images of the 1735 court records and of the sixties stenographers struggling to find a way to translate the Dutch term for sodomy. Worden (2007) argues this is already an indication that the court records are themselves a mediated construction, but one could go even further and note that language itself is a highly unstable set of signifiers. *Proteus* suggests that language is an instrument to impose power, to torture, to deceive, to disguise and to generate panic. It is an extremely moving experience owing to the performances by Rouxnet Brown and Neil Sandilands and forms part of a very small number of South African productions on homosexuality.

Another new voice to the local gay cinema is Stephen Jennings. *The Dress* (1996) follows the chance meeting of two lonely people. Shot in black and white it is a short film about an encounter between an oppressed young man and a lonely older man. The boy is obviously a victim of 'domestic violence' and after engaging in a sexual encounter with the older man, his male lover brutally removes him from the apartment. But the encounter signifies the chance for further meetings, which may even develop into a relationship that cannot be halted anymore by the abusive lover (Botha 2003b).

In an emerging gay cinema in South Africa lesbians are almost remarkably absent: *Quest for Love, The World Unseen, My Black Little Heart* and Barbara Hammer's documentary about South Africa after the 1994 elections are among the few glimpses of this hidden reality.

A landmark television series by Zackie Achmat and Jack Lewis, titled *Apostles of Civilised Vice* (1999), address the various stereotypes around gay /lesbian history in South Africa from colonial times to the post-apartheid era. Further stereotypes are addressed in *Dark & Lovely, Soft & Free* (2000), a documentary about a gay hairdresser, Zakhi. The film has been based on research by the Gay and Lesbian Archives of South Africa regarding the effect of the new constitution on the life of gay and lesbian people in small towns.

Homelessness, homosexuality and prostitution are vividly examined in *Four Rent Boys and a Sangoma* (2003). The documentary deals with the lives of five men on the streets of Johannesburg. It is a provocative and intimate glimpse into the inner lives of these five men and the social milieu they inhabit.

Lastly, the documentary *Property of the State: Gay Men in the Apartheid Military* (2003) is another milestone in the emerging gay cinema in Africa. It brilliantly and sensitively deals with the stories of the uniformed men conscripted at a tender age into a brutal war machine with severe conformity and killing as its objectives. The film explores the complex space that was the South African military for gay men under apartheid. It includes heart-wrenching testimony from aversion therapy survivors, who underwent shock therapy in military hospitals to 'cure' their homosexuality. It looks at those cases where young men tried to commit suicide and those who ended up in the psychiatric ward. And it also deals with a patriarchal society where any weakness or softness in men was condemned and where some young men were subjected to male rape.

Recent images of gay men include supporting characters in *Confessions of a Gambler* (a young male, who is an AIDS victim), *Skilpoppe, Skoonheid* and *Die Ongelooflike Avonture van Hanna Hoekom*. Despite the new constitution which prohibits discrimination against gays and lesbians, as well as a strong gay movement, South African film images of gay men and women are limited and still on the margin of the film industry. One ends up with less than 20 short films, a few documentaries and less than 10 features with openly gay and lesbian characters in the past 113 years of South African cinema!

Conclusion

In a comprehensive doctorate study of post-apartheid cinema Astrid Treffry-Goatley (2010) concluded that while the South African government's development of the South African film industry is informed by a vision of cultural diversity and an intention to empower the previously disadvantaged, an equally pervasive, if not stronger, trend of neoliberalism is also present that is sometimes at odds with this vision. Neoliberal characteristics in state policy include fiscal prudence, the avoidance of direct intervention product commodification and an emphasis on production for export. Treffry-Goatley's thesis illustrates that the current neoliberal paradigm evident in state policy has a continued impact on the production, distribution and consumption of post-apartheid cinema. Furthermore, it affects the economic, cultural and ideological development of the film industry. From a production point of view, it was found that many films are made primarily for an export market. This has a number of consequences for such works and the development of the industry as a whole.

First, these films are ostensibly more expensive to produce than those targeting local audiences, and the inflated budgets make it more difficult for such works to recoup costs. Second, in terms of distribution, an emphasis on export can be seen to curtail the creative self-expression of the artist, with there being a far greater degree of foreign involvement in productions and film-makers being required to meet internationally established casting, characterization, content, narrative structure, language and aesthetics norms. Third, there are ideological implications for this cinematic production and consumption model because, in order to comply with the expectations of foreign partners and markets, film-makers tend to perpetuate stereotypical African and South African identities rather than exploring complex, refreshing alternatives (Treffry-Goatley 2010).

Therefore, neoliberalism also has implications for racial transformation in the film industry. The development of an economically sustainable cinema in which multiple, progressive and dynamic national identities are formulated and consumed by the majority of the population requires the complete replacement of apartheid's racially biased production and consumption infrastructure. However, it is unlikely that such a transformation will occur within a paradigm that emphasizes free trade, avoids the introduction of bold interventionist measures and supports prude fiscal expenditure. Furthermore, a neoliberal approach to cinematic development can result in the voices of the historically suppressed black majority being excluded or censored to meet the commercial demands of the market (Treffry-Goatley 2010).

Nevertheless, there are a number of developments in the film industry that can be seen to challenge the dominance of neoliberalism. For example, an alternative production model exists that can potentially grant film-makers greater freedom in cinematic production and dissemination. This model makes use of digital production and distribution technology and functions with less capital, less outside assistance and has a greater focus on the local market. However, one should not view digital cinema as the 'glorious solution' to all the problems of the post-apartheid film industry. On the contrary, this should be approached as an alternative model that is most likely to run parallel to existing technologies. Moreover, it is important to recognize the challenges that limit the application of digital production/consumption technology in the post-apartheid context (Treffry-Goatley 2010).

First, it is questionable whether the current exhibition/broadcast mechanisms available for digital products penetrate a wide enough market to sustain this movement. Second, it remains to be seen whether the demographics of the audience and the film-makers themselves will expand to include a greater percentage of the black majority. Therefore, although digital technology is potentially an ideal mechanism for democratization of cinematic production and consumption in post-apartheid South Africa, it should not be viewed as a means for independent film-makers to make it alone. State support is still needed to maintain diversity and to support sustainability.

Treffry-Goatley (2010) argued that the South African film industry, like post-apartheid society as a whole, is socially and economically fragmented. This fragmentation, particularly among audiences, is arguably one of the greatest challenges to the sustainability and growth of the industry. It is evident that the neoliberal framework that has been adopted by the South African government has certain problematic implications for the sustainability and racial transformation of the film industry. Furthermore, the parallel national discourse of multiculturalism does not always sit comfortably with the freedom of expression and diversification that a democratic cinema demands. For instance, while state-run institutions such as the NFVF might preach a discourse of diversity and freedom, in practice, they tend to support a rather fixed, corrective paradigm of multiculturalism that steers away from experimentation and freedom in cinematic production. This tension between diversity and cohesion is an inherent contradiction in multicultural ideology, where the need to create unity does not always sit comfortably with diversity, multiplicity and cultural contradiction.

She suggests that perhaps a more transnational approach to cinematic production would be more appropriate, where film-makers might escape the hegemony of the state and develop hybrid styles and identities in between the margins of established norms (Treffry-Goatley 2010). However, this too has its challenges, since rather than breaking new ground, film-makers might find themselves reproducing images that mainstream audiences expect and perpetuating fixed, stereotypical representations of local identities on screen. Clearly there is not a single, simple solution to the challenge of national representation in the production of post-apartheid cinema. On the contrary, the way forward is most likely to be a dynamic, multifarious combination of approaches and methods, which would be a sound reflection of the compound, often contradictory nature of life in the global, post-apartheid context.

Notes

1. All these films and their production dates are provided in the Filmography.
2. See Pichaske (2009) for an analysis.
3. See Van Vuuren's brilliant analysis of *The Great Dance* (Van Vuuren 2007).
4. See Botha (2007) for a comprehensive discussion on marginality and post-apartheid cinema.
5. See Filmography for film titles and their production dates.
6. See Pichaske (2007; 2009).
7. An in-depth analysis of the film is provided by Rossouw Nel (2007).

8. See Marx (2010) for an excellent analysis of masculinities in post-apartheid cinema.
9. The description of *Sea Point Days* is based on notes by Francois Verster.
10. Based on the synopsis of *Sea Point Days*.
11. See Botha (2003b).
12. The Apollo Film Festival is held annually in the Northern Cape town of Victoria West and highlights achievements in independent film-making in South Africa.
13. Production notes by Dean Blumberg.
14. Interview with Harold Holscher, 2004.
15. Traditional healer.
16. An excellent discussion on old beliefs and modern lifestyles in a selection of recent South African films, including shorts, is provided by Wozniak (2007).
17. Discussion is based on information by the Foster Brothers.
18. For more on Peach's interview with Lewis, see Ricardo Peach, *Queer Cinema as a Fifth Cinema in South Africa and Australia*. Unpublished doctorate thesis, University of Technology, Sydney, Australia, 2005.
19. Interview with Peach (2005).

Bibliography

Accone, D. 'Salvation of SA film in "better govt funding"'. *The Star Tonight!*, 19 January 1990a: 1–2.

Accone, D. 'Some see new film subsidy as disaster'. *The Star Tonight!*, 1 March 1990b: 1.

Armes, R. *Dictionary of African filmmakers*. Bloomington, Indiana University Press, 2008.

Bakari, I. & Cham, M. (eds) *African experiences of cinema*. London, British Film Institute, 1996.

Balseiro, I. & Masilela, N. (eds) *To change reels: Film and film culture in South Africa*. Detroit, Wayne State University, 2003.

Barnard, C. *Paljas & Die storie van Klara Viljee: Die filmdraaiboeke*. Kaapstad, Tafelberg, 1988.

Barnes, J. *Filming the Boer War: The beginnings of the cinema in England: 1894–1901: Volume 4*. London, Bishopsgate Press Limited, 1992.

Bauer, C. 'Breaking the local no-sound barrier'. *Weekly Mail*, 2 April 1987: 21.

Bickford-Smith, V. & Mendelsohn, R. 'Film and history studies in South Africa revisited: Representing the African Past on screen'. *South African Historical Journal*, 48 (2003), pp. 1–9.

Blignaut, J. 1990. 'The distribution dilemma of local product'. *Showdata Bulletin*, 2 (1990), pp. 2–3.

Blignaut, J. & Botha, M.P. (eds) *Movies moguls mavericks: South African cinema 1979–1991*. Cape Town, Showdata, 1992.

Botha, M.P. 'Derde Wêreld-rolprentkuns en Suid-Afrika'. *The SAFFTA Journal*, 6 (1986), pp. 19–23.

Botha, M.P. 'Probleme om oplewing in S.A. film'. *Die Volksblad*, 4 January 1990: 6.

Botha, M.P. *Third cinema in South Africa?* Paper read at a meeting of the Film Commission of the Film and Allied Workers' Organisation (FAWO), Johannesburg, 6 February 1991.

Botha, M.P. 'African cinema: A historical, theoretical and analytical exploration'. *Communicatio*, 20:1 (1994), pp. 2–8.

Botha, M.P. 'The South African film industry: Fragmentation, identity crisis and unification'. *Kinema* 2:3 Spring (1995), pp. 7–19.

Botha, M.P. 'South African short film-making from 1980 to 1995: A thematic exploration'. *Communicatio*, 22:2 (1996), pp. 51–6.

Botha, M.P. 'The cinema of Manie van Rensburg: Popular memories of Afrikanerdom (Part I)'. *Kinema*, 8 Fall (1997a), pp. 15–42.

Botha, M.P. 'My involvement in the process which led to the white paper on South African cinema'. *South African Theatre Journal*, 11:1&2 (1997b), pp. 269–85.

Botha, M.P. 'The cinema of Manie van Rensburg: Popular memories of Afrikanerdom (Part II)'. *Kinema*, 8:Spring (1998a), pp. 43–56.

Botha, M.P. Overview of South African cinema. In E. Schelfhout & H. Verstraeten (eds) *De rol van de media in de multiculturele samenleving* (Brussels, VUB Press, 1998b), pp. 258–69.

Botha, M.P. 'Current film policy in South Africa: The establishment of the National Film and Video Foundation of South Africa and its role in the development of a post-apartheid film industry'. *Communicatio*, 29:1&2 (2003a), pp. 182–98.

Botha, M.P. 'Homosexuality and South African cinema'. *Kinema*, 19:Spring (2003b), pp. 39–64.

Botha, M.P. '"The song remains the same": The struggle for a South African film audience 1960–2003'. *Kinema*, 21:Spring (2004), pp. 67–89.

Botha, M.P. 'New directing voices in South African cinema'. *Kinema* 23:Spring (2005), pp. 5–21.

Botha, M.P. '110 years of South African cinema (I)'. *Kinema* 25:Spring (2006a), pp. 5–26.

Botha, M.P. '110 years of South African cinema (II)'. *Kinema* 26:Fall (2006b), pp. 5–26.

Botha, M.P. *Jans Rautenbach: Dromer, baanbreker en auteur.* Kaapstad, Genugtig!, 2006c.

Botha, M.P. (ed.). *Marginal lives and painful pasts: South African cinema after apartheid.* Cape Town, Genugtig!, 2007.

Botha, M.P. 'Short filmmaking in South Africa after apartheid'. *Kinema*, 31:Spring (2009), pp. 45–63.

Botha, M.P. 'Women on the margin of South African society: Themes in the cinema of Darrell James Roodt'. *Kinema*, 36:Spring (2011), pp. 29–40.

Botha, M.P. & Burger, F. 'A weathervane in uncertain winds'. *Weekly Mail*, 14–20 July 1989: 21, 24.

Botha, M.P. & Dethier, H. *Kronieken van Zuid-Afrika: De films van Manie van Rensburg.* Brussel, VUB Press, 1997.

Botha, M.P. & Lelievre, S. 'Promised Land ou des Afrikaners face a eux-memes'. *Cahiers d'Etudes africaines*, XLIV:1–2 (2004), pp. 441–45.

Botha, M.P., Mare, L., Langa, Z., Netshitomboni, R., Ngoasheng, K., Potgieter, J. & Greyling, M. *Proposals for the restructuring of the South African film industry.* Pretoria, Human Sciences Research Council, 1994.

Botha, M.P. & Swinnen, J. Opkomst van de representatie van lesbiennes en gays in de Zuid- Afrikaanse filmkunst: 1956–2003. In J. Swinnen (ed.) *Anders zichtbaar. Zingeving en humanisering in de beeldcultuur* (Brussels, VUB, 2010), pp. 173–207.

Botha, M.P. & Van Aswegen, A. *Images of South Africa: The rise of the alternative film.* Pretoria, Human Sciences Research Council, 1992.

Burns, Y.M. 'Censorship: Past, present and future'. *Ecquid Novi*, 11:2 (1990), pp. 148–60.

Cameron, J.T. & Spies, S.B. (eds) *An illustrated history of South Africa.* Johannesburg, Ball, 1986.

Chirol, M. The missing narrative in *Wend Kuuni* (time and space). In K.W. Harrow (ed.) *African cinema: Post-colonial and feminist readings* (Asmara, Eritrea, African World Press, 1999), pp. 115–26.

Convents, G. *Afrika verbeeld: Film en (de-) kolonisatie van de geesten.* Berchem, EPO, 2003.

Currie, W. 'Film and video workers organise'. *South African Labour Bulletin*, 14:5 (1989), pp. 7–12.

Davies, J. 'S.A. film: A brief history'. *ADA*, 6 (1989), pp. 32–3.

Davis, P. *In Darkest Hollywood: Exploring the jungles of cinema's South Africa.* Randburg, Ravan, 1996.

Davis, P. *Come back, Africa: A man possessed.* Johannesburg, STE Publishers, 2004.

De Lange, J. *The Anglo-Boer War, 1899–1902, on film.* Pretoria, State Archives Service, 1991.

Diawara, M. Popular culture and oral traditions in African film. In I. Bakari & M. Cham (eds) *African experiences of cinema* (London, BFI, 1996), pp. 209–19.

Dovey, L. 'Redeeming features: From *Tsotsi* (1980) to *Tsotsi* (2006)'. *Journal of African Cultural Studies*, 19:2 (December 2007), pp. 143–64.

Eckardt, M. *Film criticism in Cape Town: 1928–1930.* Stellenbosch, SUN PreSS, 2005.

Evans, M. Amnesty and amnesia: The Truth and Reconciliation Commission in narrative film. In M.P. Botha (ed.) *Marginal lives and painful pasts: South African cinema after apartheid* (Cape Town, Genugtig!, 2007), pp. 255–81.

Foster, C., Foster, D. & Hutchinson, M. *Africa: Speaking with earth & sky.* Claremont, David Philip, 2005.

Fourie, P.J. 'n Struktureel-funksionele model vir die formulering van 'n Suid-Afrikaanse rolprentbeleid.* University of South Africa, Unpublished PhD thesis, 1981.

Fourie, P.J. 'Interkulturele probleme in beeldkommunikasie'. *Communicare*, 3:1 (1982), pp. 60–73.

Friedberg, L. South Africa. In P. Cowie (ed.) *International Film Guide 1978* (London, Tantivity Press, 1978), pp. 278–80.

Fugard, A. & Devenish, R. *Marigolds in August and the Guest: Two screenplays*. New York, Theatre Communications Group, 1992.

Gabriel, T. Third cinema as guardians of popular memory: Towards a third aesthetics. In J. Pines & P. Willemen (eds) *Questions of third cinema* (London, BFI, 1989), pp. 53–64.

Gavshon, H. 'Levels of intervention in films made for African audiences in South Africa'. *Critical Arts*, 2:4 (1983), pp. 13–21.

Gevisser, M. & Cameron, E. (eds) *Defiant desire: Gay and lesbian lives in South Africa*. Johannesburg, Ravan, 1994.

Giliomee, H. *The Afrikaners: Biography of a people*. Cape Town, Tafelberg, 2003.

Greig, R.J. 'An approach to Afrikaans film'. *Critical Arts*, 1:1 (1980), pp. 14–23.

Gutsche, T. *The history and social significance of motion pictures in South Africa: 1895–1940*. Cape Town, Howard Timmins, 1972.

Hees, E. The birth of a nation: Contextualizing *De Voortrekkers* (1916). In I. Balseiro & N. Masilela (eds) *To change reels: Film and film culture in South Africa* (Detroit, Wayne State University, 2003), pp. 49–69.

Hees, E. *Proteus* and the dialectics of history. In M.P. Botha (ed.) *Marginal lives and painful pasts: South African cinema after apartheid* (Cape Town, Genugtig!, 2007), pp. 89–103.

Horne, F.J. 'Yesterday, AIDS and structural violence in South Africa'. *Communicatio*, 31:2 (2005): pp. 172–98.

Kannemeyer, J.C. *Die Afrikaanse literatuur: 1652–1987*. Kaapstad, Human & Rousseau, 1988.

Le Roux, A. *Screening wars: War, society, film and public perception – The case of the second Anglo-Boer War: 1899–1902*. Unpublished History Honours Dissertation, University of Stellenbosch, 2009.

Le Roux, A.I. & Fourie, L. *Filmverlede: Geskiedenis van die Suid-Afrikaanse speelfilm*. Pretoria, Universiteit van Suid-Afrika, 1982.

Louw, P.E. & Botha, J.R. Film: The captivating power of fleeting images. In A.S de Beer (ed.) *Mass media for the nineties: The South African handbook of mass communication* (Pretoria, Van Schaik, 1993), pp. 151–72.

Maingard, J.M. *Community film in South Africa as a mode of emergent cultural production*. MA dissertation, University of the Witwatersrand, Johannesburg, 1990.

Maingard, J. *South African national cinema*. London, Routledge, 2007.

Makgabutlane, S. 'Dead and forgotten'. *Tribune*, July 1989: 42–4.

Mangin, G. *Filming emerging Africa*. Cape Town, Wordsmith, 1998.

Marx, L. 'Underworld RSA'. *South African Theatre Journal*, 10:2 (1996), pp. 11–30.

Marx, L. Katinka Heyns: Questioning Afrikaans culture. In J. Levitin, J. Plessis & V. Raoul (eds) *Women filmmakers: Refocusing* (London, Routledge, 2003), pp. 330–41.

Marx, L. 'Cinema, glamour, atrocity': Narratives of trauma. In M.P. Botha (ed.) *Marginal lives and painful pasts: South African cinema after apartheid* (Cape Town, Genugtig!, 2007), pp. 283–304.

Marx, L. 'At the end of the rainbow: *Jerusalema* and the South African gangster film'. *Safundi: The Journal of South African and American Studies*, 11:3 (July 2010), pp. 261–78.

McCluskey, A.T. *The devil you dance with: Film culture in the new South Africa*. Chicago, University of Illinois Press, 2009.

Metz, C. 1990. 'FAWO'. *Showdata Bulletin*, 7 (1990), pp. 1, 4.

Metz, C. 'Film in Australia'. *Showdata Bulletin*, 8 (1991), p. 1

Moni, S. 'Italian film industry'. *Showdata Bulletin*, 9 (1991), p. 1.

Muller, B. The cinema of Gray Hofmeyr: The struggle against nature. In J. Blignaut & M.P. Botha (eds) *Movies moguls mavericks: South African cinema 1979–1991* (Johannesburg, Showdata, 1992), pp. 179–89.

Murray, J. Ethnic cinema: How greed killed the industry. In J. Blignaut & M.P. Botha (eds) *Movies moguls mavericks: South African cinema 1979–1991* (Johannesburg, Showdata, 1992), pp. 255–66.

Nathan, J. 'Movies and monopolies: The distribution of cinema in South Africa'. *Staffrider*, 9:4 (1991): pp. 61–84.

Nel, R. *The ambivalent rebellion: Tendencies in Afrikaner Counterculture*. Unpublished research essay, Centre for Film and Media Studies, University of Cape Town, 2007.

Nel, R. *Myths of rebellion: Afrikaner and countercultural discourse*. Unpublished MA dissertation, Centre for Film and Media Studies, University of Cape Town, 2010.

Ngakane, L. 'Africa in the pictures'. *Africa Forum*, 1:3 (1991), pp. 37–41.

Ozynski, J. (ed.) *Film: What the censors think*. Johannesburg, Anti-Censorship Group, 1989.

Peach, R. *Queer cinema as a fifth cinema in South Africa and Australia*. Unpublished PhD thesis, University of Technology, Sydney, 2005.

Peach, R. *Skeef* cinema *Entja*: A brief history of South African queer cinematic cultures. In M.P. Botha (ed.) *Marginal lives and painful pasts: South African cinema after apartheid* (Cape Town, Genugtig!, 2007), pp. 51–87.

Pichaske, K. Black stories, white voices. The challenge of transforming South Africa's documentary film industry. In M.P. Botha (ed.) *Marginal lives and painful pasts: South African cinema after apartheid* (Cape Town, Genugtig!, 2007), pp. 129–57.

Pichaske, K. *Colour adjustment: Race and representation in post-apartheid South African documentary*. Unpublished PhD thesis, University of Cape Town, 2009.

Pieterse, D. *Addressing the crisis in the South African film industry: The French Centre National de la Cinematographie as a model for consideration*. Johannesburg, Film and Allied Workers' Organisation, 1991.

Powell, I. 'A snip off the old film subsidy scheme'. *Weekly Mail*, 2–8 March 1990: 21–2.

Pretorius, W. Afrikaans cinema. In J. Blignaut & M.P. Botha (eds) *Movies moguls mavericks: South African cinema 1979–1991* (Johannesburg, Showdata, 1992), pp. 375–94.

Rompel, H. *Die bioskoop in die diens van die volk*. Kaapstad, Nasionale Pers, 1942.

Ronge, B. 'South Africa's film industry comes of age'. *Scenaria* (August/September 1977), pp. 1–3.

Saks, L. *Cinema in a democratic South Africa: The race for representation*. Bloomington, Indiana University Press, 2010.

Schoombie, S. 'Die pasiënt is doodsiek'. *Kalender, bylae tot Beeld*, 12 February 1990: 2.

Shepperson, A. & Tomaselli, K.G. 'South African cinema beyond apartheid: Affirmative action in distribution and storytelling'. *Social Identities*, 6:3 (2000), pp. 323–24.

Shepperson, A. & Tomaselli, K.G. 'Restructuring the industry: South African cinema beyond Apartheid'. *South African Theatre Journal*, 16 (2002), pp. 63–79.

Silber, G. Tax, lies and videotape. *The Executive*, June 1990a: 68–74.

Silber, G. 'Who killed the South African film industry?'. *Showdata Bulletin*, 4 (1990b), pp. 2–4.

Silber, G. Tax, lies and videotape: Who killed the South African film industry? In J. Blignaut & M.P. Botha (eds) *Movies moguls mavericks: South African cinema 1979–1991* (Johannesburg, Showdata, 1992), pp. 119–29.

Steenveld, L. Reclaiming history: Anti-apartheid documentaries. In J. Blignaut & M.P. Botha (eds) *Movies moguls mavericks: South African cinema 1979–1991* (Johannesburg, Showdata, 1992), pp. 301–28.

Thompson, B. 'African cinema – A well-kept secret'. *Die Suid-Afrikaan*, 42 (1993), pp. 30–5.

Thompson, L. *A history of South Africa*. New Haven, Yale University Press, 2001.

Tomaselli, K.G. *The cinema of apartheid: Race and class in South African film*. London, Routledge, 1989.

Tomaselli, K.G. 'Cultural reconstruction in South African cinema'. *Showdata Bulletin*, 5 (1990), pp. 2–4.

Tomaselli, K.G. The cinema of Jamie Uys: From bushveld to 'Bushmen'. In J. Blignaut & M.P. Botha (eds) *Movies moguls mavericks: South African cinema 1979–1991* (Cape Town, Showdata, 1992), pp. 191–231.

Tomaselli, K.G. *Encountering modernity: Twentieth century South African cinemas*. Pretoria, Unisa, 2006.

Tomaselli, K.G. & Prinsloo, J. Third cinema in South Africa. In J. Blignaut & M.P. Botha (eds) *Movies moguls mavericks: South African cinema 1979–1991* (Cape Town, Showdata, 1992), pp. 329–73.

Treffry-Goatley, A. *The representation and mediation of a national identity in the production of post-apartheid South African cinema*. Unpublished PhD thesis, University of Cape Town, 2010.

Udeman, A. *The history of the South African film industry 1940–1971: A bibliography*. Johannesburg, University of the Witwatersrand, 1972.

Unwin, C. & Belton, C. Cinema of resistance: The other side of the story. In J. Blignaut & M.P. Botha (eds) *Movies moguls mavericks: South African cinema 1979–1991* (Johannesburg, Showdata, 1992), pp. 277–99.

Van Staden, A. & Sevenhuysen, K. 'Drie vroeë Afrikaanse rolprente (1938–1949) as uitdrukking van die sosiale gewete van die Afrikaner'. *Suid-Afrikaanse Tydskrif vir Kultuurgeskiedenis*, 31:1 (2009), pp. 157–79.

Van Vuuren, L. 'An act of preservation and a requiem': *The Great Dance: A Hunter's Story* (2000) and technological testimony in post-apartheid South Africa. In M.P. Botha (ed.) *Marginal lives and painful pasts: South African cinema after apartheid* (Cape Town, Genugtig!, 2007), pp. 185–205.

Van Zyl, H. '*De Voortrekkers* (1916): Some stereotypes and narrative conventions'. *Critical Arts*, 1:1 (1980): pp. 24–31.

Van Zyl, J. 'A reeling industry: Film in South Africa'. *Leadership S.A.*, 4:4 (1985): pp. 102–06.

Wilkins, I. & Strydom, H. *The super-Afrikaners: Inside the Afrikaner Broederbond*. Johannesburg, Jonathan Ball, 1978.

Worden, N. 'What are we?': *Proteus* and the problematising of history. In V. Bickford-Smith & R. Mendelsohn (eds). *Black and white in colour, African history on screen* (Cape Town, Juta, 2007), pp. 82–96.

Wozniak, J. Interpretations of old beliefs and modern lifestyles in a selection of recent South African films. In M.P. Botha (ed.) *Marginal lives and painful pasts: South African cinema after apartheid* (Cape Town, Genugtig!, 2007), pp. 317–41.

Acts and reports

National Film and Video Foundation. *Indaba 2001: Distribution, exhibition and marketing report*. Johannesburg, NFVF, 2001.

Nel, W. Profile 2000: *Towards a viable South African film industry*. Johannesburg, PricewaterhouseCoopers, 2000.

Silver, L. *Publications Appeal Board: Digest of decisions*. Johannesburg, Centre for Applied Legal Studies, University of the Witwatersrand, 1979.

South Africa. *National Film and Video Foundation Act No. 73 of 1997*. Pretoria, Government Printer, 1997.

Filmography

The Mealie Kids (Dick Cruikshanks)
The Piccanini's Christmas (Dick Cruikshanks)
The Rose of Rhodesia (Harold Shaw)
Zulu-Town Comedies (Dick Cruikshanks)

1918

Bond and Word (Dick Cruikshanks)
The Bridge (Dick Cruikshanks)
King Solomon's Mines (H. Lisle Lucoque)
Symbol of Sacrifice (Isidore W. Schlesinger)
The Voice of the Waters (Joseph Albrecht)

1919

Allan Quartermain (H. Lisle Lucoque)
Copper Mask (Joseph Albrecht)
Fallen Leaves (Dick Cruikshanks)
The Stolen Favorite (Joseph Albrecht)
With Edged Tools (Joseph Albrecht)

1920

Isban Israel (Joseph Albrecht)
The Man Who Was Afraid (Joseph Albrecht)
Prester John (Dick Cruikshanks)
Virtue in the City (Norman V. Lee)

1921

The Swallow (Leander de Cordova)
The Vulture's Prey (Dick Cruikshanks)

1923

The Blue Lagoon (Weston Bowden)

1924

Reef of Stars (Joseph Albrecht)

1925

David Livingstone (M.A. Weatherell)

1931

Moedertjie (Joseph Albrecht)
Sarie Marais (Joseph Albrecht)

1933

'n Dogter van die Veld (J. Sinclair)

1936

Rhodes of Africa (Berthold Viertel)

1938

Die Bou van 'n Nasie/They Built a Nation (Joseph Albrecht)

1942

Lig van 'n Eeu (Andries A. Pienaar)
Newels oor Mont-Aux-Sources (Johannes J. Boonzaaier)
Ons Staan 'n Dag Oor (D.W. Uys)

1944

Donker Spore (Thomas Block)

1946

Die Skerpioen (Arthur Bennet)
Die Wildsboudjie (Arthur Bennet & Louis Knobel)
Geboortegrond (Pierre de Wet)
Pinkie se Erfenis (Pierre de Wet)

1947

Kaskenades van Dr Kwak (Pierre de Wet)
Pantoffelregering (Arthur Bennet)
Simon Beyers (Pierre de Wet)

1949

African Jim – Jim Comes to Jo-burg (Donald Swanson)
Kom Saam Vanaand (Pierre de Wet)
Oom Piet se Plaas (T.A. Wilson-Yelverton)
Sarie Marais (Francis Coley)

1950

The Adventurers (David Macdonald)
Hier's Ons Weer (Pierre de Wet)
The Magic Garden (Donald Swanson)
Zonk (Hyman Kirstein)

1951

Alles sal regkom (Pierre de Wet)
Cry, the Beloved Country (Zoltan Korda)
Daar doer in the Bosveld (Jamie Uys)
Song of Africa (Emil Nofal)
Where No Vultures Fly (Harry Watt)

1952

Altyd in my Drome (Pierre de Wet)

1953

Fifty/Vyftig (Jamie Uys)
Hans Die Skipper (Bladon Peake)
Inspan (Bladon Peake)

1954

Daar Doer in die Stad (Jamie Uys)
Die Leeu van Punda Maria (Gerrie Snyman)
'n Plan is 'n Boerdery (Pierre de Wet)
Vadertjie Langbeen (Pierre de Wet)
West of Zanzibar (Harry Watt)

1955

Geld Soos Bossies (Jamie Uys)
Matieland (Pierre de Wet)
Wanneer die Masker Val (Hennie van den Heever)

1956

Paul Kruger (Werner Grünbauer)

1957

Dis Lekker om te Lewe (Pierre de Wet)
Donker Afrika (David Millin)

1958

Die Bosvelder (Jamie Uys)
Die Goddelose Stad (Pierre Botha)
Die Sewende Horison (Franz Cloete)
Fratse in die Vloot (Pierre de Wet)

1959

Come Back, Africa (Lionel Rogosin)
The Desert Inn (Immel Botha)
Die Wilde Boere (J.O.O. Olwagen)
Ek sal opstaan (Kappie Botha)
Nooi van my Hart (Pierre de Wet)
Piet se Tante (Pierre de Wet)
Satanskoraal (Elmo de Witt)

1960

Die Bloedrooi Papawer (Cecil Whiteman)
Die Jagters (Gordon Vorster)
Die Vlugteling (Gordon Vorster)
Hou die Blinkkant Bo (Emil Nofal)
Kyk na die Sterre (Kappie Botha)
The Last of the Few (David Millin)
Oupa en die Plaasnooientjie (Pierre de Wet)
Rip van Wyk (Emil Nofal)

1961

Basie (Gordon Vorster)
Boerboel de Wet (Al Debbo)
Die Hele Dorp Weet (Kappie Botha)
Doodkry is Min (Jamie Uys)
En die Vonke Spat! (Pierre de Wet)
Hans en die Rooinek (Jamie Uys)
Spore in die Modder (James Norval)

1962

As ons twee eers getroud is (Jan Perold)
Die Geheim van Onderplaas (Al Debbo)
Die Skelm van die Limpopo (Gerrie Snyman)
Die Tweede Slaapkamer (Gordon Vorster)
Dilemma (Henning Carlsen)
Gevaarlike Spel (Al Debbo)
Jy's Lieflik Vanaand (Gordon Vorster)
Lord Oom Piet (Jamie Uys)
Man in die Donker (Truida Pohl)
Stropers van die Laeveld (David Millin)
Voor Sononder (Emil Nofal)

1963

Gee My Jou Hand (Tim Spring)
Huis op Horings (Truida Pohl)
Kimberley Jim (Emil Nofal)
Ruiter in die Nag (Jan Perold)

1964

Dingaka (Jamie Uys)
The Forster Gang (Percival Rubens)
Piet my Niggie (Jan Perold)
Seven against the Sun (David Millin)

1965

Debbie (Elmo de Witt)
King Hendrik (Emil Nofal)
Ride the High Wind (David Millin)
Voortreflike Familie Smit (Kappie Botha)

1966

All the Way to Paris (Jamie Uys)
Die Kavaliers (Elmo de Witt)
The Second Sin (David Millin)

1967

Die Professor en die Prikkelpop (Jamie Uys)
Hoor My Lied (Elmo de Witt)
Kruger-miljoene (Ivan Hall)
Wild Season (Emil Nofal)

1968

Die Kandidaat (Jans Rautenbach)
Jy is my Liefling (Dirk de Villiers)
Majuba (David Millin)
Raka (Sven Persson)

1969

Danie Bosman (Elmo de Witt)
Die Geheim van Nantes (Dirk de Villiers)
Dirkie/Lost in the Desert (Jamie Uys)
Katrina (Jans Rautenbach)
Staal Burger (Daan Retief)

1970

Die Drie van der Merwes (Dirk de Villiers)
Jannie Totsiens (Jans Rautenbach)
Lied in My Hart (Ivan Hall)
Sien Jou Môre (Elmo de Witt)
Vicki (Ivan Hall)

1971

Breekpunt (Daan Retief)
Die Banneling (David Millin)
Die Erfgenaam (Koos Roets)
Die Lewe Sonder Jou (Dirk de Villiers)
Flying Squad (Ivan Hall)
Freddie's in Love (Manie van Rensburg)
Gold Squad (Ivan Hall)
Lindie (Wallie Stevens)
A New Life (Dirk de Villiers)
Pappa Lap (Jans Rautenbach)

1972

Die Wildtemmer (Elmo de Witt)
Kaptein Caprivi (Albie Venter)
The Last Lion (Elmo de Witt)
Liefde vir Lelik (Keith Van der Watt)
Lokval in Venesië (Ivan Hall)
My Broer se Bril (Dirk de Villiers)
Salomien (Daan Retief)
Vlug van die Seemeeu (Koos Roets)
The Winners (Roy Sergeant & Emil Nofal)

1973

Aanslag op Kariba (Ivan Hall)
Afspraak in die Kalahari (Anna Neethling-Pohl)
Boesman and Lena (Ross Devenish)
Die Bankrower (Manie Van Rensburg)
Die Sersant en die Tiger Moth (Koos Roets)
Die Spook van Donkergat (Diana Ginsberg)
Die Voortrekkers (David Millin)
Die Wit Sluier (Dirk de Villiers)
Dog Squad (Tim Spring)
Groetnis vir die Eerste Minister (Bertrand Retief)
Jamie 21 (Daan Retief)
Môre Môre (Elmo de Witt)

Siener in die Suburbs (Francois Swart)
Skadus oor Brugplaas (Ray Austin)
Snip en Rissiepit (Elmo de Witt)

1974

Babbelkous en Bruidegom (Koos Roets)
Beautiful People (Jamie Uys)
Boland! (Bertrand Retief)
Catch Me a Dream (Tim Spring)
Dans van die Flamink (Ivan Hall)
Geluksdal (Manie Van Rensburg)
Gold (Peter Hunt)
Kwikstertjie (Elmo de Witt)
Met Liefde van Adele (Dirk de Villiers)
'n Sonneblom uit Parys (Sias Odendaal)
Ongewenste Vreemdeling (Jans Rautenbach)
Pens en Pootjies (Dirk de Villiers)
Suster Theresa (David Millin)
Tant Ralie se Losieshuis (Dirk de Villiers)
The Virgin Goddess (Dirk de Villiers)

1975

Daan en Doors oppie Diggins (Dirk de Villiers)
The Diamond Hunters (Dirk de Villiers)
Die Square (Manie Van Rensburg)
Eendag op 'n Reëndag (Jans Rautenbach)
e'Lollipop (Ashley Lazarus)
Ma Skryf Matriek (Franz Marx)
Maxhosa (Lynton Stephenson)
Mirage Eskader (Bertrand Retief)
My Naam Is Dingetjie (Dirk de Villiers)
Sarah (Gordon Vorster)
Ses Soldate (Bertrand Retief)
Seuns van die Wolke (Franz Marx)
Soekie (Daan Retief)
Somer (Sias Odendaal)
Ter wille van Christine (Elmo de Witt)
U-Deliwe (Simon Sabela)

1976

The Black Cat (Simon Sabela)
The Boxer (Simon Sabela)
Daar Kom Tant Alie (Koos Roets)
Die Rebel (Daan Retief)
Die Vlindervanger (Koos Roets)
The Eagle (Simon Sabela)
Funny People (Jamie Uys)
Glenda (Dirk de Villiers)
How Long? (Gibson Kente & Ben Namoyi)
Karate Olympia/Kill or Be Killed (Ivan Hall)
Land Apart (Sven Persson)
Liefste Madelein (Franz Marx)
'n Beeld vir Jeannie (Elmo de Witt)
Ngwanaka (Simon Sabela)
'n Sondag in September (Jan Scholtz)
The South Africans (Sven Persson)
Springbok (Tommie Meyer)

1977

Crazy People (Dirk de Villiers)
Die Winter van 14 Julie (Jan Scholtz)
Dingetjie en Idi (Dirk de Villiers)
The Guest (Ross Devenish)
Inyakanyaka (Simon Sabela)
Kom tot Rus (Elmo de Witt)
Kootjie Emmer (Koos Roets)
Lag met Wena (Morné Coetzer)
Mooimeisiesfontein (Elmo de Witt)
Netnou Hoor die Kinders (Franz Marx)

1978

The Advocate (Simon Sabela)
Billy Boy (Tim Spring)
Decision to Die (Dirk de Villiers)
Diamant en die Dief (Jan Scholtz)

Die Spaanse Vlieg (Dirk de Villiers)
Die Vyfde Seisoen (Gordon Vorster)
Dit was Aand en Dit was Môre (Franz Marx)
Dr. Marius Hugo (Tim Spring)
Iemand Soos Jy (Elmo de Witt)
Isivumelwano (Simon Sabela)
Ngaka (Simon Sabela)
Nicolene (Marie du Toit)
'n Seder Val in Waterkloof (Franz Marx)
Setipana (Simon Sabela)
Sonja (Daan Retief)
Witblits and Peach Brandy (Dirk de Villiers)

1979

Charlie Word 'n Ster (Dirk de Villiers)
Die Eensame Vlug (Jan Scholtz)
Elsa se Geheim (Chris du Toit)
Follow That Rainbow (Louis Burke)
Forty Days (Franz Marx)
Grensbasis 13 (Elmo de Witt)
Herfsland (Jan Scholtz)
Marigolds in August (Ross Devenish)
Ngaka (Simon Sabela)
Night of the Puppets (Daan Retief)
Plekkie in die Son (William Faure)
Pretoria O Pretoria (Bertrand Retief)
Umunti Akalahlwa (Simon Sabela)
Wat Jy Saai (Tim Spring)
Weerskant die Nag (Franz Marx)
Zulu Dawn (Douglas Hickox)

1980

April '80 (Jan Scholtz)
The Gods Must Be Crazy (Jamie Uys)
Kiepie en Kandas (Jan Scholtz)
'n Brief vir Simoné (Anton Goosen & F.C. Hamman)
Rienie (Fanie Van der Merwe)

Shadowplay (Oliver Stapleton)
Sing vir die Harlekyn (F.C. Hamman)
Skelms (Jan Scholtz)

1981

Beloftes van Môre (Daan Retief)
Blink Stefaans (Jans Rautenbach)
Nommer Asseblief (Henk Hugo)
Tommy (Simon Metsing)

1982

Blood Money (Jimmy Murray & Simon Metsing)
Die Bosveldhotel (Fred Nel)
Verkeerde Nommer (Franz Marx)

1983

Funny People II (Jamie Uys)
Geel Trui vir 'n Wenner (Franz Marx)
Kolmanskop (David Pupkewitz)
My Country My Hat (David Bensusan)
The Riverman (Ivan Hall)
Wolhaarstories (Bromley Cawood)

1984

Boetie Gaan Border Toe (Regardt Van den Bergh)
Broer Matie (Jans Rautenbach)
Die Groen Faktor (Koos Roets)
The Sandpiper (Lourens Swanepoel)
Stoney the One and Only (Rod Hay)
Torn Allegiance (Alan Nathanson)

1985

Boetie op Manoeuvres (Regardt Van den Bergh)
Die Strandloper (Lourens Swanepoel)
Eendag vir Altyd (Chris du Toit)
Love in the Wood (Lourens Swanepoel)
Magic Is Alive My Friends (Jan Scholtz)
Mamza (Johan Blignaut)
The Moment of Truth (Ronnie Isaacs)
No One Cries Forever (Jans Rautenbach)
Skating on Thin Uys (Bromley Cawood)
Skollie (Ivan Hall)
Van der Merwe P.I. (Regardt Van den Bergh)
Wie Laaste Lag (Koos Roets)
You're in the Movies (Emil Nofal)

1986

City of Blood (Darrell Roodt)
Jock of the Bushveld (Gray Hofmeyr)
Nag van Vrees (Jimmy Murray & Stanley Roup)
Place of Weeping, A (Darrell Roodt)
Tenth of a Second (Darrell Roodt)
Tojan (Johan Blignaut)
You Gotta Be Crazy (Emil Nofal)
You Must Be Joking (Elmo de Witt)

1987

City Wolf (Heinrich Dahms)
Davey (Louise Smit)
The Devil and the Song (Bromley Cawood)
Die Posman (Anthony Wilson)
Fiela se Kind (Katinka Heyns)
A Fire in Africa (Gerhard Uys)
Kampus (Etienne Puren)
Nukie (Sias Odendaal & Michael Pakleppa)
Quest for Love (Helena Nogueira)
Saturday Night at the Palace (Robert Davies)

Shot Down (Andrew Worsdale)
The Stick (Darrell Roodt)
Wêreld Sonder Grense (Frans Nel)
You Must Be Joking Too (Leon Schuster)

1988

An African Dream (John Smallcombe)
Brutal Glory (Koos Roets)
Circles in the Forest (Regardt Van den Bergh)
Dancing in the Forest (Mark Roper)
The Emissary (Jan Scholtz)
Hold My Hand I'm Dying (Terence Ryan)
The Last Warrior (Martin Wragge)
Mapantsula (Oliver Schmitz & Thomas Mogotlane)
Paradise Road (Jan Scholtz)
A Private Life (Francis Gerard)
The Shadowed Mind (Cedric Sundström)
Tyger, Tyger Burning Bright (Neal Sundström)

1989

AWOL (Neil Sonnekus)
Dark City (Chris Curling)
The Gods Must Be Crazy II (Jamie Uys)
In the Name of Blood (Robert Davies)
Jobman (Darrell Roodt)
Lambarene (Gray Hofmeyr)
The Native Who Caused All the Trouble (Manie Van Rensburg)
Oh Schucks It's Schuster (Leon Schuster)
Reason to Die (Tim Spring)
That Englishwoman (Dirk de Villiers)
Windprints (David Wicht)

1990

Agter Elke Man (Franz Marx)
Au Pair (Heinrich Dahms)

The Fourth Reich (Manie Van Rensburg)
Oh Schucks Here Comes UNTAG (David Lister)
On the Wire (Elaine Proctor)
Sandgrass People (Koos Roets)
The Schoolmaster (Jean Delbeke)
When Men Go to War (Dirk de Villiers)

1991

Die Nag van die 19de (Koos Roets)
Die Prince van Pretoria (Franz Marx)
Die Storie van Klara Viljee (Katinka Heyns)
Dust Devil (Richard Stanley)
The Good Fascist (Helena Nogueira)
No Hero (Tim Spring)
The Road to Mecca (Peter Goldsmid & Athol Fugard)
The Rutanga Tapes (David Lister)
Sarafina! (Darrell Roodt)
The Sheltering Desert (Regardt Van den Bergh)
Sweet 'n Short (Gray Hofmeyr)
Taxi to Soweto (Manie Van Rensburg)
To the Death (Darrell Roodt)
Wheels and Deals (Michael Hammon)

1992

The Angel, the Bicycle and the Chinaman's Finger (Koos Roets & Nicholas Ellenbogen)
Friends (Elaine Proctor)
'n Pot Vol Winter (Johan Bernard)
Orkney Snork Nie – Die Movie (Willie Esterhuizen)

1993

Ipi Tombi (Tommie Meyer & Don Hulette)
There's a Zulu on My Stoep (Gray Hofmeyr)

1994

Cry the Beloved Country (Darrell Roodt)
Kalahari Harry (Dirk de Villiers)
Lipstiek, Dipstiek (Willie Esterhuizen)
The Making of the Mahatma (Shyam Benegal)
Never Say Die (Yossi Wein)
Soweto Green (David Lister)

1995

Jock (Danie Joubert)
Nice to Meet You Please Don't Rape Me (Ian Kerkhof)

1996

Fools (Ramadan Suleman)
Hearts and Minds (Ralph Ziman)
Jump the Gun (Les Blair)
Panic Mechanic (David Lister)
A Woman of Colour (Bernard Joffa)

1997

Dangerous Ground (Darrell Roodt)
Kaalgat Tussen Die Daisies (Koos Roets & Dirk de Villiers)
Paljas (Katinka Heyns)
The Sexy Girls (Russell Thompson)

1998

Bravo Two Zero (Tom Clegg)
Chikin Biz'niz – The Whole Story (Ntshaveni wa Luruli)

1999

Boesman and Lena (John Berry)
Desert Diners (Francois Coertze)
Heel against the Head (Rod Stewart)
Inside Out (Neal Sundström)
The Millennium Menace (Leon Schuster)
Pure Blood (Ken Kaplan)
A Reasonable Man (Gavin Hood)
Slavery of Love (John Badenhorst)

2000

Final Solution (Chris Crusen)
Hijack Stories (Oliver Schmitz)
Kin (Elaine Proctor)
The Long Run (Jean Stewart)
Lyk Lollery (Francois Coertze)
The Second Skin (Darrell Roodt)
Styx (Alex Wright)

2001

God Is African (Akin Omotoso)
Malunde (Stefanie Sycholt)
Mr Bones (Gray Hofmeyr)
Othello (Ebulus Timothy)
Pure Blood (Kenneth Kaplan)

2002

Promised Land (Jason Xenopoulos)
Slash (Neal Sundström)

2003

Beat the Drum (David Hichson)
The Bone Snatcher (Jason Wulfson)

A Case of Murder (Clive Morris)
Pavement (Darrell Roodt)
Proteus (John Greyson)
Shooting Bokkie (Rob de Mezieres)
Soldiers of the Rock (Norman Maake)
Stander (Bronwyn Hughes)
Sumuru (Darrell Roodt)
The Wooden Camera (Ntshaveni Wa Luruli)

2004

Boy Called Twist (Tim Greene)
Dead Easy (Neal Sundström)
Dracula 3000 (Darrell Roodt)
Drum (Zola Maseko)
Forgiveness (Ian Gabriel)
Hotel Rwanda (Terry George)
In My Country (John Boorman)
Max and Mona (Teddy Mattera)
Oh Schuks I'm Gatvol (Leon Schuster & Willie Esterhuizen)
Red Dust (Tom Hooper)
Skilpoppe (André Odendaal)
The Story of an African Farm (David Lister)
Yesterday (Darrell Roodt)

2005

Crazy Monkey Presents: Straight Outta Benoni (Trevor Clarence)
Dollars and White Pipes (Donovan Marsh)
Faith's Corner (Darrell Roodt)
The Flyer (Revel Fox)
Gums and Noses (Craig Freimond)
Mama Jack (Gray Hofmeyr)
Number Ten (Darrell Roodt)
Son of Man (Mark Dornford-May)
34 South (Maganthrie Pillay)
Tsotsi (Gavin Hood)
U-Carmen eKhayelitsha (Mark Dornford-May)
Zulu Love Letter (Ramadan Suleman)

2006

Bunny Chow: Know Thyself (John Barker)
Conversations on a Sunday Afternoon (Khalo Matabane)
Don't Touch (Zulfah Otto-Sallies)
Faith like Potatoes (Regardt Van den Bergh)
Footskating 101 (Brendan Jack)
Heartlines (Angus Gibson)
Ouma Se Slim Kind (Gustav Kuhn)
Prey (Darrell Roodt)
Running Riot (Koos Roets)
Wah-Wah (Richard E. Grant)
When We Were Black (Khalo Matabane)

2007

Bakgat (Henk Pretorius)
Big Fellas (Philip Roberts)
Catch a Fire (Phillip Noyce)
Confessions of a Gambler (Amanda Lane & Rayda Jacobs)
Goodbye Bafana (Bille August)
Meisie (Darrell Roodt)
More than Just a Game (Junaid Ahmed)
Oil on Water (Peter Matthews)
Poena is Koning (Willie Esterhuizen)
The Silent Fall (Roger Hawkins)
SMS Sugerman (Aryan Kaganof)

2008

Discreet (Joshua Rous)
The Feast of the Uninvited (Katinka Heyns)
Gugu and Andile (Minky Schlesinger)
Hansie (Regardt Van den Bergh)
Jerusalema (Ralph Ziman)
Land of Thirst (Meg Rickards)
Lullaby (Darrell Roodt)
Mr Bones 2: Back from the Past (Gray Hofmeyr)
My Black Little Heart (Claire Angelique)

Nothing but the Truth (John Kani)
Skin (Anthony Fabian)
Triomf (Michael Raeburn)
The World Unseen (Samim Sarif)
Zimbabwe (Darrell Roodt)

2009

Adera (Nega Tariku)
Crime – It's a Way of Life (Savo Tufegdzic)
Darfur (Uwe Boll)
Disgrace (Steve Jacobs)
District 9 (Neill Blomkamp)
Finding Lenny (Neal Sundström)
Intonga (J.J. Van Rensburg)
Long Street (Revel Fox)
My Secret Sky – Izulu Lami (Madoda Ncayiyana)
Rainbow Skellums (André Scholtz)
Shirley Adams (Oliver Hermanus)
Tornado and the Kalahari Horse Whisperer (Regardt Van den Bergh)
Vaatjie sien sy gat (Willie Esterhuizen)
White Lion (Michael Swan)
White Wedding (Jann Turner)

2010

Attack of the Indian Werewolf (Masood Boomgard)
Bakgat 2 (Henk Pretorius)
The Bull on the Roof (Jyoti Mistry)
Die Ongelooflike Avonture van Hanna Hoekom (Regardt Van den Bergh)
Hopeville (John Trengove)
I Now Pronounce You Black and White (Oliver Rodger)
Jakhalsdans (Darrell Roodt)
Jozi Kings (Jonathan Boynton-Lee & Jamie Ramsay)
Liefling Die Movie (Brian Webber)
Life, Above All (Oliver Schmitz)
Machansa (Muntu Zwane)
Master Harold … and the Boys (Lonny Price)
Paradise Stop (Jann Turner)

Schuks Tshabalala's Survival Guide to South Africa 2010 (Gray Hofmeyr)
Skoonheid (Oliver Hermanus)
A Small Town Called Descent (Jahmil X.T. Qubeka)
Spud (Donovan Marsh)
State of Violence (Khalo Matabane)
Themba (Stefanie Sycholt)
Visa/Vie (Elan Gamaker)
White Gold (Jayan Moodley & Paul Railton)

Key documentaries 1978–2010

1978

Bara (Kevin Harris)

1979

Athol Fugard: A Lesson from Aloes (Ross Devenish)
Rhythms of Resistance (Chris Austen)
South Africa Belongs to Us (Chris Austen, Peter Chappell, & Ruth Weiss)

1980

Generations of Resistance (Peter Davis)
Isitwalandwe: The Story of the South African Freedom Charter (Barry Feinberg)
I Talk About Me – I Am Africa (Peter Chappell & Chris Austin)

1981

Awake from Mourning (Chris Austin)
Forward to a People's Republic (Tony Bensusan, Laurence Dworkin, Nyana Molete, Elaine Proctor & Brian Tilley)
Fosatu: Building Worker Unity (Laurence Dworkin)
The Stolen River (Dereck Joubert)
This We Can Do for Justice and Peace (Kevin Harris)
You Have Struck a Rock (Deborah May & Georgina Karvellas)

1982

The Right Time (Kevin Harris)
The Sun Will Rise (Tony Bensusan, Laurence Dworkin & Brian Tilley)

1983

Last Supper at Horstley Street (Lindy Wilson)

1984

And Now We Have No Land (Hennie Serfontein)
Dear Grandfather: Your Right Foot Is Missing (Yunus Ahmed)
I Am Clifford Abrahams: This Is Grahamstown (Graham Hayman, Don Pinnock & Keyan Tomaselli)
Kango (Dirk de Villiers)
Kat River: The End of Hope (Graham Hayman)
Mayfair (Tony Bensusan, Paul Weinberg & Brian Tilley)
No Middle Road to Freedom (Kevin Harris)
The Struggle from within (Kevin Harris)
Tsiamelo: A Place of Goodness (Ellen Khuzwayo & Betty Wolpert)

1985

The Anvil and the Hammer (Barry Feinberg)
Hunters (Dereck Joubert)
Indaba Ya Grievance (Kevin Harris)
The People of the Great Sandface (Paul Myburgh)
Re Tla Bona (Elaine Proctor)
The Two Rivers (Mark Newman)

1986

The End of Eden (Rick Lomba)
Journey to the Forgotten (Dereck Joubert)
Mazimbu: Behind the Lines of the Liberation Movement (Toni Strasburg)
A Moffie Called Simon (John Greyson)

The Ribbon (Harriet Gavshon & Lindy Wilson)
Song of the Spear (Barry Feinberg)
Tomorrow's Parents (Kevin Harris)
Witness to Apartheid (Kevin Harris & Sharon Sopher)

1987

A Brother with Perfect Timing (Chris Austin)
The Cry of Reason: Beyers Naudé: An Afrikaner Speaks Out (Kevin Harris & Robert Bilheimer)
David Goldblatt in Black and White (Bernard Joffa)
A Fragile Harmony (Neil Curry)
Freedom Square and the Back of the Moon (Angus Gibson & William Kentridge)
Ithuseng: Out of Despair (Lindy Wilson)
Mama I'm Crying (Bette Wolpert & Joyce Seroke)
Saga of the Silver Screen, The (Wayne Lines & Benny Machanik)
Sharpeville Spirit (Elaine Proctor)
We Are the Elephant (Glenn Ujebe Masokoane)

1988

Any Child Is My Child (Barry Feinberg)
Free Mandela (Barry Feinberg)
Frontline Southern Africa (Toni Strasburg)
Have You Seen Drum Recently? (Jürgen Schadeberg)
Knysna – The Embattled Estuary (Neill Curry)
Namibia: No Easy Road to Freedom (Kevin Harris)
Robben Island: Our University (Lindy Wilson)
Segopotso (Craig Matthew & Joelle Chesselet)

1989

Cato Manor: People Were Living There (Charlotte Owen)
Eternal Enemies (Dereck Joubert)
How I'd Love to Feel Free (Jimi Matthews)
Just an Inch Away (Andrew Bethell)
Lakutshon 'Ilanga: Beyond the Pain (Kevin Harris)
Makhaliphile: The Dauntless One (Barry Feinberg)
Mohale Street Brothers (Michael Hammon)

Nelson Mandela and the Rise of the ANC (Jürgen Schadeberg)
Out in Africa (Melanie Chait)
Singing the Changes (Angus Gibson)
Too Far Apart (Liz Fish)
Voices for Namibia (Barry Feinberg)

1990

The Comrade King (Ben Horowitz)
Conversations with Sowetan Golfers (Angus Gibson)
Fruits of Defiance (Brian Tilley & Oliver Schmitz)
Goldwidows (Don Etkind)
Homelands Belong to the Past (Teddy Mattera)
Images in Struggle (Barry Feinberg)
Keita: Destiny of a Noble Outcast (Chris Austen)
Mbira: The Spirit of the People (Simon Bright)
Namibia: Rebirth of a Nation (Kevin Harris)
Natal – South Africa's Killing Ground (George Case)
Out of the Darkness (Brenda Goldblatt)
The People's Poet: Mzwakhe (Oliver Schmitz)
War and Peace – In the Name of Mandela (Jürgen Schadeberg)
Who Was David Webster? (Mike Aldridge)
The Women of Delmas (Kevin Harris)

1991

Tamboville: One City from below (Shelley Wells)

1992

The Long Journey of Clement Zulu (Liz Fish)
The Red Flag (Stanley Ndlovu)
War and Peace: The Rise of the ANC (Jürgen Schadeberg)

1993

In Darkest Hollywood: Cinema and Apartheid (Peter Davis)
Ordinary People (Harriet Gavshon & Cliff Bestall)

A Travelling Song (Lindy Wilson)
Ulibambe Lingashoni – Hold Up the Sun (Laurence Dworkin)

1994

Countdown to Freedom (Danny Schechter)
Dolly Rathebe and the Inkspots (Jürgen Schadeberg)
Out in South Africa (Barbara Hammer)
Silwerdoekstories (Katinka Heyns)
Soweto: A History (Angus Gibson)

1995

Ernest Mancoba at Home (Bridget Thompson)
Living in a Nonsense Place (Noreen Ash Mackay)
Of Courage and Consequence (Kevin Harris)
Umuntu, Umuntu, Ngabantu (Ingrid Gavshon)

1996

Rhythm & Rights (Khalo Matabane & Oliver Schmitz)

1997

Joburg Stories (Oliver Schmitz)
Let's Hit the Streets (Michael Raeburn)
A Normal Daughter: The Life and Times of Kewpie of District Six (Jack Lewis)
Robert Sobukwe – A Tribute Integrity (Kevin Harris)

1998

Aliens or Broers (Thulani Mokoena)
Behind Bars (Kevin Harris)
Brenda Fassie: Not a Bad Girl (Chris Austin)
Cape of Rape (Derek Antonio Serra)
Certain Unknown Persons (Laurence Dworkin)

Desmond Mpilo Tutu – Man without Fear (Hennie Serfontein)
Heart and Stone – The Life and Times of Govan Mbeki (Bridget Thompson)
The Life and Times of Sara Baartman (Zola Maseko)
The Man Who Drove with Mandela (Greta Schiller)
Pavement Aristocrats – The Bergies of Cape Town (Francois Verster)
Sando to Samantha (Jack Lewis, Thulani Phungula)
Steve Bantu Biko – Beacon of Hope (Nkosinathi Biko)
What Happened to Mbuyisa? (Feizel Mamdoo)
Where Truth Lies (Mark Kaplan)

1999

Apostles of Civilised Vice (Zackie Achmat & Jack Lewis)
The Comrade King (Ben Horowitz)
Hillbrow Kids (Michael Hammon, Jacqueline Gorgen)
Isibande (Lungiswa Sithole)
JG Strijdom Is Very Very Dead (Pule Diphare)
Lady Was a Mashoza (Nokuthula Mazibuko)
A Letter to My Cousin in China (Henion Han)
The Liberal and the Pirate (Guy Spiller)
Main Reef Road (Nicolaas Hofmeyr)
The Man Who Would Kill Kitchener (Francois Verster)
Matters of Life and Death (Kevin Harris)
My African Mother (Cathy Winter)
Nat Nakasa: A Native of Nowhere (Lauren Groenewald)
Nelson Rolihlahla Mandela – An Intimate Portrait (Cliff Bestall)
A Question of Madness (Liza Key)
Spares & Besties (Jack Lewis)
The Spirit of Malombo (David Max Brown)
A Woman's Place (Catherine Steward & Patricia Van Heerden)

2000

Cape Town – Tales of a Colour'd City (Thulani Mokoena)
Dark & Lovely, Soft & Free (Paulo Alberton & Graeme Reid)
Facing Death … Facing Life (Ingrid Gavshon)
Get Down: The Kwaito Story (Ernie Vosloo)
The Great Dance: A Hunter's Story (Craig & Damon Foster)
The Gugulethu Seven (Lindy Wilson)

Had Socialism Failed Us? (Redhad Desai)
Metamorphosis (Luiz De Barros)
Please Rise (Sharon Cort)
The Second Wife (Akiedah Mohamed)
The Secret Safari (Tom Zubrycki)
White Farmer, Black Land (Aldo Lee)

2001

Cage of Dreams (Cliff Bestall)
Changing Gears (Margo Fleiser)
Ingrid Jonker – Her Lives and Time (Helena Nogueira)
Judgement Day (Kevin Harris)
My Son the Bride (Mpumi Njinge)
Ochre & Water: Himba Chronicles from the Land of Kaoko (Craig Matthew & Joelle Chesselet)
Patient Abuse: The TAC's Struggle for Treatment Access (Jack Lewis)
Scorched Earth – Verskroeide Aarde (Herman Binge)
Shouting Silent (Renee Rosen)
Tomorrow's Heroes (John W. Fredericks & Davide Tosco)

2002

Amandla! A Revolution in Four Part Harmony (Lee Hirsch)
The Black (Eddie Edwards)
Children of the Revolution (Zola Maseko)
Girlhood (Tracey Collis)
In the Shadow of Koadilalelo (Cliff Bestall)
A Lion's Trail (Francois Verster)
My Land My Life (Rehad Desai)
The Return of Sara Baartman (Zola Maseko)
Strong Enough (Penny Gaines)
The Tap (Toni Strasburg)
Very Fast Girls (Beathur Baker)
Very Fast Guys (Catherine Muller)
Voices across the Fence (Andy Spitz)
When the War Is Over (Francois Verster)

2003

Between Joyce and Remembrance (Mark Kaplan)
Body Beautiful (Omelga Mthiyane)
Casa Del Musica (Jonathan de Vries)
Close to the Heart (Dirk de Villiers)
Cosmic Africa (Craig & Damon Foster)
Doing It (Kali Van der Merwe)
A Fisherman's Tale (Riaan Hendricks)
It's My Life (Brian Tilley)
Love in the Time of Sickness (Khalo Matabane)
Memories of Rain (Angela Mai & Gisela Albrecht)
Property of the State: Gay Men in the Apartheid Military (Gerald Kraak)
Qula Kwedini – A Rite of Passage (Mandilakhe Mjekula & Jahmil XT Qubeka)
Redefining the Griot: A History of South African Documentary Film (Taryn da Canha)
A Red Ribbon Around My House (Portia Rankoane)
Simon and I (Beverly Ditsie & Nicky Newman)
Wa N' Wina (Dumisani Phakathi)

2004

All About Art (Miki Redelinghuys)
All I Want for Christmas (Jeanette Jegger)
Being Pavarotti (Odette Geldenhuys)
Belonging (Minky Schlesinger & Kethiwe Ngcobo)
Born into Struggle (Rehad Desai)
Brown (Kali Van der Merwe)
Cinderella of the Cape Flats (Jane Kennedy)
The Devil Breaks My Heart (Lederle Bosch)
Four Rent Boys and a Sangoma (Catherine Muller)
Grietjie van Garies (Odette Geldenhuys)
Hot Wax (Andrea Spitz)
Ikhaya (Omelga Mthiyane)
Jus' Call Me Tjarra (Lieza Louw)
Karoo Kitaar Blues (Liza Key)
Meaning of the Buffalo (Karin Slater)
Mix (Rudzani Dzuguda)
Nabantwa' Bam (Kulile Nxumalo)
Nikiwe (Ingrid Gavshon)
A Sentimental Journey (Liza Key)

Solly's Story (Asivhanzhi Mathaba)
Story of a Beautiful Country (Khalo Matabane)
Through the Eyes of My Daughter (Zulfah Otto-Sallies)
Transkei Holiday (Jemma Spring)
Umgidi (Gillian Schutte & Sipho Singiswa)

2005

Chasing the Ancestors (Gillian Schutte & Sipho Singiswa)
From Nkoko … with Love (Karin Slater)
The Heart of Whiteness (Rehad Desai)
The Mothers' House (Francois Verster)
My Hare Krishna Family (Frank Opperman)
My Other Mother (Diana Keam)
Pasta al La Shaik (Madoda Ncayiyana)
A Shadow of Hope (Makela Pululu)
Taking Back the Waves (Nic Hofmeyr)

2006

Beautiful in Beaufort-Wes (Walter Stokman)
Betrayal (Mark Kaplan)
Bushman's Secret (Rehad Desai)
From Cape Town with Love (Caroll Howell)
Glimpse (Dan Jawitz & Alberto Iannuzzi)
Heaven's Herds (James Hersov)
Ikaya (Elsabé Daneel)
I Mike What I Like (Jyoti Mistry)
Johnny Appels: The Last Strandloper (Michael Raimondo)
Tsietsi, My Hero (Portia Rankoane)

2007

Antarctica: Journey into the White Desert (Damon & Craig Foster)
Black Beulahs (Fanney Taimong)
Brothers in Arms (Jack Lewis)
Die Medisynesak (Lieza Louw)
En skielik is dit aand (John Lazarus)

The Glow of White Women (Yunus Vally)
Imbokodo – The Rock (Belinda Blignaut & Bridget Pickering)
In the Dock (Kevin Harris)
Keiskamma – A Story of Love (Miki Redelinghuys)
Lost Prophets (Dylan Valley)
Love, Communism, Revolution & Rivonia – Bram Fischer Story (Sharon Farr)
Masindy's Story (Sharon Farr & Lee Otten)
Mr Devious My Life (John Fredericks)
A Pair of Boots and a Bicycle (Vincent Moloi)
Revolutionaries Love Life (Riaan Hendricks)
The Spirit of the Mountain (Liz Fish)
A Truly Wonderful Adventure (Lederle Bosch)
Voëlvry (Liz Fish)

2008

Aria del Africa (Roger Lucey)
Balawa's Story (Charlene Houston)
Betrayed (Rina Jooste)
The Burning Man (Adze Ugah)
Captured (Harriet Gavshon & Rina Jooste)
Flowers of the Nation (Rina Jooste)
Forgotten (Rina Jooste)
Gorillas: A Journey for Survival (Lianne Siegh)
Hoerikwaggo, People of the Mountain (Liz Fish)
Iceman: The Lewis Gordon Pugh Story (Craig & Damon Foster)
Mountain of Ashes (Jac Williams)
Now Generation (Rina Jooste)
The Search for the Knysna Elephants (Mark Van Wijk)
The Shaman's Apprentice (Catherine Winter)
The Turtleman of Watamu (Liz Fish)
Urban Cowboy (Liz Fish)

2009

Afrikaner, Afrikaan (Rina Jooste)
Betrayed (Rina Jooste)
Captured (Rina Jooste)
Fokofpolisiekar: Forgive Them for They Know Not What They Do (Bryan Little)

A Fortunate Soldier (Nicky Crowther)
Kentridge and Dumas in Conversation (Catherine Meyburgh)
The Last Voyage (Riaan Hendricks)
Living with Bipolar Mood Disorder (Simon Barnard)
Living with Substance Abuse (Brandon Oelofse)
The Manuscripts of Timbuktu (Zola Maseko)
12 Mile Stone (Greg Fell & Dean Leslie)
The Nature of Life (Craig & Damon Foster)
The Satyr of Springbok Heights (Robert Silke)
Sea Point Days (Francois Verster)
The Silver Fez (Lloyd Ross)
Zwelidumile (Ramadan Suleman)

2010

Afrikaaps (Dylan Valley)
American Foulbrood (Carlos Francisco)
The Battle for Johannesburg (Rehad Desai)
The Black Boer (Xolani L. Gumbi)
Congo in Four Acts (Dieudo Hamadi, Divita Wa Lusala & Kiripi Katembo Siku)
The Cradock Four (David Forbes)
The Fairway (Mzimasi Gova)
Impresario (Neil Sandilands)
Into the Dragon's Lair (Craig & Damon Foster)
My Hunter's Heart (Craig & Damon Foster)
Odd Number (Marius Van Straaten)
Road to Pride (Inger Smith & Lesedi Mogoatlhe)
State of Mind (Djo Tunda wa Munga)
Surfing Soweto (Sara Blecher)
Thembi (Jo Menell)
Unhinged: Surviving Jo'burg (Adrian Loveland)

Key short films: 1980–2010

1980

Shadowplay (Oliver Stapleton)

1982

A Chip of Glass Ruby (Ross Devenish)
City Lovers (Barney Simon)
Country Lovers (Manie Van Rensburg)
Good Climate, Friendly Inhabitants (Lynton Stephenson)
Praise (Richard Green)

1984

Dear Grandfather Your Right Foot Is Missing (Yunus Ahmed)
The Mountain (Cedric Sundström)
Sales Talk (William Kentridge)

1986

Getting off the Altitude (John Hookham)
The Hidden Farms (Ken Kaplan)
The Stronger (Lynton Stephenson)

1988

The Burden (Ken Kaplan)

1990

Astor Mansions (Mark Wilby)
The Fridge (Robert Weinek)
Sacrifice (Aldo Lee & Lance Gewer)

1991

T & I (William Kentridge)

1992

Pretty Boys (Luis DeBarros)

1993

The Clay Ox (Catherine Meyburgh)
Clubbing (Luis DeBarros)

1994

The Children and I (Ken Kaplan)
Come See the Bioscope (Lance Gewer)

1995

Corner Caffie (Tim Greene)
Eating Fish (Carsten Rasch)
Heartspace (Carey Schonegevel)

1996

Angel (Barry Berk)
The Dress (Stephen Jennings)
Hot Legs (Luis DeBarros)
The Pink Leather Chair (Russell Thompson)
Stimulation (Andrew Worsdale)
Stray Bullet (Patrick Shai)

1997

Chikin Biz'nis (Khalo Matabane)
Mamlambo (Palesa ka Letlaka Nkosi)

1998

Aces (Ntandazo Gcinga)
Cry Me a Baby (Tamsin McCarthy)
The Foreigner (Zola Maseko)
Husk (Jeremy Handler)

Kap 'an Driver (Tim Greene)
Lucky Day (Brian Tilley)
An Old Wife's Tale (Dumisani Phakathi)
Portrait of a Young Man Drowning (Teboho Mahlatsi)
Salvation (Minky Schlesinger)
Stompie and the Red Tide (Tamsin McCarthy)
The Storekeeper (Gavin Hood)

1999

Christmas with Granny (Dumisani Phakathi)
Home Sweet Home (Norman Maake)
Lefifeng Bofelong Balesedi (Norman Maake)

2000

Maar Nog 'n Dooie Veerverhaal (Nicola Hanekom)

2001

Angels en Boereoorloë (Vickus Strydom)
Malpit (Johan Nel)
Note to Self (John Warner)
Raya (Zulfah Otto-Sallies)
Triomfeer (Jan-Hendrik Beetge)

2002

Azure (Meg Rickards)
Down Under (Neil Sonnekus)
'n Sprokie (Harold Holscher)
The Sky in Her Eyes (Ouida Smit & Madoda Ncayiyana)
Swing Left Frank (Johan Nel)
Ubuntu's Wounds (Sechaba Morejele)
Under the Rainbow (Dean Blumberg)
Waiting for Valdez (Dumisani Phakathi)
Western 4.33 (Aryan Kaganof)
When Tomorrow Calls (Louis du Toit)

2003

Black Sushi (Dean Blumberg)
A Drink in the Passage (Zola Maseko)
iBali (Harold Holscher)
Inja (Steve Pasvolsky)
Portrait of a Dark Soul (Thabang Moleya)
Senter (Rudi Steyn)
Skitterwit (Danie Bester)

2004

And There in the Dust (Lara Foot-Newton, Gerhard Marx)
Case 474 (Thabang Moleya)
Ever Dark (Quinn da Matta)
Flight of the Feathers (Tristan Holmes)
Killer October (Garth Meyer)
Life Is Hard (Nina Mnaya)
Lucky (Bobby Heaney)
Modder Koffie (Brett Melvill-Smith)
The One That Fits Inside a Bathtub (Inger Smith)
SA/X (Gilli Apter)

2005

Alive in Jhb (Neill Blomkamp)
Beyond Freedom: The South African Journey (Jacquie Trowell)
Bloedrooi (Quintin Wiehahn)
Considerately Killing Me (Willem Grobler)
Elalini (Tristan Holmes)
Escudo (Wolfgang Muller)
Fellini's Dreams – A Documentary (Kelli Lakey)
Hollywood in My Huis (Corné Van Rooyen)
Love Poem (Inger Smith)
The Mamtsotsi Bird (Jo Horn)
Springbokkie (Lynette Mitchell)
Tracks (Brett Melvill-Smith)

2006

Bitter Water (Garth Meyer)
Blom (Gordon Van der Spuy)
Bok (Bradshaw Schaffer)
Face Value (Gareth Bird)
The Mbulu's Bride (Justine Puren)
Milk (Jon Day)
Ongeriewe (Robin Kleinsmidt)
Sam Had Never Seen Her So Sad (Anthony Silverston)
Spyker, Pine, Pool (Ruan Smith)
Take the Cakes (Stephen de Villiers)
The Tooth Fairy (Matthew Cowles)

2007

At Thy Call (Christopher Lee Dos Santos)
Beans and a Friend (Rainer Leimeroth)
Begin (Jaco Kosie Smit)
Brothers in Arms 1978 (Dino Pappas & Christopher Lee Dos Santos)
Commando (Stephen de Villiers)
Finale (Francois Coetzee)
Freedom Days (Quinton Lavery)
Kammakastig Land (Brandon Oelofse)
Karate Kallie (Willem Van der Merwe)
'n Roos vir Mari (Louis du Toit)
Pondo Bicycle (Jan Ellis)
Réalou (Paul Speirs)
Roses & Lavender (Gareth H. Graham)
Sekalli Le Meokgo – Meokgo and the Stickfighter (Teboho Mahlatsi)
Service Pistol (Rio Allen)
The Shadow Boy (Justine Puren)
Sibahle (Joshua Rous)
Spaarwiel (Morne du Toit)
Vaderland (Desmond Denton)

2008

Breath (Mandilakhe Yengo)
Bury the Hatchet (Arthur Bacchus)
Elsie's Quota (Lee Ann Olwage)
Farm (Matthew Griffiths)
Finale (Francois Coetzee)
Friction (Aurora Drummer)
Hidden Places (Jamie Beron)
Jesus and the Giant (Akin Omotoso)
Orgie (Hein Devos)
Painting Water (Kyle Davy)
The Resident (William Nicholson)
The Shadow Boy (Justine Puren)
Three Cigarettes (Stephen de Villiers)
Transactions (Thabang Moleya)
Uhambo (Josh de Kock)
Wide Open (Michael Matthews)
Winkletown (Imran Hamdulay)

2009

Agter die Berge (Kyle Southgate)
Away from Me (Craig Cameron-Mackintosh)
Greener Grass (Zaheer Goodman-Bhyat)
Homecoming (Kershan Pancham)
In a Time without Love (Mark Strydom)
Mune – The Animation (Jesca Marisa Leibbrandt)
Out of Reach (Jade Ables)
Shaving Sheep (Carl Houston McMillan)
Shebeen Queen (Carl Houston McMillan)
The Tunnel (Jenna Bass)
Unfinished Business (Graham Shillington)
Wamkelekile (Dorotea Vucic)
We Are Home (Jessica Dawson)
Yolanda (Jo Horn)

2010

The Abyss Boys (Jan-Hendrik Beetge)
Boxcar (Bruce Paynter)
The Bullet (Michael Klein)
Cake (Philippa Caddow)
Father Christmas Doesn't Come Here (Bheki Sibiya)
The First Time (Harold Holscher)
Stay with Me (Teddy Mattera)
Sweetheart (Michael Matthews)

Note

1. The name of the director is provided next to the title of the production.

Index